THE 'IMPROPER' FEMININE

THE 'IMPROPER' FEMININE

The Women's Sensation Novel and the New Woman Writing

Lyn Pykett

London and New York

First published 1992
by Routledge
2 Park Square, Milton Park, Abingdon, Oxon, OX14 4RN

Simultaneously published in the USA and Canada
by Routledge
a division of Routledge, Taylor & Francis
270 Madison Ave, New York NY 10016

Reprinted 2000, 2001 (twice), 2002

Transferred to Digital Printing 2006

Routledge is an imprint of the Taylor & Francis Group

Typeset in 10 on 12 point Palatino by
Intype Ltd, London

British Library Cataloguing in Publication Data
Pykett, Lyn
The improper feminine: the women's sensation novel and
the new women writing.
I. Title
823.809354

Library of Congress Cataloging in Publication Data
Available on request

ISBN 0–415–04928–8

Publisher's Note

The publisher has gone to great lengths to ensure the quality of this
reprint butpoints out that some imperfections in the
original may be apparent

For Ben, Rachel and Jessica

Contents

Part III   Breaking the Bounds:
The Improper Feminine and the Fiction
of the New Woman

Introductory note

The women's sensation novel of the 1860s and the New Woman writing of the 1890s were among the chief literary sensations of their day. They were widely read, heatedly discussed in the newspaper and periodical press, imitated, parodied and, in some cases, adapted for the stage. In short, they were part of the general cultural currency of the second half of the nineteenth century. Despite (or perhaps because of) this fact, the novels and stories at the centre of this study are, on the whole, works which had disappeared from view, or had been relegated to the status of minor historical curiosities, until their rediscovery in the wake of the second-wave feminism of the 1970s. In re-examining these texts it is not my intention to insist that they should be recognised as neglected, forgotten, or suppressed masterpieces of English literature. I am not interested in adding them to the existing canon, nor in constructing an alternative female canon. However, I hope that this study will show that the female sensationalists of the 1860s and the New Woman writers of the 1890s occupy an important place in the cultural history of the nineteenth century, and played an important part in the development of fiction. In the process I hope to explore some of the ways in which these women writers (and perhaps women's writing generally) are written out of history, even as they are being written in history.

It is certainly my aim to reinsert the women's sensation novel and the New Woman writing into literary history: first by locating the women's writing of the 1860s and 1890s in its particular cultural moment, by offering readings of individual novels in relation to the specific circumstances of their production, and secondly, by bringing these two moments together for comparative analysis. One result of this process will be to *reinstate* these texts in literary history; that is to say, to make them visible. As many feminist literary historians have demonstrated, this kind of scrutiny changes the shape of literary history by subtly altering our sense of literary periodisation, and of dominant genres and modes. It also changes our perception of the canonical writers, both male and female.[1]

This double focus (and refocusing) will suggest some important interrelationships in the literary and wider culture of the mid-Victorian and *fin de siècle* periods. It will also facilitate a reassessment of some of the continuities and contrasts in women's writing, without having recourse to the idea of a female tradition deriving from a specific female subculture, or to ahistorical and essentialist notions of a female imagination or a feminine writing.

Although I focus exclusively on fiction written by women, and which is, on the whole, primarily about women, my concern is not simply with women, but with broader questions of gender definition. With this in mind I attempt to situate this women's writing in contemporary discourses on gender, and in (what I shall argue is) a gendered discourse on fiction. This latter was an important constituent or determinant of the production and mediation of the work of the female sensationalists, the New Woman writing and, indeed, the nineteenth-century novel in general.

Elaine Showalter (1991) has recently redirected our attention to George Gissing's description of the *fin de siècle* period as one of 'sexual anarchy' (3). My concern in this book is with a sexual anxiety, or, more specifically, with an anxiety about gender, which pervades the writing of much of the Victorian period. The women's sensation novel and the New Woman fiction both embody and explore, as well as acting as a focus for, this gender anxiety. They are part of, and they address, a broadly based nineteenth-century social crisis which was, in important respects, articulated as a crisis of definition of gender.

Some of the material in chapters 4–6 appears in a different form in an essay I wrote in 1987–8. Such are the delays to which multi-authored volumes are subject that publication of this essay – 'Representing the real: the English debates about naturalism, 1884–1900', in Brian Nelson (ed.) *Naturalism in the*

European Novel: Modern Essays in Criticism – will probably coincide with the publication of the present volume. Unfortunately, since I did not see Ann Ardis's *New Women, New Novels: Feminism and Early Modernism* until my own book was at a late proof stage, I was unable to make use of its perceptive findings. Ardis's discussion of the New Woman fiction can be thoroughly recommended.

Part I

The 'Improper'
Feminine

1

Gender and writing, writing and gender

A man's book is a book. A woman's book
is a woman's book.
(Christiane Rochefort 1981:183)

The canonical map of literary history represents the novel as
a primitive territory colonised and civilised by brave male
explorers. This masculinised version of the history of fiction is
particularly dominant in the case of the two decades which
are the focus of this study: the 1860s and the 1890s. George
Eliot, whose final novel was published in 1876, is virtually the
only woman writing in the 1860s to have achieved canonical
status, and it has often seemed that she secured her place in
the canon by being accepted as an honorary man – a process
encouraged by her adoption of the lofty, mandarin tone of a
masculine or gender-neutral form of address.[1] The traditional
history of the later Victorian novel is entirely dominated by
male writers: the central figure of Thomas Hardy is surrounded
by the attendant spirits of the three lesser Georges – Meredith,
Gissing and Moore.

As many feminist literary historians have pointed out,[2] the
construction of this canon has involved the filtering out of a
great deal of writing, including virtually all of the fiction produced by women. Clearly women writers were extremely
active in the production of fiction throughout the nineteenth
century, and they certainly played a very important part in
two particularly fiercely debated developments: the sensation
novel of the 1860s and the fiction variously described as the
'Fiction of Sex', the 'New Fiction', or the 'New Woman Fiction'
of the 1890s. The women's sensation novel and the New

3

Woman fiction were two of the most prominent examples of a perceived invasion of fiction by the feminine which was a major talking-point in the press throughout the Victorian period. The shocking, unconventional heroines of the women sensation writers, such as Mary Elizabeth Braddon, Ellen Wood, Rhoda Broughton and 'Ouida' (Marie Louise de la Ramée), and the daring or neurotic fictional New Women and their female creators, who included Sarah Grand, Mona Caird, Ménie Muriel Dowie, Netta Syrrett and George Egerton, were among the most widely discussed and hotly contested aspects of this 'irruption of the feminine' (Boumelha 1982:79) into fiction and the culture at large

This study aims to explore the nature of this irruption of the feminine, and its contemporary cultural significance, as well as to suggest something of its continuing interest and importance for both present-day feminists and students of nineteenth-century literature and culture. Although the cultural phenomenon denoted by the phrase 'irruption of the feminine' is not exclusively the domain of female writers,[3] my own concern will be with women's writing, and with the discursive and material conditions in which it was produced and mediated.

It is, I hope, no longer necessary to justify the project of focusing exclusively on women's writing, or of resurrecting the forgotten texts of 'bourgeois' women novelists. As Juliet Mitchell (1984) argues, 'We have to know where women are, why women have to write the novel, the story of their own domesticity, the story of their own seclusion within the home and the possibilities and impossibilities provided by that' (289). My particular justification for focusing exclusively on the women writers of the 1860s and the 1890s, rather than examining them in relation to their male contemporaries, is that this latter task has already been ably performed by others.[4] One of the problems of the existing studies, however, is that some of them tend to represent women's writing as ancillary to, or merely prefigurative of, the dominant and achieved forms of male writing.

My own focus on the production, consumption and critical mediation of the female sensation novel and the (women's) New Woman writing will enable me to raise important questions about the specificity of women's writing, about women's

4

writing *and* difference, and about women's writing *as* difference. My primary concern will be to explore an historically specific sense of difference by examining the ways in which these two forms of nineteenth-century women's writing thematise, analyse and articulate difference. I shall be looking at the women's sensation novel and the New Woman writing as (differing) forms of *écriture féminine*, but I shall want to avoid the universalism and essentialism that have sometimes been attached to this concept. The women's writing of the 1860s and 1890s, like all writing by women, is marked by the writers' specific experiences as women, and by the ways in which their biological femaleness is structured and mediated by sociocultural concepts of femininity. To this extent these women writers will be seen to reinscribe their culture's stories about femininity. However, they also participated in a rewriting of this script of the feminine, as, in various ways and to varying degrees, they self-consciously explored or implicitly exposed the contradictions of prevailing versions of femininity, or developed new styles and modes through which to articulate their own specific sense of the feminine.

At first sight nothing could appear more dissimilar than the popular sensation novel of the 1860s, with its bigamous or adulterous heroines and complicated plots of crime and intrigue, and the 'modern women's books of the introspective type' (Stutfield 1897:104), those 'portentous anthems' (Showalter 1978a:181) on the wrongs of women and the evils of men and marriage which appeared in the 1880s and 1890s. Many twentieth-century readers have readily identified the progressive social views and proto-feminism of some of the New Woman writers. Few (if any) of the female sensationalists could be regarded as either feminist or progressive. However, there are a number of reasons why it is interesting to consider these two apparently disparate kinds of fiction together. One of the most obvious is that, although they are generically different, and appear to offer radically different views of women's predicament, nevertheless both the women's sensation novel and the New Woman fiction consist mainly of works which fit W.T. Stead's (1894) description of the 'novel of the modern woman'; they are novels 'by a woman about women from the standpoint of Woman' (64). Both types of fiction are grounded

5

in women writers' attempts to find a form, or forms, in which to represent and articulate women's experience, and women's aspirations and anxieties, as well as anxieties about women. They are, therefore, particularly fertile ground for feminist investigation.

The women sensationalists and the New Woman writers both worked with forms which have usually been regarded as predominantly feminine, even when they have been used by male writers. The sensationalists brought together, in varying ways and proportions, the dominant female forms of the early nineteenth century: female gothic, melodrama and domestic realism. The New Woman writers reworked and recombined melodrama, gothic, sensationalism and the domestic, as well as developing new modes of 'feminine' writing, such as introspective reverie, dream sequences and, in some cases, a distinctive, idiosyncratic and highly wrought lyricism.

Both groups of writers focused minutely on individual women's lives, demonstrating or exploring the contradictions of the dominant ideology of the feminine, by charting the conflict between 'actual' female experience and the domestic, private, angelic feminine ideal. Both focused on marriage, rather than on the courtship which formed the main narrative trajectory of most Victorian fiction. Both constructed plots and characters which registered or interrogated the contradictions of contemporary marriage and the domestic ideal. In short, both of these genres were produced by, and were interventions in the changing debate on, the Woman Question. Both actively contested, or implicitly (but nonetheless shockingly) challenged the dominant definitions of 'woman' and her prescribed social and familial roles, and both generated critical controversies which became a focus for broader socio-cultural anxieties, particularly for contemporary anxieties about gender.

The women's sensation novel in the 1860s and the New Woman writing of the 1890s also shared the distinction of being among the main sensations of their time. A number of individual novels from each group enjoyed the brief but intense notoriety of a *succès de scandale*. Both kinds of fiction were also sensationally successful with readers. Ellen Wood's *East Lynne* was one of the bestsellers of its year (1861), and had sold over 500,000 copies by the end of the century. Mary Elizabeth Braddon's *Lady Audley's Secret* went through nine

6

editions in three months when it was issued in volume form (in 1862, after first appearing as a magazine serial), and *Aurora Floyd* was even more successful. Sarah Grand's *The Heavenly Twins*, for many the prototypical New Woman novel, sold 30,000 copies in its first year (1893), and George Egerton's *Keynotes*, which came out in the same year, went into its seventh edition by 1896.

Of course, high sales alone are not necessarily an index of the cultural significance of either individual novels or particular categories of fiction. However, these novels by and about women not only sold well, they were also widely discussed, analysed and, not infrequently, derided. The sensation novel and the New Woman fiction were both immediately constituted as distinct sub-genres, and each occasioned a kind of moral panic among its first reviewers. Indeed, the sensationalised response to both kinds of fiction is yet another example of the way in which women and women's writing are (for good or ill) cast in the role of the exotic other, or wild zone of a culture.

Both the women's sensation novel and the New Woman fiction were produced by, and productive of, controversy. They were interventions in a broader cultural debate, and also (although to different degrees and in different ways) in a cultural and political struggle. The sensation novels of the 1860s were, at least implicitly and indirectly, produced by, and to some extent reproduced, the anxieties and tensions generated by contemporary ideological contestation of the nature of woman, and of women's social and familial roles. The New Woman novels, on the other hand, were much more directly linked to contemporary controversies surrounding the Woman Question, and to the various discourses within which they were produced and mediated. Many of the New Woman novelists were also prominent contributors to the debates on 'woman' in the newspaper and periodical press, and the New Woman fiction was sometimes reviewed alongside sociological and other polemical works, as if it were part of a seamless discourse on the Woman Question.[5]

The sensation novelists and New Woman writers not only caused a sensation by generating critical controversy, they also generated controversy by being sensational. Reviewers of both groups of writers were dismayed by their tendency to dwell on physical sensation, particularly in their representation of women and women's sexual feelings. Alarmed reviewers repeatedly discussed these novels in terms of the physical sensations they produced (or were deemed likely to produce) in their readers. The *Christian Remembrancer* (1863), for example, described the sensation novel as an 'appeal to the nerves', which worked by 'drugging thought and reason, and stimulating the attention through the lower and more animal instincts'. Such fiction, it affirmed, was likely to produce both moral and social disorder by 'willingly and designedly draw[-ing] a picture of life which . . . make[s] reality insipid and the routine of ordinary existence intolerable to the imagination' (210). Youthful readers were thought to be in particular danger from the 'utter unrestraint in which the heroines of this [fiction] are allowed to expatiate and develop their impulsive, stormy, passionate characters', and to question the customary social checks on feeling (212).

Harmful effects on the young also troubled one of the first readers of George Egerton's *Keynotes*.

> [T]ake the effect on a young fellow in his student period . . . of a particularly warm description of rounded limbs and the rest. It puts him in a state that he either goes off and has a woman or it is bad for his health (and possibly worse for his morals) if he doesn't.
>
> (T.P. Gill, quoted in de Vere White 1958:23)

Their controversial subject-matter was not the only cause of the sensation these novels created among reviewers and readers. Reviewers of all persuasions were exercised by the way in which these women writers (mis)used, deviated from, or challenged traditional conceptions of novelistic practice, and of art (or Art). The women's sensation novel was usually regarded as a low form, tainted by its association with a variety of familiar popular forms; it was an ephemeral, formulaic, mass-produced commodity, 'redolent of the manufactory and the shop' (Mansel 1863:483). The New Woman writers, on the other hand, were taken to task for their failure, or refusal, to conform to traditional fictional paradigms, and to observe the formal (and other) proprieties. William Barry's (1894) review of Sarah Grand's *The Heavenly Twins* is symptomatic, attacking Grand for filling pages with 'shrieking', for inappropriately combining love affairs and ideas, and writing in a manner which is 'self-conscious, or even pedantic' (295).

In short, the New Woman novel, like the sensation novel before it, represented a threat to Art. Both types of writing were regarded as the agents and symptoms of a degenerative and improper feminisation of fiction and, indeed, of an insidious (ef)feminisation of the culture at large. Thus Alfred Austin, writing in *Temple Bar* in 1869, castigates the feminine spirit of the times, noting that 'especially in the domain of Art . . . [men] have for some time been quite as subject to women . . . as is desirable . . . [and] there can be no question that, in the region of Art, their [women's] influence has been unmitigatedly mischievous' (457). In the 1860s (according to Austin), 'we have as novelists and poets only women or men with womanly vices' (465). Similarly, when W.L. Courtney (1904) turned his attention to complaints about the aesthetic decline of turn-of-the-century fiction he attributed them to the fact that 'more and more in our modern age novels are written by women for women' (xii). This fear of the feminisation, or emasculation, of art and the broader culture is a dominant feature of the gendered critical discourse by means of which both sensation fiction and the New Woman writing were judged and mediated, and which I discuss in section 4 below.

The sensationalists and the New Woman writers alike violated (or, just as importantly, were deemed to have violated) the unwritten laws governing both women novelists and the representation of women in fiction. The chief of these rules was succinctly expressed in W. Fraser Ray's (1865) essay on sensation fiction: 'From a lady novelist we naturally expect to have portraits of women which shall not be wholly untrue to nature' (189). On the contrary, the female sensationalists and the New Woman writers either implicitly questioned or directly challenged the 'naturalness' of the prescribed role of the woman writer, and of the idealised woman who was the critics' norm.

One of the most sensational aspects of these novels, much discussed in both the 1860s and the 1890s, was the apparently and variously transgressive nature of their heroines. Sensation heroines were (or were perceived to be) criminals, madwomen and domestic fiends, while the heroines of the New Woman fiction were invariably women who – either consciously and wittingly, or through force of circumstance – trangressed, rebelled against, or were deformed by constricting social pressures. The beautiful (sometimes), self-assertive, quasi-adulterous heroine of the sensation novel became, in the New Woman fiction, the destroying and/or self-destructive seeker after truth, personal fulfilment and a measure of social and sexual equality with men. The central female characters of each genre thus disrupted both prevailing fictional and social stereotyping. Similarly, the typical sensation or New Woman plot (which usually turns on a woman's sexuality, or women's role within marriage and the family) tended to foreground the female predicament in ways which challenged and problematised definitions of the feminine or of 'woman'.

Both the women's sensation novel and the New Woman fiction registered and reacted to the unfixing of gender categories which accompanied the challenges of reformers and feminists (and the counter-challenges to them) from the 1840s onwards. However, the writers I shall examine were not simply responding to a process of destabilisation, but were participating in that process. They were (in different ways, and to differing degrees) engaged in a general struggle about the definition of woman, and also about the nature, power and function of the feminine within the culture. It was this complex engagement with, and negotiation of, the dominant definitions of the feminine and the discourse on woman, which caused the women's sensation novel and the New Woman fiction to be so vigorously debated in their own day. It will certainly be my case that the cultural significance of these novels and stories in their own time, and their continuing interest to twentieth-century readers, lie in the ways in which they reproduce, rework and negotiate[6] – or afford their readers an opportunity to negotiate – the contemporary discourses on 'woman' to which I turn next.

2

The subject of Woman

Women . . . are double. They are allied with
what is regular, according to the rules, since
they are wives and mothers, and allied as
well with those natural disturbances, their
regular periods, which are the epitome of
paradox, order and disorder.
(Cixous and Clément 1987:8)

In an age when everything seems pretty well
discovered, when one cannot preserve even
a shred of mystery to cloak the bareness of
one's own life, when the very surface of the
globe is all mapped out, and the mysterious
griffins of untraversed deserts are vanishing
from the map, it is an amazing relief to
know that an unsolved, nay . . . an insol-
uble mystery is standing on one's very
hearthrug.
(*Saturday Review*, January 25, 1868:109)

The essential and eternal mystery, the sole still point of a
turning world referred to in the second extract above is, of
course, 'woman'. In this sardonic celebration of woman's
essential sameness in and of difference, her permanence in
change, the insouciant *Saturday Review*er of 1868 sought to
erase three decades of conflicting and changing definitions of
'woman', three decades of vigorous debate about woman's
nature and woman's role, in which the *Saturday Review* itself
had played an increasingly polemical part from its inception
in 1855.[7]

11

These debates concerned women's legal status and rights, particularly within marriage; women's role within the family; and their wider social role – their participation in the world of work and public affairs, and their place in a gradually developing democracy. The debates on the Woman Question (or the Woman Problem) were instigated and orchestrated by the demands made by, or on behalf of, women for the widening of their sphere, and by resistance to those demands. All shades of opinion supported their case by appeals to a particular definition of 'woman' or 'womanliness'. This definition was extremely fiercely contested in the decades upon which this study focuses, and in succeeding sections I shall look at the women's sensation novel and the New Woman fiction in relation to two distinct moments of articulation of this contest.

Broadly speaking the contest was waged on the site of the dominant definition of the 'proper feminine' – the ideal of the domestic ideology, according to which woman was defined primarily in terms of her reproductive and domestic functions within the developing bourgeois family. The feminine norm was that 'relative creature' (Basch 1974), the middle-class wife and mother. In this dual capacity woman was charged with the responsibility of acting as the keeper of the conscience, and guardian of the spiritual and moral purity of the race.

The passionless domestic ideal, the 'Angel in the House' (as the title of Coventry Patmore's poem has it), was the creator and guardian of the newly moralised and privatised domestic haven, the middle-class home, that sanctuary from what Sarah Ellis (1845) described as 'that fierce conflict of worldly interests, by which men are so deeply occupied as to be in a manner compelled to stifle their best feelings' (22–3).[8] The development of the middle-class home and family in the nineteenth century involved a new kind of division of labour: the moral and reproductive labour of the wife and mother within the private domestic sphere, and the competitive, economic, productive labour of the husband in the public sphere of industry, commerce and politics.

This ideology of the separate spheres enshrined a theory of sexual difference based on the complementariness of, rather than competitiveness between, man and woman. Woman was to wield her influence in the domestic sphere, while man exercised his power in the hazardous, hostile, public domain.

However, since the chief duty of woman (and hence women) was to sacrifice herself to the physical and emotional needs of others and, above all, to submit to her husband, woman's power was somewhat problematic, if not entirely illusory. In fact, as many feminist historians have pointed out, there was always a gap between the domestic ideology and social practice. Both men and women were involved in both spheres, although their access to (and involvement in) them varied according to gender. It was also subject to constant negotiation and redefinition throughout the century and in a variety of discursive contexts.[9]

A plethora of conduct books in the early Victorian period,[10] and magazines and periodicals throughout the century, were deployed to reinforce the dominant definition of domestic woman, to delimit the domestic sphere, and to inculcate the fundamental truth that 'the man *naturally* governs: the woman *as naturally* obeys' (Walker 1840:129, my italics). This 'natural' state of affairs was also continually in the process of construction and reproduction in legal, medical and scientific discourses, as well as in the discourse of the new social science and anthropology. Each of these areas developed definitions of woman which arose from, and authorised the claims to power of, the bourgeois male.

In particular the rapidly developing nineteenth-century sciences constructed theories of sexual difference which justified and perpetuated existing sexual and social relations and their inequalities. Spencerian evolutionists, for example, argued that in order to ensure the maximum efficiency of her reproductive function, woman's development was arrested at an earlier evolutionary stage than that of man. Later in the century Patrick Geddes and J. Arthur Thompson (1889) also emphasised woman's lowly place in the evolutionary scheme, arguing that since the male transmits the innovative traits of the species, and the female the hereditary, the woman retains traces of its more primitive aspects. Similar evolutionary arguments were also used to account for woman's supposedly inferior brain size, a physiological feature which also allied her to the 'primitive' peoples investigated by Victorian anthropologists.[11]

Medical science, which as Foucault has argued (1979:104) was one of the chief instruments for the definition and regulation of women and sexuality in the nineteenth century, represented woman as a creature totally in thrall to biology and her body. Woman's nature and her social role were seen as the inevitable consequences of her reproductive function: the womb and the ovaries controlled the delicate organism that was woman. As Henry Maudsley (1874), one of the pioneers of British psychiatry, put it: 'the male organisation is one, and the female organisation another . . . [Woman] will retain her special sphere of development and activity determined by the performance of those [reproductive] functions' (466). This particular theory of sexual difference was used, by Maudsley and others, as an argument against girls and young women being given the same education as their brothers. The rigour of such an education was deemed to be incompatible with the rigours of the menstrual cycle, and would use up the energy which should properly be conserved for reproduction. Women, Maudsley contended, 'cannot choose but to be women; cannot rebel successfully against the tyranny of their organisation'. Thus, women's campaigns for education were seen by their opponents not merely as social rebellion, but rather as a revolt against nature. Sex, Maudsley argued, 'is fundamental, lies deeper than culture, [and] cannot be ignored or defied with impunity' (1874:467).

Many nineteenth-century commentators took the view that any attempt to ignore the 'truth' of woman's indissoluble link with nature would result in 'a monstrosity – something which having ceased to be woman is not yet man' (Maudsley 1874: 477). A woman who resisted the dominant definitions was held to be 'unwomanly', ill, or, increasingly as the century wore on, unsexed – the member of an intermediate sex.[12] As Ludmilla Jordanova (1980) has pointed out, in a period of rapid and disconcerting social change 'debates about sex roles . . . hinged precisely on the ways in which sexual boundaries might become blurred' (44). Anxieties about this blurring of gender boundaries were clearly an important component of the representations of woman and women in the women's fiction of the 1860s and 1890s. They were also a crucial part of the critical response to those representations.

In scientific and medical discourses woman was represented by means of the familiar mind–body dichotomy of western thought: woman's mind in this case being determined by the biologically maternal functions of her body. By insisting on the primacy of maternity, Victorian theorists constructed woman as a body and defined her in terms of a sexual function. At the same time, paradoxically, woman was also persistently represented as non-sexual, or asexual – disembodied. One of the most influential versions of the non-sexual or passionless woman was probably William Acton's in *The Functions and Disorders of the Reproductive Organs* (first published in 1857, but reissued in numerous editions throughout the century). Acton's representation of woman is worth quoting at length, since it proved remarkably pervasive and persistent. This is the version of woman within which, and against which, both the women sensationalists and the New Woman writers worked. It is this construction of woman which they variously reproduced, challenged, or appropriated for their own purposes.

> [T]he majority of women (happily for society) are not very much troubled by sexual feeling of any kind. What men are habitually, women are only exceptionally. It is too true, I admit, as the divorce courts show, that there are some few women who have sexual desires so strong that they surpass those of men, and shock public feeling by their consequences. I admit . . . the existence of sexual excitement terminating even in nymphomania . . . but with these sad exceptions there can be no doubt that sexual feeling in the female is in the majority of cases in abeyance, and that it requires positive and considerable excitement to be roused at all. Many persons, and particularly young men, form their ideas of women's sensuous feeling from what they notice early in life among loose, or at least low and vulgar women.
>
> (Acton 1857:133)

Of course, the gentleman protests too much. His over-insistence on the absence of sexual feeling in woman inscribes a fear of female sexuality, just as his repeated affirmation of woman's disembodiment has the effect, ultimately, of representing woman as nothing but body.

Acton constructs 'proper', normal femininity as passionless and passive. A 'modest' woman, 'as a general rule . . . seldom desires any sexual gratification for herself . . . [and] submits

15

to her husband's embraces . . . principally to gratify him . . . [and] for the desire of maternity' (134). Active and autonomous sexual feeling, on the other hand, denotes masculinity, or a deviant, 'improper' femininity. Women are either non-sexual, or they are omni-sexual, criminals, madwomen, or prostitutes.

Woman was thus inscribed in a contradictory discourse, which was organised around the concept of the 'proper' or respectable feminine. The proper feminine is a system of difference which marks off woman as essentially different from man, and whose meaning depends on a series of excluded terms. These excluded terms, the proper feminine's suppressed other, together comprised what I shall call the 'improper' feminine. The system of the proper feminine may be represented by the following set of polarities (the list is by no means exhaustive): the domestic ideal, or angel in the house; the madonna; the keeper of the domestic temple; asexuality; passionlessness; innocence; self-abnegation; commitment to duty; self-sacrifice; the lack of a legal identity; dependence; slave; victim. In the economy of the improper feminine, woman is figured as a demon or wild animal; a whore; a subversive threat to the family; threateningly sexual; pervaded by feeling; knowing; self-assertive; desiring and actively pleasure-seeking; pursuing self-fulfilment and self-identity; independent; enslaver; and victimiser or predator.

Acton's representation of respectable femininity as sexual passivity, chastity, purity, innocence and, above all, sexual ignorance, drew together a number of important strands in the Victorian construction of woman. The image of woman which emerges from *Functions and Disorders* was reproduced in a variety of cultural forms: in the conduct books (most famously in Sarah Ellis's epic series on the Mothers, Daughters and Wives of England); in sketches of modern female types, and essays on morals and manners in the magazines and journals; in the heroines of domestic fiction; in the fragile, sacrificial and nun-like images of many paintings of the 1850s and 1860s,[13] and in the poetic angels in the house, such as Owen Meredith describes in his verse novel *Lucile* (1860), whose mission is 'to watch, and to wait, / to renew, to redeem, and to regenerate/ . . . to soothe, and to solace, to help and to heal' (quoted in Djikstra 1986:15).

Some aspects of this Actonian woman proved as persistent

16

as they were pervasive. The idea of female sexual passivity survived in the writings of some of the proponents of the new science of sexology at the end of the century. Havelock Ellis, for example, took the view that while a youth spontaneously developed into a man, the maiden 'must be kissed into a woman' (quoted in Weeks 1981:69). However, medical, or socio-medical, discourse also offered a counter-representation of woman, which defined feminine purity in terms of sexual activity and knowledge, rather than sexual inertia and ignorance.

George Drysdale in *The Elements of Social Science* (1860) (first published in 1854 as *Physical, Sexual, and Natural Religion*) took issue with the mass of 'erroneous feeling attaching to the subject of sexual desire in woman', arguing that 'in woman, exactly as in man, strong sexual appetites are a very great virtue; as they are the signs of a vigorous frame, healthy sexual organs, and a naturally developed sexual disposition' (1860: 170). In Drysdale's account, healthy sexual exercise was seen as the potential source of a general improvement in the physical and emotional well-being of women, and also as a cure for specific female disorders, from chlorosis to hysteria. Drysdale effectively reversed most of the prevailing views on the conditions necessary for women's reproductive and emotional health by recommending, *inter alia*: vigorous physical exercise, a profound alteration in 'female education, and the cramping views as to female decorum' and, above all, 'solid and real knowledge . . . of the human body and the human mind' (172–5). In other words, Drysdale mobilised the categories of the improper feminine in order to provide a new definition of woman, but by doing so he remained within the terms of the discourse which his own construction of woman seemed designed to challenge.

Drysdale's version of the man and woman question also entailed quite a different view of marriage from that which underpinned the bourgeois family. Marriage, the desired goal and biological destiny of Actonian woman, and of the heroine of domestic fiction, is in Drysdale's version 'one of the chief instruments in the degradation of women' (355). Drysdale's critique of marriage and the challenges it offers to the dominant discourse on woman encapsulate many of the issues which were explored by the women sensationalists and, with even

17

greater directness, by the New Woman writers. Drysdale's critique was based on a view of marriage as the perpetuator of the 'old inveterate error' – the doctrine of the separate spheres, which he held to be 'utterly incompatible with the freedom of dignified development' of woman. Marriage is also the bedrock of the double standard of sexual morality: 'the emblem . . . of all those harsh and unjust views, which have given to woman so much fewer privileges in love than man, and have punished so much more severely a breach of the moral code in her case' (355). Marriage is a form of economic and sexual enslavement for women, which 'delivers women bound into the hands of man . . . and tempts him to abuse his gift of superior strength'. Perhaps most damning of all, and most important for the representation of marriage in the novels which I shall discuss in later chapters, marriage is, in numerous cases, *legalised prostitution*' (355).

3

The subject of Woman and the subject of women's fiction

As will be clear even from my schematised and over-simplified account of two particular examples of medical discourse, nineteenth-century discourses on woman were deeply contradictory, and they became increasingly unstable during the period spanned by this study. These contradictions and instabilities constitute the ideological matrix within which and by which the women's sensation novel and the New Woman writing were produced. Both types of fiction were involved in a complex negotiation of the categories of the proper and improper feminine, and with the (apparently) opposing versions of femininity which I have associated with the names of Acton and Drysdale.

The sensation heroine, for example, cannot easily be accommodated either to the category of normal, proper femininity, nor to that of deviant, improper femininity. Sometimes, as in the case of Braddon's Aurora Floyd, or Ellen Wood's Isabel Carlyle, she might appear to be a combination of both versions of femininity, which are put into play by the complex machinery of the sensation plot. On other occasions an apparently, or actually, 'improper' heroine may be juxtaposed with the epitome of proper femininity in such a way as to redefine both categories. Lady Audley and Clara Talboys, Aurora Floyd and her cousin Lucy, Isabel Carlyle and Barbara Hare are all used in this way. In each of these cases, as the plot unfolds, the reader is continually required to rethink her conceptions of femininity and proper feminine behaviour. Similarly some of the New Woman writers continued to problematise and blur the boundaries between these two versions of femininity, while others tended to polarise them. George Egerton, for

19

example, appropriated and celebrated Drysdale's version of femininity as the type of the New Woman. Others, like Sarah Grand, reappropriated Acton's passionless woman, but put this definition of femininity to radical new uses.

The moment of the sensation novel was also one of intense public discussion about women and the law, about the state of modern marriage, and about women's role in the family. It also saw an intensely sensational reporting of the Social Evil of prostitution, and of divorce cases with their records of marital failure and sexual transgression. These issues, and the ways in which they were reported and represented in the press, provided the sensation novel with its main preoccupations and plot situations. Women's demands for education, their changing role within the family, and their rebellion against some of the constraints of proper feminine behaviour also produced a great deal of comment in the press, sometimes apoplectic, sometimes in the form of satiric sketches of modern female types, such as Eliza Lynn Linton's 'The Girl of the Period' (1868). The sensation novel was both a response to and part of this discourse on modern femininity.

By the 1890s the tone of the debate on the Woman Question became more strident (on all sides), and its terms became more sharply polarised. Not only were women's familial, social and political roles contested by the feminists and their opponents, the very nature of femininity was at stake. Female sexuality (a prominent concern of the sensation novel) came under fresh scrutiny from a number of different perspectives. The social-purity movement and the campaigns against the Contagious Diseases Acts of the 1880s had brought the discussion of sexual matters more fully into the public domain, and had mobilised the idea of the passionless woman of the proper feminine (now figured as being involved in a holy war against the lustful male) on behalf of a new programme of social regeneration. On the other hand, the developing science of sexology challenged the proponents of female sexual innocence, and subjected female sexuality to its own microscopic gaze.

Each of these perspectives led to a renewed critique of marriage, and a reassessment of women's maternal role. In the 1880s and 1890s a cacophony of voices spoke about, or claimed to speak for, woman. The 'unwomanly' antics of the 'Wild Women', the 'Revolting Daughters' and, ultimately, the New

Woman filled the pages of the journals. The New Woman novel was itself part of this cacophony, but it also put into play the various discordant voices on the Woman Question, as a means of exploring the multiple contradictions that characterised the late-Victorian conceptualisation of the feminine.

The plot situations of the women's sensation novel and the New Woman novel, and the ways in which they represented female characters, the realities of women's lives, and relations between women and between women and men, were all produced by, and as a response to, the changing and contested discourses on woman. These novels and stories also became part of that discourse: their representation of women and of women's lot became part of the current meaning of 'woman'. Repeatedly, throughout the 1860s and 1890s commentators on the contemporary scene used the sensation novel and the New Woman novel as evidence or symptom of social movements. Sensation heroines and fictional New Woman entered the general discourse as representative types of modern femininity.

Later sections will begin to investigate how the women's sensation novel and the New Woman fiction (to varying degrees and often in contradictory ways) contested the dominant definitions of woman, mobilised counter-discourses, and explored or put into play a number of anxieties about sexual difference and gender boundaries. I shall be particularly interested in the ways in which my chosen writers (with varying degrees of self-consciousness) negotiate and, sometimes, appropriate the regime of the proper feminine.

4

Fiction and the feminine: a gendered critical discourse

[In] the gender inscriptions in the mass culture debate . . . woman is positioned as a
reader of inferior literature – subjective,
emotional and passive – while man . . .
emerges as a writer of genuine, authentic
literature – objective, ironic, and in control
of his aesthetic means.

(Huyssen 1986:46)

In the cacophony of nineteenth-century voices, both male and
female, which vied with each other to speak for or about
woman and women, the novel stands out as perhaps the most
influential and widely disseminated medium in which women
spoke on their own behalf. 'The birth of the novel', as Robert
Buchanan noted in 1862, 'has given speech to many ladies
who must otherwise have been silent' (135). However, what
women could say in fiction, and how their voices were likely
to be heard, were constrained by both the prevailing discourses
on woman, and a gendered discourse on fiction, which I shall
explore in this section. This gendered discourse was particularly important in the production and mediation of the
women's sensation novel and the New Woman fiction, both
of which were regarded as feminine or feminised forms, even
when they were produced by male writers.

From its beginnings in the eighteenth century, fiction had
increasingly been regarded as a feminised form, and this
association became even more important in shaping its production and dissemination in the nineteenth century. Paradoxically it both fostered the growth of women's writing, and

22

constituted a major problem for fiction in general and women writers in particular, since it generated a series of permissions and constraints which delimited the scope both of the novel and of women's writing. Notably, as Jane Spencer (1986) has argued (in relation to the rise of the novel in the eighteenth century), 'this feminization of literature defined [it] as a special category supposedly outside the political arena, with an influence on the world as indirect as women's was supposed to be' (xi). More contentiously, Nancy Armstrong (1987) has represented the rise of the female and/or feminised novel as the 'agent and product' of a feminisation of culture, by means of which women (and the domain of the feminine in general) produced and reproduced bourgeois patriarchy. The novel, which 'early on assumed the distinctive features of a specialized language for women', was responsible, in Armstrong's view, for a gendering of discourse which 'concealed the politics of writing' by transforming political differences into differences 'rooted in gender' (28, 30).

My own concern here is less with the gendering of the discourse *of* fiction, than with the development of a gendered discourse *on* fiction, and with the role of that discourse in the production and mediation of fiction – especially fiction by women. My interest is in the various, and variously contested, ways in which nineteenth-century critical discourse represented fiction as a feminine or feminised form, and with the various and changing meanings it assigned to the feminine. I do not see the gendered discourse on fiction (as Armstrong sees the gendered discourse of fiction) in terms of a simple binary opposition in which 'female writing – writing that was considered appropriate for or could be written by women – in fact designated itself as feminine, which meant that other writing, by implication, was understood to be male' (Armstrong 1987:28). On the contrary, I shall suggest that the gendered discourse on fiction was part of a broadly based nineteenth-century crisis of gender definition, and that the unstable, shifting and multivalent nature of the gendered terms of this critical discourse was bound up with a desire to fix gender boundaries and categories at a time of profound anxiety about the nature and fixity of those categories. I shall also suggest that the gendered discourse on fiction was a site of struggle between differently structured oppositions of masculinity and feminin-

23

ity, and between contending versions of the feminine. It should be seen (*pace* Armstrong) not as part of a process of depoliticising fiction, but rather as part of a political struggle about both the meaning of gender, and the representational authority of fiction.

Many of the complexities and contradictions of the gendered discourse on writing are evident in Alfred Austin's unsigned essay on Swinburne published in *Temple Bar* in 1869. Austin raises the spectre (increasingly familiar in the nineteenth century) of a feminine invasion of the 'domain of Art'. The golden age of the 'manly and masculine art' (463) of Scott has (in this account) been overtaken by 'the feminine temper of the times' (465), whose representative figure is Trollope: 'a feminine novelist, writing for women in a womanly spirit and from a woman's point of view' (464). Austin's analysis of contemporary writing is structured around gendered oppositions: an expansive, masculine aesthetic is opposed to a limited and limiting feminine one, and two contradictory versions of the realm of the feminine are opposed to each other.

Austin's essay provides a very clear and representative example of the way in which the nineteenth-century discourse on fiction organises the domain of art, like that of femininity itself, around the concepts of the proper and the improper feminine. The proper feminine (of which Trollope is the exemplar) is domestic. Its locus is the nursery or the drawing room, its main topic 'the sentimental love of youths and maidens, of coy widows and clumsy middle-aged men, beginning in flirtation and ending in marriage . . . pretty, pious, half-comical domestic love – love within the bounds of social law' (Austin 1869:467). The improper feminine, on the other hand, denotes the domestic ideal's dangerous other. It is 'the feminine element at work when it has ceased to be domestic; when it has quitted the modest precincts of home, and courted the garish lights of an intense and warm publicity' (469). The fictional terrain of the improper feminine (which, to compound the impropriety, is occupied in the main by women novelists) is 'the love – had we better call it the lust? – which begins with seduction and ends in desertion . . . whose agreeable variations are bigamy, adultery, and, in fact, illicit passion of every conceivable sort' (467–8).

The 'improper feminine' does not simply denote what is

24

represented but, more importantly, describes a mode of representation. It not only treats of sexual promiscuity, but it is also characterised by promiscuous forms of representation. 'It is the feminine element . . . unrestrainedly rioting in any and every area of life in which an indiscriminating imagination chooses to place it' (469). Austin's 'proper feminine' also denotes the separate feminine sphere to which, from the eighteenth century onwards, novels by or for women were usually assigned. The dominant forms of this feminised fiction in the nineteenth century were moral, didactic and domestic, and it habitually focused on private experience. Women's writing in its proper feminine mode was associated with, indeed supposedly derived from, woman's affective nature and familial role. Women writers were to provide a 'happy and improving influence' in all those branches of literature which are 'most nearly connected with the welfare of mankind, and tend to dignify and exalt our nature'. Such writing was deemed to be particularly suited to the circumstances of domestic woman, since its 'successful exercise demands little or none of that moral courage which more public avocations require' (these quotations Parkes 1865:121).

Even when its subject-matter or form was romance, the prevailing or preferred mode of the proper feminine was realistic. On the whole, contemporary reviewers and theorists of fiction considered realism (and especially domestic realism) to be peculiarly appropriate for women writers, as it supposedly reflected or acted as the vehicle for their limited experience, and their particular limited powers. Robert Buchanan equated the rise of the female novel with the rise of realism.

> Realism has served at least one admirable purpose – that of bringing women prominently before the public as book writers. The lady-novelists are the most truthful of all aesthetic photographers. Narrow as their range necessarily is, they have been encouraged to describe thoughts and emotions with which men are of necessity unfamiliar . . . Disciplined in a school of suffering, closely observant of detail, and painfully dependent on the caprice of the male sex, they essay to paint in works of art the everyday emotions of commonplace or imaginative women,

25

and the domestic experience of sensible daughters, wives and mothers.

(Buchanan 1862:134–5)

Feminine realism and, by extension, domestic realism in general were thus defined in terms of woman's nature and woman's social role. Given the prevailing views of woman, and also the actualities of women's lives, it is not surprising that feminine realism was repeatedly defined as a lack. According to R.H. Hutton (1858), for example, women were realists *faute de mieux*, as a consequence of the 'main deficiency of feminine genius' which 'can observe . . . recombine . . . [and] delineate' (474), but can go no further. In short, the contemporary discourse on realism characterised representation by women as the representation of surfaces. Women writers were deemed capable of submitting everyday events to minute scrutiny, but lacked the power of 'generalization' and 'reasoning' (*London Review* 1860:137). Men 'have more imagination and can generalize character better than women but they often fail in detail', whereas 'a passion for the detail is the distinguishing mark of nearly every female novelist' (Courtney 1904:x). Women's superior powers of observation were, however, crucially limited by the fact that they 'can describe, or rather transcribe with success only those scenes and characters which come under their observation' (*Fraser's* 1860:213).

Women's writing and the fiction of the proper feminine were thus contained within and constrained by a limiting aesthetic of realism, which was also, in part, a limiting aesthetic of feeling. Both the qualities and the limitations of feminine surface realism were directly attributed to categories in which the essential and the contingent were elided. The limited qualities of domestic realism were attributed to (what were seen as) essential properties of the feminine, such as woman's 'greater affectionateness, her greater range and depth of emotional experience' (Lewes 1852:131). These limited qualities were also, at the same time, the product of the contingent particularities of women's subordinate social role; for example, that 'marvellous faculty of sympathy and intuition' which supposedly enabled woman to 'divine much which she cannot discover, and to conceive much which she has never seen and heard'

26

is a faculty 'given to those who have felt profoundly and suffered long' (Greg 1859:49).

The economy of the improper feminine was similarly associated with feeling, in this case with the excessive or 'effeminate' feeling of a potentially uncontrollable feminine emotionalism. Like the proper feminine, the improper feminine was also defined in terms of an over-reliance on detail. One of its main characteristics was said to be a sensuous surrendering to detail, particularly in the representation of physical sensation and sexual feeling. The gendered critical discourse thus perpetuated two main ways of viewing women's writing, or feminine writing: it was seen either in terms of a limited detailism – a world of surfaces and sympathy – or as a riot of detail and promiscuous emotion.

The association of female writers and, by analogy, domestic realism in general with surfaces, detail and emotion, rather than with depth and significant pattern, persisted into the 1890s, when realism had become more firmly established, more scientific, and more masculinised. A *Quarterly Review* article on the New Woman fiction in 1894 reiterated the idea that feminine realism derives from woman's affective nature and her subordinate social position.

> [Women] observe minute traits of conduct; they spy unconsciously upon the men their masters, and learn the signals which betoken storm and sunshine . . . when a woman sits down to write a story, she is exercising the same kind of faculties that enable her to overcome mere strength by delicacy of interpretation and natural tact.
>
> (Barry 1894:305)

The resulting fictional form is said to be disagreeable and unscientific. Female observation, it is argued, produces works of instinct rather than 'exact mensuration', and the 'aboriginal' in woman 'accordingly will never be scientific; it will be passion seizing the weapons of the male and brandishing them for stage effect' (296).

Naomi Schor (1987) has recently gone so far as to suggest that there is a gendered aesthetic of the detail in European culture. Schor traces the process by which woman, largely because of her childbearing role, is first aligned with a devalorised nature (as opposed to the masculine realm of culture);

27

then with mimesis, since 'her close association with nature means that she cannot but replicate it' (17); and finally with the details of representational art. Schor suggests that in western aesthetics 'unvalorised' feminine detailism is associated with both the homely plainness of (for example) the Dutch school of painting (the proper feminine) and, paradoxically, with the ornamental style (another version of the improper feminine perhaps), which is seen as profuse and lacking in 'masculine' clarity, rigour and rational severity.

Schor argues that, particularly in nineteenth-century France, there was a 'remarkably coherent discourse on the detail' in which,

> the totalizing ambitions of a realism that claims to account for the entire domain of the visible are deplored . . . the loss of difference between the insignificant . . . is . . . lamented . . . [and] the invasion of the arts by an anarchic mass of details is pronounced the unmistakeable sign of cultural dissolution.
>
> (Schor 1987:43)

Although pervasive, this discourse on the detail was, in England at least, far from coherent. Its contradictions are evident in the conflicting and contested values attached to particular gendered terms. For example, in the debates about naturalism (which I explore below) its opponents habitually associated the naturalist project either with the limited feminine, or with a debased masculinity; the latter was expressed either as effeminacy or as a coarse and brutal virility (or sometimes as a combination of the two). On the other hand, naturalists and their supporters, both male and female, attempted to empty the detail of its limiting feminine connotations, or alternatively to endow it with value by incorporating it in a masculine discourse of judgement, professionalism, labour, system and science.

Contradictions and incoherence notwithstanding, the gendered discourse on the detail was clearly an important component of the discourse on fiction in nineteenth-century England. It is central to the mid-century debates on realism and verisimilitude which coincided with the moment of the sensation novel, and it is also an important element in the later debates on naturalism and the New Realism within which the New

28

Woman fiction was produced. The next two sections attempt a brief analysis of the operations of this gendered discourse in the mediation of the women's sensation novel and the New Woman fiction.

5

Fiction, the feminine and the sensation novel

In the moral panic that surrounded the debate about sensation fiction, the gendered discourse on fiction intersected with a materialist or, more properly, a frustrated idealist discourse.[14] One of the chief objections to sensation fiction was that it was (at least in the opinion of middle-class reviewers) a commodity, produced (and deformed) by market forces, and directed at the appetites of consumers. 'Its object is an intensely commercial one', wrote Robert Buchanan in 1862. 'It appeals not to the sympathies of the educated few, but those of the general public' (136).

The form, style and content of sensation fiction were seen as being directly shaped and determined by contemporary changes in literary production and distribution. In particular, the spread of periodicals, and their development of the 'violent stimulant of serial publication' (Oliphant 1862:569) were widely condemned as being responsible for the 'perverted and vitiated taste' for extravagant and sensational plots (*Fraser's* 1863:262). The most detailed elaboration of this thesis came from Henry Mansel in a *Quarterly Review* article which attributed an inevitable lack of aesthetic integrity to a specific mode of literary production (the periodical) which 'from its very nature, must contain many articles of an ephemeral interest, and of the character of goods made to order'. One of the chief evils of the periodical was the stimulus it allegedly provided for the production of tales of 'the marketable stamp, which, after appearing piecemeal in weekly or monthly instalments, generally enter upon a second stage of their insect-life in the form of a handsome reprint under the auspices of the circulating library' (Mansel 1863:484). Mansel had the usual highbrow's disdain for this latter institution, which he described as a 'hot-bed for forcing a crop of writers without talent and readers without discrimination', and (mixing his metaphors) as a kind of department store for women shoppers: '[I]t is to literature what a *magasin des modes* is to dress, giving us the latest fashion and little more' (ibid.). The growing practice of 'railway reading' was also seen as a significant element in the shaping of the literary market-place. Mansel was not alone in identify-ing the sensation novel as the typical offering of the railway bookstall, which enticed the 'hurried passenger' with 'some-thing hot and strong', promising 'temporary excitement to relieve the dulness [*sic*] of the journey' (Mansel 1863:485).[15] In short the style, form, subject-matter and, above all, the quality of sensation fiction are over-determined by the ephemerality built into its production and distribution.

This emphasis on mechanistic, commercial production, and passive, appetitive consumption, marked the sensation novel as a feminine form, irrespective of the gender of the particular sensation author. Mass-produced for mass-consumption, based on repeated and hence predictable formulae, sensation fiction was by definition 'feminine', according to the terms of a gen-dered critical discourse in which the masculine (positive) term was reserved for work that offered itself as the unique expression of individual genius. For example, both sensation fiction and Spasmodic poetry[16] were concerned with 'convul-sive throes in the soul'. However, in terms of the prevailing critical discourse, Spasmodic poetry (a form associated exclus-ively with male writers) is 'art' (or Art) because the poet 'writes to satisfy the unconquerable yearnings of his soul'. Sensation fiction, on the other hand, is inferior art, or not art at all, because only 'the market-law of supply and demand' presides over its birth, and it is tainted by 'a commercial atmosphere . . . redolent of the manufactory and the shop' (all quotations Mansel 1863:483). The sensation debate is thus, in part, an example of that process of stratification along gender lines which Andreas Huyssen (1986) has noted as a feature of the categorisation of mass culture: 'The notion . . . gained ground during the nineteenth century that mass culture is somehow associated with woman while real, authentic culture remains the prerogative of men' (47). The role of the feminine in demar-cating the division between high and low culture may be seen as a function of the marginality of women and the feminine within patriarchy. Julia Kristeva has argued that women's marginal position in patriarchal society places them at the borderline of the symbolic order.[17] Viewed thus, woman becomes the frontier between the order of man and chaos. In this particular case woman and women become the borderline between the order of high art, and the chaos of the endlessly proliferating products of a mechanised culture. Woman's position at this cultural borderline, as at others, is shifting and ambivalent. Neither inside nor outside the frontiers of high culture, she is always in danger of receding into the chaos that lies beyond its gates.

Although many of the main critical anxieties about sensation fiction can be traced to the way in which the gendered discourse on fiction marks it as implicitly feminine, most contemporary reviewers found the prominence of actual women in its production and consumption even more alarming than this covert femininity of the form. Despite the success and greater critical visibility of male sensation writers such as Wilkie Collins and Charles Reade, sensation fiction was perceived mainly as a feminine phenomenon. Many, perhaps most, of the reviewers' objections to the genre, and their anxieties about it, derive from their perception of it as a form written by women, about women and, on the whole, for women. 'This is the age of lady novelists', wrote E.S. Dallas in *The Times* (November 18, 1862:4), and the lady novelists and especially the sensation novels they wrote gave a new (and to many reviewers an undue) prominence to the role and point of view of the female characters. In doing so they transformed the fictional representation of women. 'If the heroines have the first place,' as Dallas noted, 'it will scarcely do to represent them as passive and quite angelic, or as insipid – which heroines usually are. They have to be high-strung women, full of passion, purpose and movement' (ibid.). Sensation fiction was also in many cases clearly *addressed* to women. M.E. Braddon's and Ellen Wood's narrators in particular often use a woman-to-woman address, and assume or invoke a shared feminine experience. Although this was a common feature of women's fiction it was a particular source of anxiety to reviewers of the sensation novel because of the 'fast' nature of its main characters and situations, and because of the particular type of female experience which it represented.

The contemporary reviewers' perception of sensation fiction as a feminine or feminised form exposes many of the contradictions of the gendered discourse on fiction. Indeed the debate about the sensation novel reveals the fragmentation of mid-Victorian conceptions of the feminine. One of the central paradoxes of the sensation debate was its tendency to define the sensation novel as a form which was both characteristically feminine, and profoundly unfeminine, or even anti-feminine. According to one set of the terms of the contemporary discourse on fiction, sensation fiction was stereotypically feminine because it was produced by women writers working within their 'natural' feminine limitations as minute, faithful observers of everyday domestic settings in plots focusing on family life. Sensation fiction thus belonged to the domain of the proper feminine, to the feminised, detailistic 'coat and waistcoat' school of realism (Lewes 1865:187). *East Lynne*, for example, although condemned for its extravagant plotting and false morality, was praised for its faithful recording of 'the gossip and petty squabbles of a country town', which 'are evidently sketched from nature' (*Fraser's* 1863:253). However, despite their faithful transcriptions of the surfaces of provincial life, sensation novels were seen as deviating from the realist criteria of the proper feminine because they disappointed the 'natural' expectation that 'a lady novelist' would produce 'portraits of women which shall not be wholly untrue to nature' (Ray 1865:189). Here, once more, we encounter a discourse on realism which prescribes both how women may represent and how woman may be represented. Mary Elizabeth Braddon was censured for defying these unwritten rules of representation in her portrayal of Lady Audley. 'In drawing her, the authoress may have intended to portray a female Mephistopheles; but if so, she should have known that a woman cannot fill such a part' (Ray 1865:186).

Sensation fiction was seen not simply as a failure of realistic representation, but also as an (injudicious) attempt to extend the domain of fictional representation. It was part of 'the tendency of the present age towards investigation' and towards 'the morbid analysation of mere sensation' (*Fraser's* 1860:210). This attempted extension of the field of representation (like that of the naturalists in the 1880s and 1890s) was seen as a misrepresentation, because it presented the extraordinary as typical. The sensation novel was also seen as a 'reaction against realism' (Buchanan 1862:136) in its mixing of 'the incredible' and the documentary, its refusal to stay within the proper sphere of acceptable character types in domestic settings, and its habit of transporting 'lurid people' from 'the universal gaze' of 'our courts of law, and the communicative columns of the daily papers' to 'our domestic hearths' (Buchanan 1862: 424, 422).

Sensation fiction was thus both *dismissed* as *merely* a feminine form and also feared and censured as a non- or even anti-feminine form – a form which was not only deviant, but also threatening and dangerous. Both the subject-matter of sensation fiction, and its dominant modes of representation, transgressed socially acceptable norms of the proper feminine. Margaret Oliphant (1867), for example, found it profoundly ironic that the sudden increase in women novelists should have resulted in 'a display of what in woman is most unfemi-nine' (259). For many critics the sensation novel most obviously entered the transgressive domain of the improper feminine in its treatment of sexuality, particularly female sexuality. In this respect sensation novels were doubly transgressive. They did not simply portray women as sexual beings; they also dwelt on the details of women's sexual response in a 'very fleshly and unlovely record' (ibid.).

> [The sensation heroine] waits now for flesh and muscles, for strong arms that seize her, and warm breath that thrills her . . . and a host of other physical attractions . . . The peculiarity of it in England is that it is oftenest made from the woman's side – that this intense appreci-ation of flesh and blood, this eagerness of physical sen-sation, is represented as the natural sentiment of English girls.
>
> (Oliphant 1867:259)

This is more than just the predictable moralising objection to the fact of the representation of sexuality. It is also an objection to the nature of that representation, to the proliferation of sensuous detail and the detailed representation of physical sensation. In the critical response to sensation fiction, the gendered discourse on the detail referred to earlier (pp. 27–8) is deployed to focus on the sensation novel's detailed representation of the female body. Many of these 'fast novelists' were alleged to be 'deeply enamoured of the female form', which they present 'as seductively as the nature of their art will admit of' (Austin 1870a:184). Braddon's tendency to anatomise the female body was a subject of particular discussion and ridicule – W. Fraser Ray (1865) was just one of the critics who had great fun cataloguing the number and nature of the references to the hair of her heroines. In short, contemporary reviewers repeatedly identified sensation fiction as a form of writing the body, and hence as a deviation from the proper feminine. The sensation novel was also assigned to the domain of the improper feminine because of the way it *read* the body, or *produced a reading* in the body, by its 'appeal to the nerves rather than to the heart' (*Christian Remembrancer* 1863: 210), to the animal passions and instincts rather than to the reason:

> This lower level, this drop from the empire of reason and self-control, is to be traced throughout this class of literature, which is a constant appeal to the animal part of our nature, and avows a preference for its manifestation, as though power and intensity come through it.
>
> (ibid.: 212)

6

Representation and the feminine: engendering fiction in the 1890s

Naturalism and the New Realism, two of the main areas of
fictional innovation in the late nineteenth century, were in
some ways attempts to masculinise the novel.[18] From George
Henry Lewes's ironic complaints about 'the melancholy fact
. . . that the group of female authors is becoming every year
more multitudinous and more successful' (1850:189), and
George Eliot's satiric diatribe against 'Silly novels by lady
novelists' (1856), to George Moore's animadversions on the
power of the circulating libraries (1885), and Edmund Gosse's
on the 'tyranny of the novel' (1892), writers and critics (male
and female) complained about the dominance of women as
producers and consumers of fiction, and of feminine concerns
in the novel.

Gaye Tuchman and Nina Fortin have recently gone so far
as to represent the history of fiction in the nineteenth century
as a battle of the sexes in which feminine forms and female
writers were progressively 'edged out' by masculine forms and
norms (Tuchman 1989). Although their account has a certain
dramatic appeal, it is, I think, a radical over-simplification. The
nineteenth-century battle of the books was not simply a battle
of the sexes, although it increasingly became part of the sex
war. It was rather a battle that was waged on the terrain of
gender; it was part of a contest about the meaning of gender,
and about how and by whom gender is to be defined.

The controversies within which the New Woman fiction was
produced cannot be separated from the controversies surrounding the new naturalism and the Fiction of Sex. The New
Fiction debate was also part of a broader panic about degeneration which was, to a great extent, articulated as a set of

responses to literary texts. These debates in the 1880s and 1890s were the site of a contest about representation in which questions of aesthetic representation – who or what might be represented in fiction, in what manner, by whom and for whom – were deeply enmeshed with debates about political representation, about gender and the representation of gender, and also with pervasive anxieties about cultural and political authority and control.

The debates were conducted in terms of a changing discourse on representation and the feminine, and were part of a more general contest in which the question of women's right to self-representation played an increasingly important part. For example, in the 1880s the male writer's success as a realist might be gauged by his 'unequalled knowledge of the mysterious workings of woman's mind and heart . . . and truth to nature' (Norman 1883:834–5). Alternatively, the naturalist's decadence was linked to his 'almost unholy knowledge of the nature of woman', which made the reader feel 'intrusive and unmanly' (Lang 1887:537). As female writers increasingly questioned the authority by which any male writer might claim to know and represent the truth of woman, the authority of female experience was invoked against the authority of 'masculine' modes of representation. In 'A dialogue on novels', for example, Vernon Lee claimed a privileged authority for actual female experience over the claims of French naturalism to know and represent the real meaning of a particular 'immoral' woman: 'I have known such a woman,' her young Englishwoman asserts, 'known the full meaning of such a woman . . . I understood that woman's real meaning' (Lee 1885:401). The representation of a woman's real meaning became particularly contentious in the production and reception of the New Woman fiction in the 1890s.

The late nineteenth-century controversies about realism, naturalism, the representation of woman and the representation of sexuality were also, in part (as was the debate about sensation fiction), debates about the organisation of the book trade, and about censorship. All of these issues raised important questions about cultural authority; indeed they arose from a crisis of cultural authority. Several *causes célèbres* of the 1880s – the responses of the press to Zolaism; its treatment of the trials of Henry Vizetelly, the publisher of English translations

37

of Zola; the debate on censorship initiated by George Moore in the *Pall Mall Gazette* in 1884, and in his *Literature at Nurse* (1885) – turned on the question of the franchise of fiction: to whom and on behalf of whom might it speak? What subjects might it address? Who might determine and control its dissemination?

These debates were shaped by attitudes to emerging political groups, notably women and the newly literate masses. George Moore, a champion of naturalism and opponent of censorship, explicitly defined his project for reforming fiction in terms of extending its franchise beyond its usual constituency of 'young girls and widows of sedentary habits' (Moore 1976 [1884]:28). As D.H. Lawrence was later to do, Moore equated the extension of the range of representation in fiction with the extension of the franchise. He declared that the realisation of his desire for a more inclusive fiction representing the 'nervous passionate life' of the nineteenth century 'would be as far reaching in its effects, as the biggest franchise bill ever planned' (Moore 1976 [1885]:22).[19]

The debate about the New Fiction's extension of the franchise of fiction was also a debate about changing social relations and shifts of cultural authority, and this debate was, in turn, bound up with continuing anxieties about the rising power of the market-place and of a mass readership. Proponents of the new writing claimed the cultural authority of an artistic integrity which they saw as being threatened by the repressive philistinism of commercialism, and by the material conditions of the production and distribution of fiction. Opponents deplored the fact that, despite condemnation by critical authorities, some of the new writing sold in large quantities. In both cases the market and readers were seen as usurping the authority of artists and/or existing critical institutions.

Issues of gender and class figured prominently in this contest over cultural authority. George Moore, for example, objected to the fact that a 'mere tradesman' dared 'question the sacred right of the artist to obey the impulses of his temperament' (Moore 1976 [1885]:7), and protested that 'those who would press forward towards the light of truth' (16) were impeded by an alliance of philistine commercialism and a particular version of the feminine. A feminised commercialism, and the authority of 'the taste of two ladies in the country' (whose objection to a scene in Moore's *A Modern Lover* led to its withdrawal from Mudie's list) were said to produce a feminised literature: 'a kind of advanced school book, a sort of guide to marriage and the drawing room' (Moore 1976 [1884]:32).

> Instead of being allowed to fight with and amid, the thoughts and aspirations of men, literature is now rocked to an ignoble rest in the motherly arms of the librarian . . . that from which he turns the breast dies like a vagrant's child.
>
> (Moore 1976 [1885]:18)

While the advocates of the New Fiction protested against the limitations placed upon fiction by its consumption (and, in the case of women writers, its production) within the domestic space, its opponents claimed the authority to prevent the invasion of the domestic space (specifically those domestic spaces housing women, children and the lower orders) by 'pernicious literature'.

The role of fiction's predominantly female audience in the delimitation of the representable was foregrounded in the 'Candour in English fiction' discussion in the *New Review* (1890), in which Walter Besant defended the views of 'philistine', 'Average Opinion' and the 'cultured class of British Women' against 'your literature of free and adulterous love' (7), and (on the other side) Eliza Lynn Linton and Thomas Hardy argued that 'fiction should not be shackled by conventions concerning budding womanhood' (Hardy 1890:20). Reversing the purity campaigners' fears about the feminisation that might result from wanton representation, Linton argued that it was 'the repressive power of the British matron' that would produce an 'emasculation' of the fiction of a 'strong-headed and masculine nation' (Linton 1890: 10).

Ultimately Linton and Hardy argued for a kind of proportional representation: superior minority fiction for sophisticated mature readers. Both writers, in effect, restated the case for separate spheres of fiction based on sexual difference: on the one hand, the domestic, feminine sphere of novels suitable for women and young persons; on the other, the wider, public sphere of 'masculine literature'. Besant's theories of fiction and his view of the limits of the representable also derived from theories of sexual difference. His contribution to the 'Candour' discussion figured the world as a gendered book, in which masculine life is simultaneously fuller but less open to representation than that of the proper feminine. 'Certainly', he wrote, 'there is a chapter in the lives of many men which they would not publish . . . [but] as for women – those above a certain level – there is never any closed chapter at all in their lives' (Besant 1890: 11). In the 1880s and 1890s, in the social purity campaigns, in medical discourse and in fiction – above all in the New Woman writing – the closed chapters of male life and the supposedly missing chapters of female life were increasingly rendered representable, and opened to view.

By the mid-1890s the gendered terms of the discourse on fictional representation became increasingly unstable and contested. Arthur Waugh's 1894 essay 'Reticence in literature' argued that the style and the substance of the New Fiction of the 1890s were the result of a fusion of two developments of realism. These he represented in terms of a narrative of the convergence of debased gender stereotypes: the effeminate and the coarse and brutal masculine; the sensual and the 'chirugical'; 'the language of the courtesan' and the language of the 'bargee' (217). This analysis contested the naturalists' attempts to appropriate realism for a 'masculine' science. In Waugh's account realism is simultaneously masculine (applying the microscope in the study) and effeminate.

Art . . . claims every subject for her own . . . Most true. But there is all the difference in the world between drawing life as we find it, *sternly* and *relentlessly* surveying it all the while from outside with the *calm, unflinching gaze of criticism*, and, on the other hand, *yielding ourselves to the warmth and colour of its excesses, losing our judgement* . . . becoming in a word, *effeminate*.
(Waugh 1894:210, my italics)

Despite the fact that many writers of the New Fiction employed non-naturalistic modes and eschewed the naturalist stance of scientific objectivity, discussions of the 'modern woman novel' recapitulated and recirculated many of the terms of the discourse on naturalism. Attacks on the 'super-subtlety', 'microscopic self-examination', and 'worship of ugliness' of the New Woman fiction reproduced the discourse of the earlier

40

attacks on naturalism. However, as Penny Boumelha (1982) has pointed out, some of the terms of this discourse changed their value in the 1890s, as 'the vocabulary of realism, itself seen comparatively recently as outrageous, was rapidly pressed into service to accuse these new writers of disproportion in their emphasis on the sexual' (68). J.A. Noble's (1895) condemnation of Sarah Grand's *The Heavenly Twins* for its 'flagrant violation of the obvious proportion of life' typifies this process. Noble argued that 'the new fiction of sexuality presents . . . a series of pictures painted from reflections in convex mirrors, the colossal nose which dominates the face being represented by one colossal appetite which dominates life' (492–3). Critics like Noble did not simply appropriate the vocabulary of realism, they also appropriated key elements of the anti-realist discourse of the 1880s: for example, its condemnation of realism's failure to select, and of its morbid, tasteless inclusiveness of range; and also the idea that to include everything is to distort, to bring everything within the field of representation is to misrepresent.

The representation and misrepresentation of women were central to the controversy on the New Woman fiction. Champions of the 'novel of the Modern Woman', like W.T. Stead, linked women's fictional self-representation directly to progressive social change. Others, such as Hugh Stutfield (who conducted a one-man crusade against the New Woman and all her works), contested and undercut women's claims to fictional self-representation. For Stutfield, as for many of its critics, the New Woman writing was an articulation of the obsessional interiority and self-scrutiny of late nineteenth-century woman in general, and of feminism in particular. In the New Fiction, woman 'turn[s] herself inside out'; she does not simply bare her soul but dissects it, 'analysing and probing into the innermost crannies of her nature . . . for ever examining her mental self in the looking-glass' (Stutfield 1897:105). Like many commentators Stutfield makes it clear that this is a distorting mirror.

If the New Woman writing was a distortion of reality, the woman writer was a distortion of nature. Within the terms of a discourse which defined her as a mere copyist or detailist, a woman could only become an artist by throwing off 'the habit of her sex' (Waugh 1894:210). Thus by aspiring to be an

41

artist, rather than merely a woman writer, a woman automatically unsexed herself.

> The man lives by ideas; the woman by sensations; and while the man remains an artist so long as he holds true to his own view of life, the woman becomes one as soon as she throws off the habit of her sex, and learns to rely upon her judgement, and not her senses. It is only when we regard life with the untrammelled view of the impartial spectator . . . that we approximate to the artistic temperament. It is unmanly, it is effeminate, it is inartistic to gloat over pleasure, to revel in immoderation.
>
> (ibid.)

The gendered discourse on fiction thus attempts to contain women's writing within a limiting aesthetic of feeling: women's writing is a literature of the nerves, it is hysterical, 'intuitive rather than intellectual', and it owes 'nothing whatever to the reason or the research of man' (Stutfield 1897:110). This linking of the feminine in writing with intuition and feeling simultaneously limits women's writing and renders it threatening. There is a constant fear that feminine feeling will erupt and invade the masculine domain of judicious impartiality. Thus the main danger posed by the French writer – that longstanding bogeyman of degeneracy – was his possession of a 'kind of feminine intuition . . . which brings with it the dangers of all excited feeling' (Barry 1892:482).

Like French (or French-influenced) naturalism, the New Woman novel was seen as the literary expression of destabilising democratic tendencies, or even of revolutionary excess. It was part of a general invasion of the culture by the feminine, a symptom and cause of degeneration, disease and effeminacy, and a threat to the nation's safety. Continental influence was blamed for the 'predilection for the foul and repulsive' in the pathological novel, and for generating that hysteria which, 'whether in politics or art, has the same inevitable effect of sapping manliness and making people flabby'. As in the earlier debates on naturalism, British manliness was offered as the antidote to feminine and continental decadence: '[I]n this country, at any rate, amid much flabbiness and effeminacy there is plenty of good sense and manliness left' (all quotations Stutfield 1895:843).

Nowhere are the contradictions of the gendered discourse on fiction more evident than in its figuring of women as both cause and cure of the New Fiction. On the one hand, women were characterised as neurotic, hysterical, morbidly introspective, slaves of the sensuous and sensual, and the producers (or, in some less direct way, originators) of a pathological fiction which threatened to undermine healthy, rational, male civil society. Women were the chief culprits in spreading the modern spirit of revolt through their 'booming of books' which are 'close to life'. On the other hand, since 'in all matters relating to decency and good taste men gladly acknowledge the supremacy of women' (Stutfield 1895:844), women were called upon to exercise their moral superiority and form an alliance with the philistines to discourage the production and circulation of such books.

The gendered discourse I have been outlining yearns nostalgically for the stability of 'the old ideals of discipline and duty, of manliness and self-reliance in men, and womanliness in woman' (Stutfield 1895:845), but is riven with anxieties about the very possibility of a stable discourse on gender. This desire to affix particular stable values to each gender category, and the accompanying anxiety about the possibilities of stability, are not only characteristic of the discourse on fiction in the last two decades of the nineteenth century, they are also prominent features of much of the fiction of the 1890s, especially of the New Woman novel.

Part II

The Sentimental and Sensational Sixties: The Limits of the Proper Feminine

7

Historicising genre (1): the cultural moment of the woman's sensation novel

> Genre is a socio-historical as well as a formal entity. Transformations in genre must be considered in relation to social changes.
>
> (Todorov 1984:80)

The sensation novel was perhaps the chief sensation of the 'sensational sixties'. Contemporary reviewers of the mid-Victorian literary scene described it as an entirely new form of fiction, which burst dramatically upon an unsuspecting but eager public, dislodging the domestic novel – the stereotypical fictional form of the proper feminine – from its position of dominance. 'Two or three years ago', lamented the *Edinburgh Review* in 1864, 'nobody would have known what was meant by a *sensation novel*. Yet now the term . . . [is] adopted as the regular commercial name for a particular product of industry for which there is just now a brisk demand' (quoted in Tillotson 1969: xi). Later investigators of the sensation phenomenon (such as Kathleen Tillotson, P.D. Edwards and Winifred Hughes) have echoed this rather sensationalised version of literary history, in which the sensation novel is figured as a disruption of the comparative calm of a middle-class fiction market dominated by domestic tales with a moralising bent. The distinctive features of this new novelistic mode were its passionate, devious, dangerous and not infrequently deranged heroines, and its complicated, mysterious plots – involving crime, bigamy, adultery, arson and arsenic. Perhaps most shocking of all was the fact that these 'fast' novels of passion and crime were all set in the context of the otherwise mundane domestic life of a contemporary middle-class or aristocratic

47

English household, and that they were both read and written largely by women.

Although women, as producers, consumers or subjects, were at the centre of the sensation debates, comparatively few contemporary commentators addressed the interesting question of why women should have played such a key role in the rise of the sensation novel. Margaret Oliphant was one who did, arguing that female sensation fiction was, among other things, the woman writer's protest against the double standard on the issue of sexual purity. However, she was chiefly interested in condemning rather than analysing this fact, and took the view that women's reading and writing of sensation fiction were a betrayal of both their essential womanhood and their womanliness.

> It is a shame to women so to write; and it is a shame to the women who read and accept as a true representation of themselves and their ways the equivocal talk and fleshly inclinations herein attributed to them. Their patronage of such books is in reality an adoption and acceptance of them. It may be done in carelessness. It may be done in that mere desire for something startling which the monotony of ordinary life is apt to produce; but it is debasing to everybody concerned.
>
> (Oliphant 1867:274–5)

The Victorians' comparative silence on the nature of the attractions of the genre for both women writers and readers has been filled by a great deal of discussion and analysis by later feminist critics. In one of the earliest feminist rereadings of the women's sensation novel, Elaine Showalter (1978a) responded to Oliphant's condemnation of women's complicity in its production with the rejoinder that 'the flood of popular books by women sensationalists in the 1860s and 1870s shows that readers *recognised themselves in the outspoken heroines*' (175, my italics). Showalter's rereading, although suggestive, presents a number of problems, at least two of which are to be found in the sentence just quoted. The first is the question of the reader's self-recognition, a point to which I will return later. The second is her characterisation of the sensation heroine as 'outspoken', a move which seems to collapse the differences between individual sensation novels and sensation heroines.

In fact most of the major sensation heroines are not particularly outspoken – indeed they are significantly silent and unable to articulate their feelings and desires at crucial points in the narrative. Moreover, several of them are more striking for what they *do* than what they *say*.

In general terms Showalter's influential reassessment saw the women's sensation novel as fulfilling a wide range of needs for both women writers and readers: it supplied readers with some of the excitement missing from their middle-class lives; it gave writers more or less off-the-peg formulae for the satiric subversion of literary conventions and social codes; it drew upon and reinforced a community of values shared by women writers and readers; and, perhaps most importantly, it articulated suppressed female emotions and expressed women's covert anger at the limitations of their social and domestic circumstances. Add to this the sensation novel's development of a 'new kind of heroine . . . who could put her hostility toward men into violent action' (160) – by pushing them down wells or setting fire to them, for example – and thus function as a kind of fantasy avenger of the wrongs of women, and one begins to wonder why Showalter places the women sensation novelists at the end of the second or 'feminine phase' of women's writing, rather than as part of the 'feminist phase' towards which her march of the female literary mind progresses. The reason for this placing lies in what Showalter sees as a failure of nerve and a failure of literary form. The women sensation novelists, she argues (180), ultimately compromised their radical and subversive impulses; they were trapped by their own conventionality (the fear of appearing 'morbid, unnatural, and unfeminine') and ensnared by literary conventions and generic constraints:

> Typically, the first volume of a woman's sensation novel is a gripping and sardonic analysis of a woman in conflict with male authority. By the second volume guilt has set in. In the third volume we see the heroine punished, repentant, and drained of all energy . . . the very tradition of the domestic novel opposed the heroine's development.
>
> (Showalter 1978a:180)

Showalter's reading derives from a somewhat inflexible

concept of genre, and also reveals the problems of concentrating too much on endings at the expense of the more complex middles of novels.[1] It also demonstrates the limitations of reading the women's writing of the past simply in the light of our own political concerns, especially if this involves scanning the texts for 'messages' whose sexual politics can simply be read off and graded as 'radical', 'subversive' or 'conservative' by our own standards of progressiveness. Showalter's early, feminist-inspired desire to see women and women writers transcend the historical conditions of their oppression left her insufficiently interested in, or alert to, the ways in which the women's sensation novels rework and negotiate, as well as simply reproduce, the contradictions of those conditions.

Equally problematic would be a feminist reappropriation of women's sensation fiction which would simply celebrate its focus on female emotions and sensations as a form of emotionally rich womanspeak articulating female power and feeling (female power *as* feeling?), or as a form of *écriture féminine* which inscribes both the female body and a feminine subjectivity. This would be to risk reinscribing essentialist notions of the feminine, and to replicate the gendered critical discourse of the nineteenth century through which sensation fiction was mediated – the only difference being that in such a celebration the improper feminine becomes the positive and valued, rather than the negative and marginalised term.

A feminist analysis of sensation fiction should also be a properly historical analysis of the sensation novel as a popular cultural form. Such an analysis needs to take account of the processes by which the products of the fiction market are sifted and stratified into high and low forms. It will also involve an understanding of genre as a flexible and historically developing set of codes rather than as a fixed formula or category, as 'a socio-symbolic message' (Jameson 1981:141) and a social practice as well as a literary category. We shall also need to work towards an historicised awareness and understanding of the cultural meaning of feeling in sensation fiction. We need to see it not simply as either the transgressive or subversive field of the improper feminine, or the contained, conservative domain of the proper feminine. Instead we should explore the sensation novel as a site in which the contradictions, anxieties and opposing ideologies of Victorian culture converge and are

put into play, and as a medium which registered and nego-
tiated (or failed to negotiate) a wide range of profound cultural
anxieties about gender stereotypes, sexuality, class, the family
and marriage. With this aim of historicising genre I will look
briefly at the cultural moment of the women's sensation novel.

The enormous popularity of sensation fiction with the reading
public was in almost directly inverse proportion to the apoplectic response it induced in the numerous reviewers who were
at pains to comprehend the phenomenon and diagnose its
significance. From the time of its first appearance the sensation
novel became a focus of controversy on a number of important
issues in contemporary fiction and culture. The middle-class
periodicals designated it a collective 'delusion' of the reading
public (Mansel 1863:514), an endemic comparable with the
'Dancing Mania and Lycanthropy of the Middle Ages'
(*Westminster Review* 1866:269). Many reviewers treated sensationalism, as they did realism and later naturalism, as evidence of a cultural disease of which it was both a symptom
and cause. 'Works of this class', argued Henry Mansel in an
early vituperative attack on the genre, belong:

> to the morbid phenomenon of literature – indications of
> a widespread corruption, of which they are in part both
> the effect and the cause; called into existence to supply
> the cravings of a diseased appetite, and contributing
> themselves to foster the disease, and to stimulate the
> want which they supply.
>
> (Mansel 1863:482–3)

Whether it was figured as a form of disease or decline, or as
a palliative for cultural ill-health,[2] the sensation novel was seen
as *the* characteristic fictional form of a modern, high-speed,
industrialised culture. Margaret Oliphant, who wrote a number
of influential reviews on the sensation phenomenon, argued
that the 'depth of effect and shock of incident' of sensation
fiction was expressive of the spirit of the modern age which
'has turned out to be one of events' (1862:565). The sensation
novel, 'however extravagant and unnatural' was 'a sign of the
times – the evidence of a certain turn of thought and action,
of an impatience of old restraints, and a craving for some
fundamental change in the working of society' (*Christian*

Remembrancer 1863:210). To moral conservatives the sensation novel was a deeply transgressive form, subversive of an incontrovertible social and moral order. On the other hand, the freethinking *Westminster Review* welcomed its 'rebellion' against the 'prudish conventionalities of our present English style' as a 'much needed practical protest, more or less direct and bold, against the tacit arrangement by which fiction in our day is expected to ignore all the perplexities, dangers and sufferings springing from the relations between man and woman' (McCarthy 1864:46).

As well as being a focus for moral debate, the sensation controversy also became the focus for a 'range of distinct, though interrelated tensions about wider and longer-term transformations that were taking place in middle-range and middle-class publishing and literary culture' (Taylor 1988:5). The cultural moment of sensation fiction coincided with a period in which the literary market was both expanding and becoming more stratified. In particular there was an exponential increase in the production of fiction and the number of novelists, as Margaret Oliphant noted in a comment which contrived to equate the growth in novel production with democratisation, massification and feminisation:

> At no age, as far as we are aware, has there existed anything resembling the extraordinary flood of novels which is now pouring over this land. There were days when an author was a natural curiosity . . . stared at because of the rarity of the phenomenon . . . [but] nowadays . . . most people have been in print one way or another . . . stains of ink linger on the prettiest fingers and to write novels is the normal condition of a large section of society.
>
> (Oliphant 1863:168)

As reading and, to a lesser extent, writing became more widespread and more widely diffused throughout the classes, the boundaries between high culture and low culture – high art, low art, and no art – were constantly being redrawn and redefined. Many commentators saw this process of redefinition as a pernicious invasion of middle-class culture by lower-class forms. Others regarded the sensation novel's role in the expansion of the market for fiction as an important means of cultural renovation. Wilkie Collins (1858), for example, welcomed sensation fiction's appropriation of ephemeral lower-class forms as a means of creating a new audience for the novel. Even Margaret Oliphant, no admirer of the genre, saw it as a refreshing challenge to the hegemony of the 'domestic histories' of the 1840s and 1850s, which, 'however virtuous and charming', had been failing to provide that primary narrative pleasure that kept readers reading. Before the advent of sensation fiction, she noted, 'the well-known stories of readers sitting up all night over a novel had begun to grow faint in the public recollection' (1862:565).

Although the debate about sensation fiction was, in part, a debate about the drawing of boundaries, the sensation novel itself was concerned in all sorts of ways with the unfixing and transgression of boundaries. Formally it is a 'mixed mode' (Hughes 1980:16), demotic in origin and democratic in its appeal. Its roots lie in popular forms such as the stage melodrama, street literature and penny dreadfuls.[3] The narrator of M.E. Braddon's *The Doctor's Wife* notes the mongrel nature and demotic origins of a genre that had been in existence for much longer than its name.

> That bitter term of reproach, 'sensation,' had not yet been invented for the terror of romancers in the fifty- second year of this present century; but the thing existed nevertheless in divers forms, and people wrote sensation novels as unconsciously as Monsieur Jourdain talked prose . . . [These] highly-spiced fictions enjoyed an immense popularity amongst the classes who like their literature as they like their tobacco – very strong . . . a public that bought its literature in the same manner as its pudding – in penny slices.
>
> (DW I:10–11)

Clearly much of the energy and excitement of the sensation novel derives from its appropriation of the conventions and preoccupations of lower-class genres which had developed independently of middle-class forms, and outside of the constraints and controls of middle-class moral management. This phenomenon was noted by a *Fraser's* reviewer, who remarked that:

The growing independence of the young people of the present day, and the very slight supervision exercised by parents or guardians over what they read . . . render such books as we allude to even more dangerous than they would have been twenty years ago.

(*Fraser's* 1860:210)

The development of the sensation novel was also complexly interlinked with the development of sensational newspaper journalism, particularly with the vogue for lurid reporting of divorce cases following the 1857 Matrimonial Causes Act, and of trials concerning domestic murder and domestic crime in general. Sensational narratives of actual murders were the staple daily reading diet of Victorians of all social classes, and the plots of many sensation novels were directly indebted to specific details and situations from actual cases as reported in particular newspapers.[4]

The vogue for both sensational crime reporting and sensation fiction was part of a wider preoccupation within Victorian culture, with the nexus of social, legal, financial, emotional and sexual relationships involved in changing and conflicting views of marriage and the domestic ideal. In the fields of journalism and of fiction the question of woman was central to the representation of this nexus. The sensationalised divorce cases, the sensation novel and the wider sensation debate all turned on the question of woman, and all put woman in question. They were part of a mid-century explosion of discourse on woman – an explosion that, to borrow Jacqueline Rose's phrase, 'made a spectacle' of woman, a spectacle which was repeated 'across a range of discourses' (Rose 1986:112), in which women and the subject of woman were examined, scrutinised and looked at. The next section will look briefly at some of the ways of staging that spectacle which were of particular importance in the production of the sensation novel.

8

Surveillance and control: women, the family and the law

The sensation novel's intense focus on marriage and domestic relations, on bigamy and adultery (or quasi-bigamy and adultery), and its extensive use of plots depending on missing wills and legal intricacies, may be seen as a fictional mediation of the heightened awareness, from the 1830s onwards – but particularly in the 1850s and 1860s – of the anomalies in women's legal status, especially within marriage. As Justin McCarthy (1864) noted in his review of 'Novels with a purpose', 'The institution of marriage might almost seem to be . . . just now upon its trial' (40). The mid-Victorian contest over women's legal status and identity, and the changing discourse in which it was conducted were important components of sensation fiction in general and the women's sensation novel in particular.

The mid-century campaigns for reforms in women's legal position and for reform of the marriage and divorce laws were an extension, in slightly (but significantly) different terms, of the campaigns initiated by Caroline Norton and others in the late 1830s. Those earlier campaigns, and the opposition to them, were supported by appeals to particular definitions of 'woman' and 'womanliness', which were constructed within a broadly stable if contradictory discourse. Lady Caroline Norton's campaign for maternal custody (which resulted in the Infant and Child Custody Bill of 1839),[5] and the opposition to it, were both based on the dominant view of woman as a naturally dependent, self-sacrificial, nurturing, maternal creature. The contradictions involved in this version of woman with her supposed power in the domestic sphere were clearly demonstrated in the arguments used by Norton's opponents.

55

Within the prevailing domestic ideology woman was figured as the queen of the drawing room or parlour, the priestess of the domestic temple and the nurturer and moral guide of the coming generation. However, within the social and legal framework of the patriarchal family she had only duties, and not rights. As John Kemble, a leading opponent of the bill, affirmed in the *British and Foreign Quarterly Review*:

The great fundamental law of society [is] the law of paternity . . .
This sole and absolute power over the children, to the exclusion of everyone else, is a fundamental right vested in the man, as man and father, from the beginning.
(Kemble 1838:358)

Any questioning of this 'oldest and most sacred right belonging to a man' (ibid.) was held to be a threat to the very foundation of the family, and hence of society. Should a woman go further than mere questioning, and 'desert her husband's house, the sphere of her duties, and . . . the only proper home of his children' (280), she was deemed automatically to forfeit the care of her children. As will become clear in my later discussion, especially of Ellen Wood's *East Lynne*, women's legal subjugation within marriage and particularly their lack of legal rights over their children, generated the narrative and emotional tensions of many sensation novels.

Within the patriarchal family, of which she was supposedly the cornerstone, woman was defined in terms of the discourse of the proper feminine, as meekly submissive, the very model of and for decorum and propriety. However, as Kemble's *Quarterly* article demonstrates, the proper feminine was itself always defined in terms of its contradictory other, the improper feminine, which surfaces in his vision of women as 'so many wild beasts', whose lusts and licentiousness run riot 'when you have unbarred [their] cages' (381). In other words, the improper feminine could only be contained within the patriarchal family, an institution which it also constantly threatened to dissolve or destroy. This discourse of containment and threat, which was used to reinforce masculine control of both women and the family, also became an important component of the discourse of the sensation novel.

The discourse of containment was neatly deconstructed by

56

Harriet Taylor in a *Westminster Review* article of 1851, which sought to show how the moral mission and spiritual superiority generally attributed to (proper, middle-class) women, and which gave them 'a position apart' as a sort of 'sentimental priesthood', also worked to exclude them from the common public sphere. Taylor unmasked the tyranny which conventionally masqueraded as protection, by demonstrating whose interests were best served by positioning women as delicate, dependent creatures.

> The real question is, whether it is right and expedient that one half of the human race should pass through life in a state of forced subordination to the other half. If the best state of human society is that of being divided into two parts, one consisting of persons with a will and substantive existence, the other of humble companions to these persons . . . for the purpose of bringing up *his* children, and making *his* home pleasant to him; if this is the place assigned to women it is but kindness to educate them for this; to make them believe that the greatest good fortune which can befall them is to be chosen by some man for this purpose; and that every other career which the world deems happy or honourable, is closed to them by the law, not of social institutions, but of nature and destiny.
>
> (Taylor 1851:300–1)

Since its beginnings, the novel has, of course, played a very important part in persuading women (and men) of this special female destiny. It is a message which is variously inscribed or undercut (sometimes both at once) in sensation novels.

The issue of woman's status as a legal subject returned to the centre of cultural debate with the publication in 1854 of a widely circulated pamphlet by Barbara Leigh Smith (later Bodichon), *A Brief Summary in Plain Language of the Most Important Laws Concerning Women, Together with a Few Observations Thereon*. This pamphlet focused on the severely circumscribed nature of the legal position of single and married women alike. As far as married women were concerned, their condition had not changed from that described by William Blackstone in his *Commentaries on the Laws of England* (1765–9); that is to say, married women had no separate legal existence.

A man and wife are one person in law: the wife loses all her rights as a single woman, and her existence is entirely absorbed in that of her husband. He is civilly responsible for her acts; she lives under his protection or cover, and her condition is called coverture.

(Leigh Smith 1854:4)

In other words, as this reformulation of Blackstone makes clear, a married woman could not be a subject, but only an object who was subject to the absolute authority and control of her husband. The husband owned his wife's personal property, her earnings, her children, and even her body (she was in his custody, and he could enforce his right by a writ of *habeas corpus*). These particularities of women's legal subjection within marriage and the family generated both the plot situations and much of the emotional force of sensation novels.

If in strictly legal terms (as far as women were concerned) marriage was a subject state, it was also a state of subjection from which it was extremely difficult for women to extricate themselves. At the time of Leigh Smith's pamphlet there were two kinds of divorce: 'Divorce *a mensa et thoro*' and 'Divorce *a vinculo matrimonii*'. The first was a separation which could be pronounced by the Ecclesiastical Courts on the grounds of adultery, 'Intolerable Cruelty' or 'Unnatural Practices'. The second was 'an entire dissolution of the bonds of matrimony' which could be effected only by Act of Parliament on the grounds of 'adultery in the wife, and in some cases of *aggravated adultery on the part of the husband*' (Leigh Smith 1854:10). This legal institutionalisation of the sexual double standard embodied in the divorce laws was debated with fresh vigour during the late 1850s and 1860s, the period immediately preceding and coinciding with the high point of the production of sensation fiction, and is clearly an important element in the sensation novel's representation of marriage and of relations between the sexes.

Leigh Smith's pamphlet, the petition circulated by 'the country's first real feminist committee' (Holcombe 1980:9), and the parliamentary debates on the resulting Married Women's Property Bill of 1857 all provoked fierce controversy in the press. Opposition to the bill was conducted in a discourse in which the stability of the family, and hence of society, was

58

predicated upon the traditional definition of the married woman as both subjected and invisible, that is to say legally non-existent. Any attempts to change this definition of woman, according to Sir Richard Bethell, the Attorney General, 'must involve a material change in the social and political institutions of a nation', by placing woman 'in a strong minded and independent position' which 'the most amiable women' did not desire (3 Hansard, CXLV, 1857:276).

One such 'amiable' woman was Margaret Oliphant, prolific essayist, novelist and (on most issues) defender of the status quo (although she became somewhat more reform-minded over the Married Woman's Property Act in the 1860s). Oliphant's (1856) response to Leigh Smith's 'very serious and well-meaning pamphlet' (381) simultaneously engaged with and demonstrated the ideological operations of language. Oliphant took issue with the 'unchancy' nature of words and terms, and sought to redefine those used by Leigh Smith by opposing the literary to the legal, and appealing to nature and common sense to supply the inadequacies of both kinds of language.

> It is hard to enter upon this subject [women's legal status] without falling into the automative hardness of legal phraseology, or the sweet jargon of poetic nonsense, on one side or the other. 'The wife loses her rights as a single woman, and her existence is entirely absorbed in that of her husband,' says this *Brief Summary in Plain Language* of the formal law. 'His house she enters,' says the poet,
>
> > A guardian angel o'er his life presiding,
> > Doubling his pleasures, and his cares dividing.
>
> The one utterance is somewhat humiliating, and the other unquestionably poetry, and both fail the truth. Lawyer and poet alike survey the surface and external aspect of the question – common experience pronounces a fuller verdict.
>
> (Oliphant 1856:381)

The 'fuller verdict' offered by 'common experience' involves the reader's *recognition* of what Oliphant offers as self-evident truths. First, that 'It is no fallacy of the law to say that [man and wife] . . . are one person; it is a mere truism of nature'

59

(280), and secondly, that as *every man and every woman knows*, with the most absolute certainty . . . a household divided against itself cannot stand' (381, my italics). Oliphant here requires the reader to recognise marriage as an indissoluble unity of difference which fuses discrete, but complementary, gendered roles or duties. In short she reaffirms the ideology of the separate spheres. 'The man is at once the *natural* representative of his wife in one set of duties', that is to say, those of the public sphere. On the other hand, 'the wife is the *natural* representative of the husband in the other' (381, my italics), the domestic sphere.

As well as demonstrating the ideological operations of language, Oliphant's essay implicitly reveals the ideological work done by literature. The lines of poetry which she opposes to Leigh Smith's legal language are not simply another way of saying the same thing; in masking the 'automative hardness of legal phraseology' they also say something different. The poetic utterance transforms the material and legal power relations of marriage by representing the legal subordination of women as a form of moral and spiritual power.

In a more direct, if tongue-in-cheek, reference Oliphant's essay implicitly demonstrates that literature both masks inequality and is also produced or served by it:

> The injuries of women have long been a standing subject of animadversion. Woman's rights will never grow into a popular agitation, yet *women's wrongs are always picturesque and attractive*. They are indeed *so good to make novels and poems about, so telling as illustrations of patience and gentleness, that we fear any real redress of grievances would do more harm to the literary world than it would do good to the feminine.*
>
> (Oliphant 1856:379, my italics)

The picturesqueness and attractiveness of women's wrongs are central to most sensation novels, particularly those by women. Sensation fiction is both produced *by* and is *about* the injuries of women. Among the things I shall want to investigate in more detail in later sections are the various ways in which different sensation novels produce, reproduce and resolve the injuries of women, and how women and their injuries are rendered 'picturesque'.

Female suffering was both perpetuated and made more picturesque (in the sense of increasingly becoming the object of public spectacle) by developments in the reform of the marriage and divorce laws. The Married Women's Property Bill of 1857 was unsuccessful, and campaigning on this issue continued throughout the sensation decade. However, some limited reform of the marriage laws was effected by the passing of the Divorce Act of 1857 (the Matrimonial Causes Act), which improved the property rights of married women and transferred all matters concerning the dissolution of marriage from the Ecclesiastical Courts to a new secular court – the Court of Divorce and Matrimonial Causes – which had the power to grant both judicial separations and divorces. The new legislation perpetuated the existing institutionalisation of the double standard on sexual conduct: a husband could divorce his wife simply on the grounds of her adultery, but a wife was required to prove adultery plus an additional misdemeanour, such as desertion (for more than two years), bigamy, cruelty, rape, incest or bestiality.

Although the inequitable nature of the 1857 Act made it of limited usefulness to women, it was, in Margaret Oliphant's terms, extremely useful to and productive of literature. The activities of the new Divorce Courts, and the reporting of these in such publications as the *Divorce News and Police Reporter*[6] produced a whole new sensational literature. The developing genre of reportage of divorce cases not only provided the sensation novelists with plot incidents, it also fed a taste for marital scandal, and an interest in the complexities of marital discord which provided a ready-made market for sensation fiction. As one of Ouida's fashionable young blades remarks in *Under Two Flags*, 'everybody goes through the DC [Divorce Court] somehow or other . . . It's like the Church, the Commons and the Gallows, you know – one of the popular institutions' (40).

61

9

Spectating the Social Evil: fallen and other women

The year 1857 was not only that of the Matrimonial Causes Act, it also marked one of a series of high points in the press agitation about the 'Social Evil' of prostitution. The 'private shame of divorce' and the 'public shame of prostitution' (Trudgill 1976:179) were thus brought together under the same spotlight. The result was the production of a moral panic about both male and female sexuality, the institution of marriage, and 'immorality as a pervasive social fact' (ibid.). This moral panic was clearly an important factor in the sensation novel's representation of sexuality (especially female sexuality), and a source of its particular preoccupation with marriage and with various kinds of extra-marital relationships.

There was, and still is, much discussion and disagreement about the extent of prostitution, and the degree to which (sexual) immorality was, and is, a *pervasive* social fact. There can be little doubt, however, that both prostitution and immorality were pervasive facts of discourse throughout the 1850s and 1860s, and indeed throughout the latter half of the nineteenth century, a period in which, as Jacqueline Rose has argued, 'morality makes a spectacle of itself':

> Something has to be looked at which has not been looked at before, vice must be rooted out, and the woman must be inspected because . . . it is the woman who [supposedly] is the immediate and visible cause of social decay . . . The prostitute therefore becomes the publicly sanctioned image against which society measures its moral consciousness of self.
>
> (Rose 1986:112)

By 1860, as the *Saturday Review* noted, 'the Social Evil question' had become 'too popular by half' (October 6, 1860:417). In offering his own analysis of how the discourse of the Social Evil was constructed, this particular reviewer also exemplifies the wider discursive framework within which prostitution was constituted as a social fact and a social disease. The reviewer's own language assigns the prostitute to active membership of the 'dangerous classes', but the essay also points to an alternative discourse in which the prostitute is passive – a victim of social and economic circumstance or sexual temptation. The reviewer deplores the prevalence of modern euphemism, which has become as great a social evil as that which it is used to describe, and insists on the 'old fashioned language of the "streetwalker" '.

> 'Unfortunates,' and 'fallen sisters,' are the language of the sentimental . . . [and even] patrician matrons and aristocratic maidenhood allude to the subject with more simpers than blushes. The fact is that we have familiarized ourselves too much with the subject. There is a subtle indelicacy and a refined coarseness in a good deal of our sentimental sympathies with 'the fallen' and there are evils – and social evils, too – growing up around the subject, which are as bad as what is technically known as the Social Evil itself.
>
> (*Saturday Review* 1860:417)

The fundamental anxiety underlying this article is one which, in various forms, pervaded middle-class culture throughout the latter half of the nineteenth century. It is, in part, an anxiety about shifts in the terminology relating to moral and behavioural categories but, more importantly, it is an anxiety about the instability of these categories themselves. Definitions of the prostitute and attitudes towards prostitution were multiple, fragmented and frequently contradictory. In the great press debate of the late 1850s and the 1860s (in both middle-class newspapers and the specialist medical press) prostitution and proper or 'respectable' femininity were habitually defined against each other. Respectable femininity was womanhood in its normal, healthy and (many argued) asexual state of married motherhood. The prostitute, on the other hand, was deviant femininity, the negation of the womanly norm. Sexually depraved and mentally and physically diseased, the prostitute was the bearer of contagion into the sanctuary of the middle-class home.

However, as the *Saturday Review* article indicates, there was a counter-discourse that defined the prostitute not against, but *within* the terms of the respectable or proper feminine. Within this discourse of the 'fallen woman', prostitutes were victims, not predators; they were economically and morally vulnerable women who fell prey to a rapacious society, and to male economic and sexual power. This counter-discourse on the prostitute both exposed the problems of women's social and economic dependence within the family and, at the same time, reinforced it. Women's dependence and vulnerability were seen both as a cause of prostitution and a sign of the need to contain women within the family. It was precisely this slippage between the fallen woman as predator and the fallen woman as victim which was such a disturbing feature (to contemporary reviewers) of the sensation heroine.

Paradoxically, marriage and proper femininity were seen both as being threatened by prostitution, and also as its cause. The middle-class custom of delaying marriage until a husband could support a household of normative bourgeois gentility, combined with the ideology of proper feminine asexuality to produce that 'fractured sexuality' which gave rise to the 'psychopathological demand which prostitution satisfied' (Nield 1973:Introduction). Middle-class marriage customs, and in particular the 'growing and morbid luxury' (Greg 1862:446) of genteel marriage, were the subject of much press comment in the 1850s and 1860s. They were persistently linked to what was perceived to be the growing preference among middle-class men for keeping mistresses rather than, or in addition to, marrying. Many commentators (male and female) also linked this practice to the insipidity of the innocent feminine ideal, noting that the inoffensive passivity encouraged in middle-class women served to render the middle-class wife considerably less attractive than a mistress. The women of the demi-monde were seen not only as being more sexually attractive than their respectable counterparts, but also as more lively and interesting, and hence more suitable companions for educated middle-class men. Among male commentators, the arrival of the 'fast woman' in the 1860s to challenge the domi-

64

nance of the respectable ideal of the proper feminine, and to blur the boundaries between respectable society and the demi-monde, served only to increase the attractions of the latter sphere. As W.R. Greg noted:

> Society – that is, the society of great cities and of culti-vated life – high life – has for some years been growing at once more expensive and less remunerative . . . All this time, while the *monde* has been deteriorating, the *demi-monde* has been improving . . . The ladies *there* are now often clever and amusing, usually more beautiful, and not infrequently (in external demeanour at least) as modest, as their rivals in more recognised society.
>
> (Greg 1862:453)

By mid-century and throughout the sensation decade the con-tradictions in the dominant versions of marriage and bourgeois femininity were becoming increasingly apparent. The plots and central dilemmas of the sensation novel were generated by these contradictions and by the anxieties they produced amongst the middle classes. Marriage was represented as a sanctuary from female sexuality, but also as threatened by it, and especially by the Social Evil of prostitution, which marriage had helped to create. The dominant discourses on marriage and respectable femininity were further destabilised by a tend-ency to see contemporary marriage as itself a form of prosti-tution. For those who defined the feminine in terms of the absence of sexual desire, marriage and prostitution involved a similar joyless and/or shameful exchange of sex for money or financial security. In his *Westminster Review* article of 1850 W.R. Greg saw the same painful sacrifice in the first sexual act of both prostitute and wife. He defines prostitution in economic terms, arguing that most prostitutes take up their trade through economic necessity rather than from lust or love of luxury. Indeed 'the unfortunate women who come upon the town' through love of finery 'are far from being the chief or most numerous delinquents. For one woman who thus, of deliberate choice sells herself to a lover, ten sell themselves to a husband' (458).

The sensation novel frequently echoed Greg's terms in its satirical treatment of the marriage market and in its focusing on the situation of the purchased wife. In the women's sensation novel the satirisation of contemporary marriage through commercial metaphors (which is found in the work of earlier writers such as Thackeray) is replaced by an emphasis on the experiencing of marriage as a commercial transaction. Rhoda Broughton's *Cometh Up as a Flower*, for example, focuses sharply on a wife's view of marriage in these terms by dwelling minutely on the sensations produced in her heroine by the embrace of the husband to whom she has been married for financial reasons.

> His arm is round my waist, and he is brushing my eyes and cheeks with his somewhat bristly moustache as often as he wants to . . . for has he not bought me? For a pair of first-class blue eyes warranted fast colour, for ditto super-fine red lips . . . he has paid down a handsome price on the nail . . . [T]hat accursed girdling arm is still around me – my buyer's arm – that arm which seems to be burning into my flesh like a brand.
>
> (CUF:325)

10

Reviewing the subject of women: the sensation novel and the 'Girl of the Period'

> No-one who studies the present temper of women can shut his eyes to the fact that there is a decided diminution among them in reverence for parents, trust in men, and desire for children.
>
> (*Saturday Review*, September 9, 1871:335)

The contest over the definition of woman, and the ideological work of repairing the fractures within the dominant discourse of the proper feminine, filled the pages of the newspaper and periodical press throughout the sensation years. Women (or 'woman') became a public spectacle, the object of discourse and the subject of numerous articles and essays. By the mid-1860s the increasing stridency of the tone of some of these essays indicates that there was indeed a crisis of definition, a panic over the instability of established gender norms and categories.

The struggle over the meaning of woman was particularly fierce in the pages of the *Saturday Review*, as will be clear from the nature of various examples I have already given. I want to look, finally, at a series of important articles, published in 1868, which drew together and thus (so to speak) retrospectively illuminate many of the concerns and anxieties about the upheavals of the sensation decade. These essays (most of which were written by Eliza Lynn Linton) made a concerted effort to stabilise the discourse on gender, by reinstating a nostalgically evoked domestic ideal of the womanly woman, and by ridiculing and satirising any deviations from this norm.

In doing so they reveal a great deal about the nature of what was at stake in the sensation novel.

The *Saturday*'s chief anxieties derived from a concern with the disruption of difference. For example, 'What is woman's work?' (February 15, 1868) represents a world turned upside down by women, whose incursions into the public sphere of work have disrupted tradition, continuity and the natural order, all of which were posited on the gendered division of labour.

> Professions are [now] undertaken and careers *invaded* which were formerly *held sacred to men*, while things are left undone which, for all the generations that the world has lasted, have been *naturally and instinctively* assigned to women to do . . .
>
> . . . From the savage squaw gathering fuel . . . to the lady giving up her keys to her housekeeper, house-keeping has been one of the primary functions of women. The man to provide, the woman to dispense . . . and *any system which ignores these divisions of labour, and confounds these separate functions, is of necessity imperfect and wrong.*
>
> (*Saturday Review* 1868b:197, my italics)

This reviewer was exercised by the apparent paradox that the disruption of difference in terms of the gendered division of labour had served to reinforce difference in other respects. Most notably it had had the effect of developing an unprecedentedly 'wide division between the interests and sympathies of the sexes' (ibid.). This sense of a growing division between men and women, husbands and wives is central to the sensation novel's representation and investigation of modern marriage. One symptom of this new division, and of a perceived crisis in modern marriage, was the 'unreasonable disrepute [into which] active housekeeping – woman's first natural duty – has fallen in England' (ibid.). The *Saturday Review* also attacked the developing tendency for middle-class marriage to be based on woman's economic redundancy in her role as decorative object and conspicuous consumer. Instead it reasserted the traditional gendered division of labour, insisting that women should reapply themselves to domestic labour and the moral and emotional nurturing of the providing male who, in his turn, must endure the monotony of City labours.

The toiling, preoccupied husband, and the idle, inefficient, or simply redundant wife are, of course, often found in sensation fiction, where they play an important part in the genre's problematisation of the wifely role, and of gender roles within marriage. Such pairings are at the heart of the main narratives of Wood's *East Lynne* and Braddon's *Eleanor's Victory*. Elsewhere (in *Lady Audley's Secret*, for example) anxieties about the increased instability of middle-class social and marital roles are displaced into narratives of the plight of the socially mobile woman (or, more exceptionally, man) in the aristocratic family.

The most widely known of the *Saturday Review* articles on modern woman is Eliza Lynn Linton's essay 'The Girl of the Period', published on March 14, 1868, which was described by Merle Bevington as 'perhaps the most sensational middle article the *Saturday Review* ever published' (Bevington 1941:110). In coining what came to be known as the 'GOP', Linton retrospectively gave a name to a version of femininity that was a major source of narrative disturbance in the sensation novels of the early 1860s, and also provided a label for the 'deviant' woman of the 1870s and beyond. Linton's satiric portrait of the freakish GOP was constructed from a network of anxieties which circulate through the 1860s debates about woman, and which are prominent in the sensation novel: the belief or fear that women are inherently duplicitous; that femininity implies and involves acting; and that women are primitives, savages, hysterics, or whores. In addition, Linton's critique of the self-concern of modern women also plays upon the fears of female self-authorisation and of women's resistance of male control and regulation, which are an important undercurrent in the sensation novel.

The GOP (like some sensation heroines) is virtually produced to embody these fears. Her fashionable freakishness is likened to the savage, to Madge Wildfire (the madwoman), and to the demi-mondaine or prostitute. The GOP is a freak because her 'uselessness at home, [and] dissatisfaction with the monotony of ordinary life and horror of all useful work' (Linton 1868a:340) resist or negate the domestic virtues usually thought to be embodied in woman. Her attitude to marriage also foregrounds aspects of the domestic ideology which are usually suppressed. The sexual politics of female economic dependence in marriage, and its similarity to prostitution (noted by W.R. Greg above), are exposed by the GOP's

69

supposed view of marriage as 'the legal barter of herself for so much money, representing so much cash, so much luxury and pleasure' (Linton 1868a:340).

Perhaps the most interesting aspect of Linton's rhetoric is the way that the norm from which the GOP supposedly deviates can only be recalled nostalgically, as a race memory which at some future date, 'when the national madness has passed', may once more have its day. Linton's respectable, domestic norm is a fiercely nationalistic vision of a fair young English girl, 'the most essentially womanly in the world', a 'creature generous, capable and modest . . . franker than a Frenchwoman, more to be trusted than an Italian, as brave as an American but more refined, as domestic as a German and more graceful' (ibid.). This epitome of England, home and beauty is innately pure, dignified and non-competitive. In other words she knows and accepts her place. She does not compete with men, but defers to them. In short she is the very model of the Ruskinian ideal, who makes her husband's house 'his home and place of rest, not a mere passage-place for vanity and ostentation to go through; a tender mother, an industrious housewife, a judicious mistress' (ibid.). This ideal forms a constant (sometimes satiric) point of reference for defining the feminine in sensation fiction.

The qualities of this feminine ideal are further elaborated in the womanly alternative to '*La femme passée*', the title of another of Linton's contributions to what looks like a concerted attempt on the part of the *Saturday Review* to (re)construct and put into circulation a strong and stable version of the respectable feminine.

> All children and all young persons love [the ideal woman of middle age], because she understands and loves them. For she is essentially a mother – that is a *woman who can forget herself, who can give without asking to receive* . . . There is no servility, no exaggerated sacrifice in this, it is simply a *fulfilment of woman's highest duty* – the expression of that *grand maternal* instinct which need not necessarily include the fact of personal maternity, but which must find utterance in *some line of unselfish action with all women worthy of the name*.
>
> (Linton 1868c:50, my italics)

Mid-century commentators on the subject of woman (like many of their counterparts in the 1890s) were particularly exercised by the alleged decline of the 'grand maternal instinct' in the Girls of the Period.

> It is rare to find a woman, boasting herself of advanced culture, who confesses to an instinctive love for little children, or who would condescend to any of that healthy animal delight in their possession which has always been one of the most beautiful and valuable constituents of feminine nature.
>
> (*Saturday Review* 1871:335)

In its articles on modern feminine types, the *Saturday Review* attempted to re-establish fixed gender categories by means of a sharply polarised binary definition of the feminine, which opposed a normative feminine ideal to a non- or anti-feminine deviation that reversed all the positives of the norm. This attempt was, however, riven with contradictions – contradictions which the sensation novel also revealed and put into play. Many of these articles from the 1860s reveal both the *desire* to fix the category of the feminine, and the *fear* that it cannot be fixed, owing to woman's chameleon nature. Linton's satiric piece on 'Feminine affectations' represents femininity as a role to be acted, emphasising women's self-consciousness about their roles, and exploring the numerous and contradictory roles constructed for and by women. Linton appears to want both to fix and categorise woman, and to make feminine multiplicity appear deviant, and thus recallable to the norm of 'the thoroughly natural and unaffected woman . . . who is truthful to her core, and who would as little condescend to act a pretence as she would dare to tell a lie' (Linton 1868b: 777).

'Feminine affectations' does not simply ridicule commonly recognised deviations from the feminine norm (such as the Bluestocking, Poetess, or the 'mannish woman'), it also seeks to delimit and control the feminine by ridiculing women's autonomous development of their socially assigned gender roles. Thus it mocks those women who attempt to extend the moral dimension of the feminine ideal by assuming the 'antiseptic' role of 'spiritual beadledom'(ibid.). It is equally scathing of the self-consciously staged 'intensive womanliness'

71

adopted by 'certain opposers of the prevalent fast type', who 'in every action of their lives . . . see themselves as pictures, as characters in a novel' (776). In fact this essay implicitly points to a real problem in women's self-perception in a culture which surrounds them with potent but self-contradictory images – a problem which is viewed from a variety of perspectives in the female sensation novel.

11

Historicising genre (2): sensation fiction, women's genres and popular narrative forms

> Twentieth-century critics have taught generations of students to equate popularity with debasement, emotionality with ineffectiveness, religiosity with fakery, domesticity with triviality, and all of these, implicitly, with womanly inferiority.
>
> (Jane Tompkins 1985:123)

The evaluative system and its attendant process of cultural sifting described by Jane Tompkins (above) have not only played a crucial role in writing the women's sensation novel out of literary history, but were also important components of the contemporary critical response to sensation fiction, and constitutive elements of the genre itself. However, a variety of recent historical and theoretical work on popular forms and genres (particularly narrative forms by and for women) has enabled us to rethink the equations Tompkins outlines, and to reassess both the contemporary cultural meaning of sensation fiction, and its subsequent changing significances.

Of particular importance in this respect has been what Andrew Higson and Ginette Vincendeau (1986) have described (with reference to contemporary film studies) as 'The feminist-inspired desire to focus on texts traditionally popular with female audiences (and derided by male critics)' (3). This focus on women's genres has not only brought 'low' genres into critical view, but has also led to a rethinking of the concept of genre itself; instead of conceptualising it as 'a structure (of binary oppositions, of iconographies and themes)', there has been a move towards seeing it as 'a processing of narrative point of view, subject position and desire' (Higson and Vincendeau 1986:3). Much of this work attempts to build into its analysis of text and genre an account of the pleasures and desires of readers, and the various reading or spectating positions offered to the audience.

For example, Tania Modleski's work on 'mass market fantasies for women' in *Loving with a Vengeance* (1984) invites us to rethink the relationships between the women's genres of the past, and to analyse them in terms of the complex and contradictory pleasures they offer to both women writers and readers. Using Modleski's analysis of eighteenth- and nineteenth-century fiction by or for women, one might argue that the sensation novel, like gothic – the subversive fictional form of the late eighteenth and early nineteenth centuries – is 'somewhat continuous with' domestic fiction. Sensation novels, like gothic novels, 'are "domestic" novels too, concerned with the (often displaced) relationships among family members and with driving home to women the importance of coping with enforced confinement and the paranoid fear it generates' (Modleski 1984:20). Like these earlier women's genres, sensation fiction engages in an intense focus on the domestic space of the marital home – the desired goal of the domestic heroine – which becomes in the sensation novel (as in gothic) the locus of passion, deception, violence and crime. This is one of the key areas in which sensation fiction represents and (variously) negotiates the contradictions of the domestic ideology. The home, in Ruskinian orthodoxy, 'the shelter, not only from all injury, but from all terror, doubt and division' (Ruskin 1880 [1865]:92), becomes instead the site of terror, doubt and division. However, in the sensation novel, unlike gothic, it is a woman who tends to be the origin or cause of the terror, doubt and division.

Like their domestic and gothic predecessors, sensation novels are usually family romances whose narrative trajectory derives from the dynamics of (sometimes concealed) family relationships. This concern with the domestic scene and the dynamics of the family is also one of sensation fiction's many points of connection with the popular melodrama, from which many of its plot situations, character types and rhetorical devices were borrowed. Indeed the women's sensation novel seems to display most of the characteristics which Peter Brooks discerns in melodrama: 'The indulgence of strong emotional-ism; moral polarization and schematicization; extreme states of being, situations, action; overt villainy, persecution of the good, and final reward of virtue; inflated and extravagant expression; dark plottings, suspense, breathtaking peripety' (Brooks 1976:11–12).

As Brooks argues in his important study of the melodramatic imagination in European culture, melodrama is usually most popular in periods of intense social or ideological crisis, in which (depending on the particular historical circumstances and ideological pressures) it functions either subversively, or as escapist entertainment. Melodrama was certainly a pervasive aspect of Victorian culture, appearing in a number of different forms throughout the period. In all of its guises – as Martha Vicinus (1981) has observed – nineteenth-century melodrama invariably served as both a 'cultural touchstone' for those classes or social groups which were confused by major social changes and ambivalent about their own role in the new order, and as a 'psychological touchstone' for the poor, the powerless and 'those who felt themselves to be "helpless and unfriended" ' (128). Clearly this aspect of melodrama had particular resonance for women. Melodrama addressed the contradictions of women's lives and, through its habitual deployment of motifs of rebellion and self-sacrifice, spoke to a 'recurrent underlying emotional tension' (Vicinus: 1981:133) in those lives.

The sensation novel of the 1860s (especially the work of Mary Elizabeth Braddon and Ellen Wood) was perhaps the dominant mid-Victorian form of domestic melodrama for women. The similarities between the women's sensation novel and other melodramatic forms are, of course, well docu-mented. Sensation fiction's close connection with stage melodrama is evident in its extravagant plotting, its emotional intensity and linguistic excess, and also in its characteristic displacement of anxieties about social and political issues into intersubjective dramas focused on the family.

However, the differences between the two forms are just as important as the similarities, and in my own analysis of par-ticular sensation novels (in the next two sections) I shall sug-gest that the women sensationalists put the emotional and linguistic excess of melodrama to new uses. I shall also attempt to show that in the women's sensation novel the family was both the site and origin of an even more profound tension than was the case in the stage melodrama. In the female sensation novel the family was not simply a refuge from change (as Vicinus argues in relation to stage melodrama), but also, more emphatically, the site of change. It was not only an arena in which an abstract moral 'struggle between good and evil' (Vicinus: 1981:131) was played out, it was itself both the cause and site of a struggle in which those abstract moral categories were destabilised.

In short, I suggest that the representation of the family in the women's sensation novel was more conflicted and ambiguous than in the popular stage melodrama of the earlier nineteenth century. Indeed one of the most interesting aspects of the sensation novel (and, no doubt, a primary source of narrative interest for contemporary readers) is the way in which it problematises the family, explores women's contradictory roles within it and articulates their complex and contradictory feelings about it. In this respect, as in others, the women's sensation novel does not merely reproduce generic conventions and ideological codes, but rather reworks and develops them.

The theoretical and historical work on nineteenth-century melodrama by critics such as Brooks and Vicinus has combined with psycho-political analyses of the operations of melodrama in modern mass-culture forms (particularly film) to produce, in effect, the recovery of a cultural field. It has also led to the reassessment of a category which had previously been written out of cultural history in that process of sifting by which the components of a culture become stratified into a hierarchy of value. In this case the process resulted in melodrama being 'constituted as the anti-value for a critical field in which tragedy and realism became the cornerstones of "high" cultural value, needing protection from mass, "melodramatic" entertainment' (Gledhill 1987:5). The recovery and reassessment of melodrama have been crucial in establishing new ways of reading and understanding a wide range of melodramatic forms, including the sensation novel. As I suggested earlier, feminist analyses have played a particularly important role in bringing this ' "woman's area" into critical view' (Gledhill 1987:2). They have also posed far-reaching questions about gender, genre and culture, which have led to a rethinking of the categories

76

habitually used to separate 'art' and 'entertainment', the 'serious' and the 'trivial'.

Recent feminist work on contemporary mass-market romance has been particularly productive in generating fresh perspectives on women's genres such as the sensation novel. For example Tania Modleski's (1984) reading of contemporary 'gothics' and Harlequin romance offers a suggestive analysis of the semiotics of the popular romance text and the cultural meaning of genre, which discovers 'elements of protest and resistance underneath highly "orthodox" plots' (25). Such narratives, she argues, both enact and contain strategies of resistance to women's (usually) subservient familial and social roles. Janice Radway's work on Harlequin romance and its readers (1987), Alison Light's (1986) exploration of the readerly pleasures of women's popular romances, and Bridget Fowler's (1991) study of 'the alienated reader' of romance have also (from quite different perspectives) developed analyses which have questioned the orthodox view of romance text as inherently conservative, and romance reading as a process of merely passive and appetitive consumption.

Radway, for example, combines reader-response theory, ethnographic analysis of actual readers and reading communities, and feminist psychoanalysis to produce a view of the romance-reading experience as deeply contradictory. She maintains that female readers (at least temporarily) resist and escape from the limiting conditions of their social and familial roles, in the very act, paradoxically, of becoming immersed in narratives which make an idealised version of those roles the object of desire.

One consequence of Radway's work (as of much of the recent work on modern mass-market romance) has been to overturn the view that popular romance forms depend on the reader's simple identification with the heroine, or, indeed, with any other single figure in the text. On the contrary, both theoretical and empirical work suggest that the romance text offers a range of positions and identifications for the reader, and that the female romance reader's presumed surrender to the narrative pleasures of the formulaic text does not necessarily involve her surrender to, or acceptance of, its (usually) conservative ideology. Women romance readers, as Radway (most strikingly) has shown, do not merely passively consume their chosen texts but commonly read against the grain, negotiating a variety of positions of spectatorship, and appropriating the text and its messages to their own perspectives and for their own purposes.

Clearly we cannot hope to replicate Radway's analysis of actual reading practices in relation to nineteenth-century texts and audiences. Nevertheless her analysis of the psychology of romance reading and the structure of the romantic narrative can be usefully appropriated. Instead of analysing actual readers and reading practices, students of the sensation novel must focus on the implied reader(s) constructed and addressed by the discourse of sensation fiction, and on the specific historical and cultural contexts of reading and writing. This will require careful analysis of the tone and address of particular sensation novels, and of the rhetorical strategies of individual writers, as well as (and in conjunction with) an informed historical analysis of the discursive contexts in which the sensation genre was produced.

Work on other modern mass-culture narrative forms for women, such as soap opera, family melodrama and 'the woman's film' (and the theoretical positions which inform this work)[7] is also extremely useful for developing an analysis of the 1860s sensation novel. Of particular importance here are the debates about the gendered pleasures of narrative; the text's positioning of its female readers and feminine addressees, and the kind(s) of femininity it constructs for them; the relationship between the specific gendered identities constructed within and by the text; the codes of gender which operate within its wider cultural context; the various forms of spectatorship involved in textual consumption – particularly the debates around what Christine Gledhill (1988) describes as the 'largely negative accounts of female spectatorship, suggesting colonized, alienated or masochistic positions of identification' (66); and the ways in which contradictions are foregrounded and spaces created for oppositional readings.

Clearly the conditions of production of nineteenth-century sensation fiction were very different from those within which modern mass-market romances, soap opera and the woman's film have developed. It would therefore be unwise simply to transfer analytic models from one medium to another, or from one historical conjuncture to another. However, as I hope my own analysis of the early (1860s) novels of Mary Elizabeth

Braddon and Ellen Wood will show, some aspects of this recent work on theories of representation, and the cultural production and consumption of modern mass-culture forms, can be usefully applied to a popular women's genre of the nineteenth century. Literary criticism has much to gain from an engagement with the theoretical and methodological debates within film and media studies.

For example, the broad theoretical framework developed by Annette Kuhn's work on television soap opera and film/television melodrama offers a useful model for a flexible study of genre as an historically specific social practice. Kuhn's emphasis on the importance (in analysing popular representations) of developing a complex awareness of the relationship between specific forms and codes, the cultural freight and currency of particular images, and the way in which specific spectators in a specific historical and cultural location might work and rework those images, is particularly useful for the analysis of a formula genre such as the sensation novel.

Kuhn's reading of how the mass-culture text (in this case television soap opera and the film melodrama) actively produces a 'feminine' point of view in the socially constructed female audience which it addresses is of particular relevance to an analysis of the operations and effects of the woman-to-woman address, and the shifting point of view of the women's sensation novel. Kuhn argues that the construction of gendered audience and spectator in and by the woman's text is a contradictory process, involving an 'interplay of masculine and feminine subject positions'.

> Culturally dominant codes inscribe the masculine, while the feminine bespeaks a 'return of the repressed' in the form of codes which may well transgress culturally dominant subject positions, though only at the expense of proposing a position of subjection for the spectator.
>
> (Kuhn 1987:347–8)

By being positioned as the spectator (especially of a female character) the female reader is offered a culturally masculine 'position of mastery'. (I would argue that in sensation fiction this mastery is also an effect of the specularity of the melodramatic style, especially its tendency to fetishise the female body.) At the same time (or by turns), the reader is placed 'in a masochistic position of . . . identifying with a female character's renunciation' (Kuhn 1987:347), submission, or subjection. It is this contradictory process (and the opportunities that it offers to readers to negotiate contradictions) which opens a space for oppositional readings and the subversion of the dominant discourses.

In fact, it is by no means clear (even in *East Lynne*) that the reader of the sensation novel is placed unequivocally in a 'masochistic' position of identification with the suffering heroine. Indeed, in much sensation fiction the reader might be said to 'spectate', rather than to identify with female suffering. Nevertheless the idea of a (potentially subversive or oppositional) gap between a functionally masculine reading position (of mastery) and the woman reader's customary subservience remains a useful one. Moreover, Kuhn's account of how the woman's text articulates women's anxieties about and resistances to their situation, and simultaneously manages and contains them, offers a pointer towards a way of thinking through the relationship between the subversive and conservative elements of the women's sensation novel. This thinking-through requires a different kind of critical attention from that which sensation fiction has usually received. Instead of merely identifying themes and types, and labelling the elements of a formula, we must engage in close textual analysis which pays particular attention to the rhetorical strategies and devices employed, and to the specific texture of the writing.

One of the defining characteristics of the sensation novel, as of the woman's film, is 'its construction of narratives motivated by female desire and processes of spectator identification governed by female point-of-view' (Kuhn 1987:339). In earlier feminist analyses of sensation fiction, such as Showalter's (1978a and 1978b), female desire and spectator-identification were seen in terms of the female reader's repressed anger and presumed identification with an active and, usually, transgressive heroine. Using some of the perspectives on the spectator and the shifting point of view to which I have referred, one might arrive at a different interpretation of the sensation heroine; although she is of central importance in the sensation novel, the heroine is not necessarily or uniformly the central point of, and for, the reader's identification. Indeed, both Braddon and Wood employ a complex manipulation of point of view, and offer their readers a variety of perspectives and positions within the text which permit a dispersal of narrative identifications: the female reader may, at various points, identify with or share the perspective of the heroine, other female characters, or various of the male characters.

The shifting point of view also produces a number of (varyingly distanced) perspectives on the heroine, ranging from active identification with the transgressive heroine, to a potentially masochistic identification with her sufferings; from sympathy with her plight, to outright condemnation of her transgressions. The reader, by turns, recognises herself in the heroine and views the action through her eyes; is made into a spectator of the heroine, who becomes the fetishised object of her gaze; is addressed by the narrator, or co-opted to a narrative perspective which involves a moral judgement of the heroine. As a consequence of these shifting perspectives the female reader has the complex narrative pleasure (simultaneously or by turns) of spectating and participating in an exciting deviance, and in the moral judgement of that deviance, as well as spectating and participating in the punitive social and emotional consequences of transgression.

Unlike some earlier rereaders of Braddon and Wood (Winifred Hughes, for example), I shall not attempt to account for the popular success or the cultural meaning of their sensation novels simply in terms of their differing degrees of transgression, or sentimental conservatism. Instead I shall suggest that neither novelist offers a single ideological perspective nor, indeed, a coherent and unified range of perspectives, whether radical or conservative. Rather, their novels contain a variety of contradictory views on gender, sexuality, class, marriage and the family. In this respect, they both embody and work through (while remaining within) the ideological battles, contradictions and confusions of the mid-Victorian period.

I shall also suggest that the sensation 'heroine' herself offers a complex and contradictory range of significations, and is not simply the iconic embodiment of transgressive femininity, or a fantasy version of a feared or desired female power, as some critics have argued. If the sensation heroine embodies anything, it is an uncertainty about the definition of the feminine, or of 'woman'. Woman, or a woman, whether as heroine or as villainess (or, as is usual in sensation fiction, as a

81

combination of these two roles), is almost always at the centre of the sensation novel. However, her role in the narrative structure and sexual and familial economy of the novel is fraught with contradictions. In particular it involves 'a conflict between the aesthetic requirements of plot and the conventional social role assigned to women' (Hughes 1980:45). To put a woman at the active centre of a sensation plot was to make her functionally trangressive, because such an active and assertive role conflicted with accepted views of the proper feminine. E.S. Dallas was quick to note the way in which the sensation heroine destabilised established gender categories: 'When women are thus put forward to lead the action of a plot, they must be urged into a false position. To get vigorous action they are described as rushing into crime, and doing masculine deeds' (Dallas 1866:297). However, the key opposition in the sensation novel is not between the 'masculine' woman and the 'feminine' woman, but between conflicting versions of femininity, in particular the proper and the improper feminine. In the sensation plot the shifting and disputed category of the feminine is itself almost always the origin of narrative; the improper feminine functions as the narrative return of those forces which are repressed in and by the social construction of the proper feminine. As Braddon's narrator observes in *Aurora Floyd*: '[I]f she had been faultless she could not have been the heroine of this story; for has not some wise man of old remarked, that the perfect women are those who leave no histories behind them . . .' (AF: 330).

12

Mary Elizabeth Braddon: the secret histories of women

[Sensation novelists] wanted to persuade people that in almost every one of the well-ordered houses of their neighbours there was a skeleton shut up in some cupboard; that their comfortable and easy-looking neighbour had in his breast a secret story which he was always going about trying to conceal.

(Ray 1865:203)

Had every creature a secret, part of themselves, hidden deep in their breasts, like that dark purpose which had grown out of the misery of her father's untimely death – some buried memory, whose influence was to overshadow all their lives?

(EV I:3)

This fearful question, asked by Eleanor Vane, heroine of *Eleanor's Victory*, lies at the heart of the sensation novel. It both exposes and plays on the fear of respectable Victorian society that social and familial normality had some dark secret at its core. The secrets of the family and the secret histories of families are the source of the typical sensation plot, which, as Henry James noted, is concerned with 'those most mysterious of mysteries, the mysteries that are at our own doors' (1865:594). Indeed, the power of sensationalism, as Elaine Showalter has pointed out, derives 'from its exposure of secrecy as the fundamental enabling condition of middle-class life' (1978b:104). As both Showalter and Anthea Trodd (1989) have demonstrated, the sensation novel's characteristic preoccupation with domestic crimes is the focus of a range of anxieties about the nature and structure of the family, and the problematic relationship of this private (feminine) sphere with the public (masculine) domain.

In particular, the sensation novel habitually focuses on the secrets and secret histories of women. All of Mary Elizabeth Braddon's early novels are structured around women with a concealed past: women who, for a variety of reasons, conceal their present motivations and desires, and who have a hidden mission which drives their lives. In most cases these feminine concealments both result from, and foreground, a tension between the proper and the improper feminine. The secret at the heart of Braddon's novels usually involves a former transgression of the bounds of the proper feminine, or it involves a guilt by association, which taints or threatens the heroine's respectability. The concealment most often results from a conflict between a particular woman's self-appointed mission and the accepted codes of the proper feminine, or from the necessity for women to act by stealth, and often through male agents, in a society which casts them in a passive, dependent role. Except in the case of Braddon's two best-known novels, the secret involves a conflict between the heroine's mission to avenge a wronged father (or father-substitute) and that code of the proper feminine which defines woman as self-sacrificing, loving and forgiving. Revenge thus serves as a generalised metaphor for a commanding secret passion, a hidden desire which motivates a woman's actions.

Often, several forms of secrecy converge to generate a particular narrative. In *Eleanor's Victory*, for example, Eleanor Vane conceals and bears the guilty burden of her impoverished past with a dissolute father who is addicted to gambling. Although this 'guilty' past (and its convergence with the family secrets of others) is the origin of the story, it is Eleanor's own deliberate concealments which sustain – and provide the necessary complications for – the narrative trajectory. In the earlier part of this novel Braddon rewrites *The Old Curiosity Shop*, tempering Little Nell's preternatural goodness, which is all suffering and endurance, with a more realistic sense of the moral and psychological consequences of the experience of observing and being involved in the downward spiral of the obsessive gambler. The secret of Dickens's heroine is an ultra-'feminine', passive goodness which passes all understanding, and which cannot survive in this fallen world. Eleanor's secret, on the other hand, is her 'unwomanly' desire for revenge and her active pursuit of the man who has driven her father to suicide.

A similar set of secrets lies at the centre of the particularly complex (even cumbersome) plot and sub-plots of *Run To Earth*, whose heroine, Jenny Milsom, is literally rescued from the gutter (where she has been earning a precarious living as a street-singer) by Sir Oswald Eversleigh, who renames her and remakes her as a genteel woman. Jenny/Honoria's secret history is her ignoble birth (she is the daughter of a desperado called Black Milsom), her association with low-life criminals, and her dark knowledge of hideous crimes. However, an even darker secret sustains the second half of the novel; Honoria compromises her 'womanly' nature by apparently forsaking her infant daughter in order to unravel the secret of (and avenge) her husband's death.

The sins of the father also lie at the root of the concealments of Margaret Wilmot/Wentworth in *Henry Dunbar*. Margaret not only bears the taint of her father's criminality and poverty, but is also implicated in his guilt through her dutifully filial concealment of his murder and impersonation of his former employer. The plot of *Henry Dunbar*, like those of several of Braddon's novels, turns on women's position as 'relative creatures' (Basch 1974) and on the complexities and contradictions resulting from their conflicting loyalties as daughters, wives and mothers. This conflict is repeatedly foregrounded in direct comments by the narrator. In *Eleanor's Victory*, for example, we are told that Eleanor's life 'had fashioned itself to fit that unwomanly purpose [of avenging her father]. She abnegated the privileges, and left unperformed the duties of a wife' (EV II:152); or again, 'She had neglected her duty as a wife, absorbed in her affection as a daughter; she had sacrificed the living to the dead' (EV III:173). Unsurprisingly, the narrative trajectory of this novel, as of most of Braddon's fictions, is directed towards the proper feminisation of the heroine. The 'victory' of the title turns out 'after all' to be 'a proper womanly conquest, and not a stern, classical vengeance. The tender woman's heart triumphed over the girl's rash vow' (EV III:321). Ultimately Eleanor declines to exact her long-desired retribution

85

from her father's destroyer, and wholeheartedly embraces her wifely and womanly role. However, as in other women's sensation novels, without the heroine's 'unwomanly purpose' there would have been no story.

Family secrets and the secret histories of women are most spectacularly present in *Lady Audley's Secret* and *Aurora Floyd*. It is significant that Braddon's most successful novels should each involve the secrets of a woman's own transgressive past, rather than her concealments of the guilty secrets of others. In fact, Braddon's most famous heroines are actually criminals; both are bigamists, and one attempts, and the other is suspected of, murder. Like a number of sensation heroines, Lady Audley and Aurora Floyd are used both to exploit and explore the fear expressed by another bestselling woman novelist, that all women 'possess a sleeping potentiality for crime, a curious possibility of fiendish evil' (Ouida 1895:324).

Aurora Floyd, Braddon's second bestseller, is built around the simplest and most commonplace of secrets: that of an impetuous and misspent youth. According to the double standard of sexual morality such a secret in a man's life may be of little interest; there is no story, unless it be in the return of the repressed feminine, as in Bertha's embodiment of Rochester's past in *Jane Eyre*. In the case of a woman, however, the secret of youthful trangression is the origin of a proliferation of narratives. Aurora, the motherless and hence improperly socialised and improperly feminised heroine of the novel, has extended her masculinised interest in horses and racing to her father's groom, Conyers, with whom she elopes. Rumours of her youthful misdemeanours subsequently prevent her marriage to Talbot Bulstrode, a scion of the Cornish aristocracy. The need to conceal this early misjudgement is compounded (and plot complications proliferate) when, erroneously believing Conyers to be dead, Aurora subsequently marries John Mellish, only to discover that her first husband is still alive, and indeed has come to work on her second husband's estate.

It is worth noting, incidentally, that all of Braddon's heroines (indeed the heroines of most sensation novels) share Aurora's lack of a mother. As the speaker of Florence Nightingale's fragment 'Cassandra' observes: 'the secret of the charm of every romance that ever was written . . . is that the heroine has *generally* no family ties (almost *invariably* no mother), or, if she has, these do not interfere with her entire independence' (quoted in Strachey 1978:397). It is certainly a defining characteristic of the sensation heroine that she has not been 'educated to that end [of the good wife] by a careful mother' (AF:41). As in so many nineteenth-century novels by women, the motherless heroine is both more vulnerable and more assertive than was the norm for the properly socialised woman. Socially sanctioned mothering, as an extended horticultural metaphor in *Aurora Floyd* has it, is required to 'train and prune' the 'exuberant branches' sometimes found in women in their natural state, so that they may be 'trimmed and clipped and fastened primly to the stone wall of society with cruel nails' (AF:42).

Aurora Floyd moves from hidden transgression to concealed criminality more by accident than by design, as a result of her inadvertent bigamy. Lady Audley's secret criminality is, apparently, a matter of cold calculation. Helen Talboys, disguised as Lucy Graham, marries Sir Michael Audley knowing that she is still legally married to George Talboys. When she learns of Talboys's imminent return from Australia she carefully stage-manages the death by consumption of 'Helen Talboys', and places an obituary announcement in *The Times*. Accidentally discovered by her first husband, she pushes him down a well – she assumes to his death – and subsequently attempts to dispose of her second husband's nephew, Robert Audley, whom she fears will reveal her guilt.

These two women, each possessed of a secret past which compromises the marriage on which they embark in the narrative present, become the focus of a range of questions and tensions about the nature of femininity, the domestic ideal, women's role in marriage, and the state of modern marriage, which were central preoccupations in sensation fiction in general. I want to look first at some of the ways in which Braddon's two bestselling novels represent femininity.

STAGING THE FEMININE: BRADDON'S MELODRAMATIC STYLE

Most critics were and are agreed that the power of *Aurora Floyd* and *Lady Audley's Secret* lies in their transgressive heroines. Indeed, both contemporary reviewers and later readers have focused on the transgressive nature of these heroines rather than on their criminality.This tends to reinforce the view that the bigamy novel was used either to develop the adultery plot in a displaced form, or as a way of representing a sexually active female character whilst keeping within that framework of law and custom which was designed to regulate female sexuality. In what ways are Braddon's best-known heroines transgressive? What does their transgressiveness signify? How does it function within the narrative economy of the text?

The characterisations of Aurora Floyd and Lady Audley both involve an elaborate play with fictional female stereotypes. Both characters, in different ways, embody the contradictory discourse on woman (discussed in I, 2 above) in which woman is figured as either a demon or an angel. The two heroines embody and exploit the fear (which pervaded middle-class culture) that women are 'wild beasts' whose lusts and licentiousness run riot if unconstrained by the patriarchal family.[8]

Aurora Floyd is represented from the outset as very obviously transgressing the boundaries of the proper feminine. Her physical appearance is itself a sign that she belongs to the category of the dangerous, improper feminine. Moreover, like her creator, Aurora (in James's memorable phrase) 'knows much that ladies are not accustomed to know' (1865:593). She is represented as a prototypical 'Girl of the Period': her behaviour is generally fast, she uses coarse language, and has a passion for (and unwomanly knowledge of) horseracing. The verve with which this stereotype is represented in Braddon's novel has the paradoxical effect of portraying the culture's demon, the masculinised 'unwomanly' woman, as the desirable and desired feminine. However, Aurora's secret (as revealed in the rapidly unfolding narrative) is that beneath this racy and, apparently, criminal exterior beats the eternal heart of domestic, maternal woman. Aurora's story is the story of the gradual taming of the wild beast of the improper feminine.

On the other hand (an irony not lost on her contemporary readers), Braddon's first *femme fatale*, the bigamous, murderous and possibly insane Lady Audley, seems, at least on the surface, to be contained within the boundaries of the proper and respectable feminine. This feminine ideal is elaborated and, it appears, celebrated in an early descriptive passage:

Wherever she went she seemed to take joy and brightness with her. In the cottages of the poor her fair face shone like a sunbeam. She would sit for a quarter of an hour talking to some old woman, and apparently as pleased with the admiration of a toothless crone as if she had been listening to the compliments of a marquis; and when she tripped away, leaving nothing behind her (for her poor salary gave no scope to her benevolence), the old woman would burst out into senile raptures with her grace . . . For you see Miss Lucy Graham was blessed with that magic power of fascination by which a woman can charm with a word or intoxicate with a smile.

(LAS:5–6)

The direct narratorial address of this extract, with its familiar, even banal, formulae for feminine charms, involves the reader in shared assumptions about the nature of feminine fascination. A typical example of Braddon's descriptive technique, this passage (which continues in the same vein for some length) engages in an excess of description and an over-emphasis on Lucy's embodiment of the feminine ideal, with the effect of making her the object of the reader's gaze. Thus, at the level of textual or narrative representation, Lucy Graham is staged as spectacle, just as within the narrative the character is staging herself. This latter kind of performance is central to Braddon's novels, since, like Lucy Graham, virtually all of her heroines have something to hide, and are to that extent actresses.

Lady Audley shares with a number of Braddon heroines the 'shame' of an ignoble father and humble and impoverished family circumstances. To this is added a more fundamental fear about her parentage: the fear that she may have inherited her mother's madness. This taint, passed on from mother to daughter like a mark of Eve, represents an association between madness and the feminine which was pervasive in nineteenth-century culture.[9] In fact the question of Lady Audley's madness (is she mad, or is she simply clever and/or wicked?) becomes one of the key secrets of the narrative. The repeatedly postponed uncovering of the mystery of Lady Audley is one of the major sources of narrative pleasure, as the main plot of this novel persistently promises to get at the hidden truth of its heroine/villain, and of woman.

As far as the character of Lady Audley herself is concerned, her fear of her secret destiny adds another dimension to the determining conditions of a woman's life. The habits of self-surveillance developed by Helen Maldon/Lady Audley in response to her fears of inheriting her mother's madness are an exaggerated form of that self-scrutiny enjoined upon every woman by prevailing ideas of the proper feminine. Braddon's emphasis on her heroines' concern to protect their secrets, like her habitual minute focus on their sensations and feelings, is in part a foregrounding of the process of self-surveillance endemic in a culture in which the 'supremacy of the woman's moral nature and her potential degeneracy were the twin poles of a representation which had already transposed a panic about the social body – its ordered regulation and reproduction – into moral terms' (Rose 1986:111).

In fact 'Lucy Graham' and 'Lady Audley' are both roles played by Helen Maldon, who has repeatedly remade her identity with each rise in the social scale from the impoverished daughter of a disreputable half-pay naval officer; to the wife of George Talboys, heir to a considerable fortune (from which he is disinherited as a result of his father's displeasure at his imprudent marriage); to Lucy Graham, the quiet, respectable governess. In her final incarnation as Lady Audley, 'every trace of the old life [is] melted away – every clue to identity melted and forgotten', as marriage to Sir Michael promises to put an end to 'dependence . . . drudgery . . . [and] humiliations' (LAS:12).

Braddon not only shows Lady Audley adopting a series of different roles, but also focuses on the way her heroine plays a number of different parts within one apparently stable role. That of 'Lady Audley', the respectable gentlewoman, child-bride of a wealthy baronet, is itself fraught with contradictions; it is a kind of masquerade. By foregrounding Lady Audley's impersonation of proper femininity, the novel does more than simply focus attention on the feminine duplicity in which the entire narrative originates. It also explores and exploits fears that the respectable ideal, or proper feminine, may simply be a form of acting, just one role among other possible roles. Even more seriously, the representation of Lady Audley, like

90

that of some of Braddon's other heroines, raises the spectre that femininity is itself duplicitous, and that it involves deception and dissembling.

Such fears are exploited in one of Braddon's favourite narrative procedures – the construction of a narrative of unmasking. This strategy is most frequently used in a process of progressive revelation of the 'real' nature of a particular female character. In *Lady Audley's Secret* the unmasking narrative is found in its most extreme form in Robert Audley's attempt to expose his uncle's wife. One of the key points in this narrative of the contest between Lady Audley and her husband's nephew – the viewing of Lady Audley's portrait in Chapter 8 – is worth looking at in some detail, since it is a very good example of the way in which Braddon's narratives habitually stage the feminine as spectacle. The strategy is one in which the excess of the melodramatic style is extremely important (I shall return to both of these points shortly).

In his eagerness to improve upon his 'imperfect notion of her face' Robert Audley, accompanied by his friend George Talboys, gains entry to Lady Audley's private rooms, which contain her unfinished portrait. The men's method of entry (by a secret passage) has clear sexual overtones, and the scene is presented as a stealthy, illicit, masculine invasion of a feminine domain. The reader is invited to share in the voyeuristic male gaze upon the exotic and intimate feminine space of Lady Audley's dressing room. The *mise-en-scène* is extremely elaborate and detailed, and emphasises sexual difference. On glimpsing his bearded face in the mirror, Talboys 'wondered to see how out of place he seemed among all these womanly luxuries' (LAS:69). The room, 'almost oppressive from odours', is full of flowers, exquisite china, jewels and gorgeous dresses carelessly abandoned (and suggesting a feminine abandon); all are traces of the feminine presence of the absent Lady Audley.

The scene builds to its climax as the male invaders proceed from the boudoir, through the dressing room, to the ante-chamber and approach Lady Audley's portrait. Unlike the other objects in her apartments the portrait is not just a sign or trace of Lady Audley, it is representation as revelation. The objects in the room are signs of the absent female body, but signs too of the social masquerade which that body adopts. The discarded clothes function both as erotic traces of femininity and as the abandoned costumes of the actress. The portrait, on the other hand, represents the body itself as sign. In viewing the portrait the characters in the narrative acquaint themselves with Lady Audley's face, while the readers are granted access to the secrets of her being. In this scene readers are positioned as spectators of the portrait which is both displayed to their gaze and 'read' for them. Our gaze is fixed firmly on the Pre-Raphaelite detail, while the narrator both satirises Pre-Raphaelitism and appropriates its sensuous and sensual gaze.

The elaborate description and reading of the painting suggest that, just as Audley and Talboys (and hence the reader) have glimpsed something of Lady Audley's inner, private self through their penetration of the recesses of her private rooms, so too the painter has penetrated the inner recesses of her identity and revealed its awful truth (and, perhaps, a feared truth about the nature of femininity): the inner reality that lies behind the mask of respectable femininity.

> It was so like and yet so unlike; it was as if you had burned strange-coloured fires before my lady's face, and by their influence brought out new lines and new expressions never seen before in it . . . [It] had something of the aspect of a beautiful fiend.
>
> (LAS:71)

The portrait scene prefigures the progressive narrative exposure of Lady Audley's secrets. In the narrative, as in the portrait, the angel in the house is revealed as the demon in the house. Long before the end of the novel the domestic idyll of Audley Court is unmasked as a hollow sham, and through this unmasking the economic and power relations of an aristocratic marriage (and the passions it represses) are also exposed. Ultimately the transgressive Lady Audley, too, is unmasked and 'Buried Alive' (to quote the title of the chapter which narrates this event) in a *maison de santé* (a madhouse) in the appositely named Belgian town of Villebrumeuse. Her incarceration and her subsequent death after a prolonged *maladie de langeur* (which is reported in a chapter ironically entitled 'At Peace') are the means by which the trangressive heroine (and the improper feminine) is expelled from the narrative.

However, the improper feminine remains as a repressed trace in the text's narration, in the linguistic excess of the

92

melodramatic style. The physical manifestation of the improper feminine – Lady Audley's body – which has persistently been represented and read as spectacle, is finally represented simply by means of the Pre-Raphaelite painting that had promised to yield up her secrets. In the final paragraphs of the novel the reader's attention is directed once more to this portrait, now hidden behind a curtain from the prurient gaze of 'the inquisitive visitors . . . [who] admire my lady's rooms, and ask many questions about the pretty fairhaired woman, who died abroad' (LAS:446). The curtain which hangs before the portrait is at once a shroud which hides the improper feminine from the society whose equilibrium it has threatened, and also a veil which tantalisingly conceals and maintains the improper feminine's alluring mystery. Thus, even after her death, Lady Audley remains as a disturbing presence.

Lady Audley's Secret deliberately blurs the issue of whether its heroine's acting – her process of self-construction – is the product of her madness, or the result of cool calculation. In either case it is explicitly associated with the process of self-fashioning required by any respectable Victorian girl seeking to make her way in the world. (This is equally true of the way in which Aurora's dissembling is represented in *Aurora Floyd*.) Lady Audley's self-proclaimedly heartless attitude to her situation is, from one point of view, simply a more than usually honest assessment of the nature of the choices open to the would-be genteel woman:

> I had learnt that which in some indefinite manner or other *every schoolgirl learns sooner or later* – I learned that my ultimate fate in life depended upon my marriage, and I concluded that if I was indeed prettier than my schoolfellows, I ought to marry better than any of them.
>
> (LAS:350, my italics)

The reader is also implicated in this common-sense view of Lucy's situation (and thus aligned with the views of a criminal and/or madwoman) through those representative characters 'the simple Dawsons' (Lucy's employers), who encourage her marriage to Sir Michael and who 'would have thought it more than madness in a penniless girl to reject such an offer' (LAS:9). The notion that normal, sane femininity is built upon prudential calculations of this kind is endorsed by Dr Alwyn

Mosgrave, the medical expert called in by Robert Audley in his attempts to deal with the problem of Lady Audley. When in possession of only part of Lady Audley's story – the part relating to her bigamous deception of Sir Michael – Mosgrave delivers a medical verdict that is unequivocal:

> She ran away from her home, because her home was not a pleasant one, and she left it in the hope of finding a better. There is no madness in that. She committed the crime of bigamy, because by that crime she obtained fortune and position. There is no madness there. When she found herself in a desperate position, she did not grow desperate. She employed intelligent means, and she carried out a conspiracy which required coolness and deliberation in its execution. There is no madness in that.
>
> (LAS:377)

Robert Audley's definitions of the feminine are more conventional and less capacious than Mosgrave's. Audley seeks to prove Lady Audley's madness partly to save his friend and his uncle's family from scandal, but largely because his notions of the feminine cannot reconcile *sane* femininity with the criminally duplicitous behaviour of which he intuitively knows Lady Audley to be guilty. The readers' definitions of sane femininity are destabilised by the way in which they are invited, by turns, to share Mosgrave's and Robert Audley's view of the heroine. The readers' view of normal, sane femininity is similarly challenged by their changing emotional investments in the character, which are engineered by the narrator's constantly shifting point of view.

When acquainted with the full extent of Lady Audley's crimes, the expert on insanity agrees to incarcerate her, not because she is mad, but because she is 'dangerous'.

> There is latent insanity! Insanity which might never appear; or which might appear only once or twice in a life-time . . . The lady is not mad; but she has the hereditary taint in her blood. She has the cunning of madness, with the prudence of intelligence. I will tell you what she is, Mr. Audley. She is dangerous!
>
> (LAS:379)

Lady Audley is dangerous because she is not what she appears to be, because she cannot be contained within the bounds of the proper feminine. Mosgrave's diagnosis seems to hold the key to an understanding of the way in which Braddon uses madness in her novels.

Braddon structures several novels (most notably *Lady Audley's Secret* and *John Marchmont's Legacy*) around characters who are, appear to be, or become mad or deranged. In each of these novels madness is used as a way of figuring the dangerous, improper feminine, which is both formed by and resists the management and control of the middle-class family and the self-regulation which is the internalisation of those broader social forms of control. *Lady Audley's Secret* and *John Marchmont's Legacy* both raise the question of whether female insanity may simply be 'the label society attaches to female assertion, ambition, self-interest, and outrage' (Showalter 1987:72). In addition *John Marchmont's Legacy* asks whether madness is, in fact, a *symptom* of bourgeois femininity.

Lady Audley is represented in terms of a contemporary medical discourse in which women's behaviour is related to the vagaries of the female body: her strange career dates from the birth of her son, and the onset of puerperal fever.[10] The figure of Lady Audley – the angel in the house turned domestic fiend – is also produced within and by a socio-medical discourse in which the image of female purity always contains within itself the antithetical image of female vice. Such a figure represents and explores fears that (actual, historical) women cannot be contained within dominant definitions of 'woman', or of normal femininity.

Olivia Arundel, the female villain in *John Marchmont's Legacy*, is in some ways an even more interesting representation of the feminine and of madness, or indeed of the feminine as madness, since her insanity seems to be actively produced by the norms of respectable femininity. Like Lady Audley, Olivia is used to raise the question of whether the proper feminine is a cover for, or the cause of, madness (the improper feminine). Lady Audley's story ends with her incarceration in an asylum modelled on the bourgeois household in order that the domestic ideology and its definitions of femininity may be defended. Olivia's story, on the other hand, is the story of a woman's incarceration within and by that ideology and those definitions. On a number of occasions the narrator focuses directly on this aspect of Olivia's predicament.

Olivia Arundel had lived from infancy to womanhood . . . performing and repeating the same duties from day to day, with no other progress to mark the lapse of her existence than the slow alternation of the seasons, and the dark hollow circles which had lately deepened beneath her grey eyes . . .

These outward tokens, beyond her own control, alone betrayed the secret of this woman's life. She sickened under the dull burden which she had borne so long, and carried out so patiently. The slow round of dull duty was loathsome to her. The horrible, narrow, unchanging existence, shut in by cruel walls, which bounded her on every side, and kept her prisoner to herself was odious to her. The powerful intellect revolted against the fetters that bound and galled it. The proud heart beat with murderous violence against the bonds that kept it captive.

(JML I:135-6)

I have quoted this passage at such length because it is outwardly a direct and open analysis of 'the problem' of the frustrations and constraints of the domestic woman's lot. However, closer scrutiny (and the narratorial perspective is all about *close scrutiny*) reveals Olivia's situation not as a generalised female predicament but as one which is peculiar to the woman of 'powerful intellect'. This aspect of the representation of Olivia reveals, once again, the sensation novel's preoccupation with the blurring and instability of gender categories. The combination of passively endured suffering and the latent aggression of the murderous violence of her captive heart is precisely not what any *normally gendered* woman was supposed to feel about the frustrations of a dull life. The secret of Olivia's predicament seems to be that she is like a man. She is a 'mistake of nature', who has 'the brow of an intellectual and determined man' (JML I:125); she lacks the 'tenderness which is the common attribute of a woman's nature. She ought to have been a great man' (JML III:54).[11]

The above passage also provides another interesting example of the functions and effects of the melodramatic style. The omniscient narrator appears to be in complete control of the

96

character, whose inner secrets are fathomed and anatomised with forensic care and detail. However, Olivia is also constituted as a disturbance, and thus beyond anatomisation and control. As the agent of disruption and confusion she is a disturbance in the narrative, but she is also a disturbance at the level of narration. The stance of narratorial control is disrupted by the melodramatic excess, not only of Olivia's actions, but also of the way in which she is represented in and as language. The narrator's forensic representation is overwhelmed by the melodramatic style, and the anatomising stance is abandoned at the end of the long passage quoted earlier.

> *How shall I anatomise* this woman, who, gifted with no womanly tenderness of nature, unendowed with that pitiful and unreasoning affection which makes womanhood beautiful, yet tried, and tried unceasingly, to do her duty, and to be good . . .?
>
> (JML I:136, my italics)

Anatomising is replaced by display. As is so often the case in Braddon's fiction, the narrator announces the difficulty or impossibility of articulating a particular example of the feminine, only to embark on a surplus of articulation.

THE MELODRAMATIC STYLE AND THE SPECTACLE OF WOMAN

This melodramatic excess is one of the hallmarks of Braddon's style, as it is of the sensation novel in general. It is an irruption into narration of that feeling (particularly the erotic feeling) which is repressed in the narrative. This excess – as Jane Feuer (1984) argues of television melodrama – opens up a 'textual space, which may be read against the seemingly hegemonic surface' (8). It appears in its most highly wrought form in set-piece scenes and dramatic tableaux which stage the heroine/villainess as a spectacle; she may be presented as the object of a public gaze within the text, or the scene may be staged directly for the reader. In such scenes the female body becomes a sign (or system of signs) which is imperfectly read, or misread, by the characters within the text, but which is legible to the narrator, and hence to the reader – even if what is legible is finally the sign's elusiveness.

Again and again in Braddon's novels female characters are represented by means of an intense focus on their physical appearance. For example, the mystery of Olivia's failure to conform to the feminine ideal is both 'explained' and inscribed in this description of her hair (a passage which, incidentally, typifies Braddon's habitual fetishisation of women's hair):

> Those masses of hair had not that purple lustre, nor yet that wandering glimmer of red gold, which gives peculiar beauty to some raven tresses. Olivia's hair was long and luxuriant; but it was of that dead, inky blackness, which is all shadow. It was dark, fathomless, inscrutable, like herself.
>
> (JML I:141)

Braddon's women rise up from the page like the heavily sensualised female subjects of Pre-Raphaelite paintings, and are offered as the object of the reader's rapt gaze. This staging of a particular version of the feminine for the gaze of the reader is also prominent in *Aurora Floyd*. Aurora's mother, who plays no part in the narrative present of the novel (she died at Aurora's birth), is, nevertheless, a powerful narrative presence, and provides a way of representing and viewing the feminine which anticipates the presence of the heroine herself.

> The banker's wife was a tall young woman, of about thirty, with a dark complexion, and *great flashing black eyes* that lit up a face, which might otherwise have been *unnoticeable*, into the splendour of absolute beauty.
>
> (AF:7, my italics)

Noticing this flashing incandescence is precisely what the text requires readers to do, as the narrator invites them to gaze admiringly at Eliza. As in the description of Olivia's hair, the passage works by addressing and invoking a particular cultural awareness of the female body. The reader is co-opted into the role of co-creator of the spectacle.

> *Let the reader recall* one of those faces, whose chief loveliness lies in the glorious light of a pair of magnificent eyes, and *remember* how far they surpassed all others in

their power of fascination. The same amount of beauty frittered away upon a well-shaped nose, rosy pouting lips, symmetrical forehead, and delicate complexion, would make an ordinarily lovely woman; but concentrated in one nucleus, in the wondrous lustre of the eyes, it makes a divinity, a Circe.

(AF:7, my italics)

The speaking presence of the body in the text was a much-discussed aspect of sensation fiction. Their tendency to dwell on the (female) body was generally regarded as one of the improprieties of sensation novels; the intense physicality of their representation of the heroine was the source of their perceived transgression. Braddon's deployment of a familiar repertoire of physical traits and ways of describing the seductive feminine was one of the formulaic aspects of her novels which were much criticised by reviewers. Since these formulae are such a prominent feature of her work, one can only assume that such writing was also an important source of pleasure to readers, and hence that it is worth examining more closely.

As I have suggested, the reader is repeatedly required to *notice* Braddon's central female characters. Aurora, for example, is first brought to notice (although it is not the first time she appears in the text) when she is the object of the fascinated gaze of Talbot Bulstrode, to whom she appears as, 'A divinity! imperiously beautiful in white and scarlet, painfully dazzling to look upon, intoxicatingly brilliant to behold' (AF:29). The rest of this passage simultaneously indulges in and satirises the practice of spectating femininity, by representing Bulstrode's fluctuating and contradictory reponses to (and revisions of) his vision, before it is punctured by the bathetic 'reality' of Aurora's enquiry about the result of a horse race.

Aurora is sometimes presented as the direct object of the reader's gaze, and sometimes mediated through a male gaze, while at other times the reader spectates a more or less public spectating of the character. Several of these perspectives are present in the following scene, which stages Aurora's arrival at Mellish Park upon her marriage to its owner:

They [the Yorkshire servants] could not choose but admire Aurora's eyes, which they unanimously declared

99

to be 'regular shiners;' and the flash of her white teeth, glancing between the full crimson lips; and the bright flush which lighted up her pale white skin; and the purple lustre of her massive coronal of plaited hair. Her beauty was of that luxuriant and splendid order which has almost always most effect upon the masses, and the fascination of her manner was almost akin to sorcery in its power over simple people.

(AF:110)

This passage moves from physically displaying Aurora to the reader through the eyes of the Yorkshire servants, to implicating the reader directly in the process of spectatorship. The feminine power of the character not only bewitches simple people (like the servants) but also (by the end of the passage) intoxicates the discriminating narrator: 'I lose myself when I try to describe the feminine intoxications, the wonderful fascination exercised by this dark-eyed siren' (AF:111). Aurora Floyd possesses the text. The effect is one of simultaneously exploiting and satirising those mid-Victorian 'regimes of representation' which 'signify in the historical process of redefinition of woman as *image, as visibly different*' (Pollock 1988:120).

Like Lady Audley, Aurora Floyd is continually presented as spectacle, as a speaking picture of power, pride and beauty. The reader is repeatedly invited to join a character (usually a male character) in a voyeuristic spectating of the unwitting heroine – as when John Mellish discovers his wife asleep in her dressing room:

Aurora was lying on the sofa, wrapped in a loose white dressing-gown, her masses of ebon hair uncoiled and falling about her shoulders in serpentine tresses that looked like shining blue-black snakes released from poor Medusa's head to make their escape amid the folds of her garment.

(AF:227)

Here, the heroine is 'pictured' in the 'sleeping-woman' pose much favoured by male artists of the later nineteenth century. She is represented by a heavily sexualised word-painting which is typical of Braddon's sixties novels. This aspect of Braddon's melodramatic style, like the paintings it replicates, offers a representation of woman as simultaneously 'an object of erotic desire and a creature of self-containment, not really interested in, and hence not making any demands upon, the viewer's participation in her personal erotic gratification' (Djikstra 1986:69).[12]

The effect is a representation of female sexuality as voyeuristic spectacle, which offered both male and female readers pleasurable images of female erotic power. The potential danger of this power is defused through the fetishisation of the text's gaze, and through the melodramatic style. As in the portrait scene from *Lady Audley's Secret* (see pp. 91–2) and in numerous other passages in Braddon's novels which represent female figures in private female spaces (especially boudoirs and dressing rooms),[13] such writing (like the painting styles it both replicates and satirises) combines sexual frisson with the promise of a privileged access to feminine interiority.

Braddon's writing both panders to a contemporary taste created by Rossetti and his followers and, at the same time, foregrounds in its satiric excess the way in which the Pre-Raphaelites figured woman as fantasy, the 'sign of masculine desire' (Pollock 1988:21). As Griselda Pollock has suggested, the Pre-Raphaelite representation of woman as difference was a direct intervention in the complex process of renegotiation of gender roles which was taking place throughout the latter half of the nineteenth century.

In the visual sign, woman, [which was] manufactured in a variety of guises in mid-nineteenth-century British culture, this absolute difference is secured by the erasure of indices of real time and actual space, by an abstracted . . . representation of faces as dislocated uninhabited spaces which function as a screen across which masculine fantasies of knowledge, power, and possession can be enjoyed in a ceaseless play on the visible obviousness of woman and the puzzling enigmas, reassuringly disguised behind the mask of beauty. At the same time, the face and sometimes part of a body are severed from the whole. Fetish-like they signify an underlying degree of anxiety generated by looking at this sign of difference, woman.

(Pollock 1988:123)

101

The cumulative effect of those scenes in which Braddon writes the body is complex. Ultimately, however, they work to destabilise the category of the feminine by simultaneously reinscribing and satirically undercutting conventional codes for describing and representing the female body.

The staging of the heroine as spectacle is also the site of another important destabilising factor in Braddon's novels, and a source of their subversive potential. Within the narrative economy of a particular text, the heroine usually has a functionally trangressive role as subject or agent. However, this active trangression is undercut or negated at the level of narration, where the heroine is the passive object of the text's gaze, placed in a specular relationship to the reader, who, in turn, occupies a position of mastery *vis à vis* the heroine. On the other hand, the frequent changes in point of view involve the reader in constantly shifting power relations with the heroine. The reader moves from spectating her as the object of the text's or narrator's gaze, to seeing her through the eyes of one or more of the other characters, to sharing her own perspective, or being co-opted by the narrator to a moral judgement or sympathetic understanding of her heroine. These constant shifts tend to keep the heroine's meaning and significance in a state of flux. As in the contradictory or double discourse on woman, Braddon's heroines constantly shift from being active agents to passive sufferers, from transgressors to victims.

MASCULINITY, THE FEMININE IDEAL, AND MODERN MARRIAGE

Although most of Braddon's sixties novels, especially *Lady Audley's Secret* and *Aurora Floyd*, focus on different kinds and differing degrees of feminine transgression, they are not simply stories of the thrills and spills of errant femininity (or, as it would sometimes seem, stories about reforming or expelling it). Rather they use the transgressive woman as both a trigger and a focus for a range of narratives of uncertainty about gender, class, marriage and the family.

Uncertainties about gender are not confined to the definitions of femininity, but are also demonstrated in the representation of masculinity. Braddon's novels habitually reproduce and satirise contemporary anxieties about the blurring of gender boundaries and gender functions. Robert Audley in *Lady Audley's Secret* is used to focus attention on the social construction of gender as he progresses from a period of 'feminised' indolence to a fully 'masculinised' role as head of the bourgeois family. Audley plays a crucial role in *Lady Audley's Secret*: the unmasking of a duplicitous female by a feminised male. This unmasking provides the novel's central narrative dynamic – the cat-and-mouse game in which Robert tries to penetrate and unmask the secrets of his aunt, and she tries first to ensnare him sexually and then to kill him. Both ploys are equally threatening to Robert's masculine identity.

The parrying relationship between nephew and aunt both focuses on gender instabilities, and ultimately stabilises them. Robert's suspicions of his aunt are represented as a privileged insight into her nature, which derives, in part, from his quasi-incestuous attraction to her. His insight into Lady Audley's secrets is also associated with his own feminised identity. The Robert Audley of the early stages of the narrative is a version of the improper masculine, that is to say, he has not been properly socialised into an acceptable masculine role. Audley is an example of that recurring spectre of Victorian fiction, the young man whose active energies and purpose are sapped by 'expectations' and by the lack of a necessity to earn his own living. His brooding, sensitive nature is formed by his 'feminine' habit of reading decadent French novels; his lack of vocation or employment supplies him with extensive leisure in which to brood on the situation at Audley Court with the heightened sensitivity and imagination produced by this reading.

In his pursuit of the secret of Lady Audley, Robert discovers manhood and his vocation. He embarks on a chivalric quest, to solve the mystery of George Talboys's disappearance and Lady Audley's role in it. This chivalric quest is transformed into bourgeois epic as, in his detective role, Robert increasingly develops the legal skills which had merely bored him when he was ostensibly practising at the Bar. Robert's obsessive knightly detective quest, a central strand of the narrative, derives, in part, from a masculine camaraderie and loyalty to George Talboys. However, more importantly for the narrative and sexual economy of the novel, Robert's quest is also (and increasingly) motivated by his love for George's sister Clara. This relationship functions to some extent as a displacement of the homoerotic bonding of Robert and George. (There is a great deal of narratorial insistence on Robert's attraction to Clara's close physical resemblance to her brother.) However, its main function is its role in the novel's investigation and satirisation, as well as reproduction and naturalisation, of a particular social construction of masculinity. The movement from male bonding to male–female bonding is presented as part of a process of maturation and socialisation. As both motivator and reward of the novel's bourgeois epic, the transparent Clara becomes the foundation of Robert's emergence into a properly socialised masculinity; his quest to unmask and expel Lady Audley becomes the route to that destiny.

Clara is the true embodiment of the domestic ideal which Lady Audley merely impersonates. She also embodies many of its contradictions. Robert's discovery of Clara comes at a crucial stage in the repression and expulsion of his attraction to the dangerous, duplicitous femininity of the *femme fatale* in Lady Audley. It also plays a vital part in his conversion to the roles of defender of the proper feminine, and of the patriarchal, aristocratic family from the threat of dissolution.[14] In this last respect Robert acts as his uncle's proxy as well as Clara's. In fact Robert's quest ends in a subtle displacement and merging of aristocratic and bourgeois values, which is complex in its effects. Robert does indeed expel the disrupter of his uncle's household but, significantly, his actions do not result in the restoration of equilibrium, or the reinstatement of the aristocratic family. The patriarch Sir Michael retires from the scene, a broken man, and Audley Court remains empty.

The aristocratic family is not so much restored as remade, in the genial companionate union of Alicia Audley (Sir Michael's daughter) and Sir Harry Towers. The main focus of the novel's closure, however, is the bourgeois, suburban idyll 'in a fairy cottage . . . between Teddington Lock and Hampton Bridge' (LAS:445), where Robert becomes the head of an idealised affective family and a rising man of the legal profession. The idealised family of Robert, Clara, George and their respective offspring not only replaces the aristocratic one of Sir Michael Audley, but is also a renewal of the bourgeois family, in which warmth and affection replace the cold formality of the mother-less family of Harcourt Talboys.

The concluding idyll of Lady Audley's Secret is partly a fantasy resolution of the contradictions of the Victorian bourgeois family: a patriarchal institution which is, nevertheless, persistently represented as a private feminised space. The Thames-side cottage is a feminised domestic world in which, paradoxically, men can be men. It is a world purged of the improper feminine of illegitimate desire, passion and French novels. However, Braddon's use of the conventional closure of a marriage which reinstates the order of the bourgeois family and the domestic ideal, also foregrounds the contradictions of that institution and that ideal, and destabilises them through satire. The beginning of the novel's concluding chapter has an element of self-conscious excess, of over-perfection, as the redeemed and redeeming younger generation eat strawberries and cream in 'pretty rustic harmony', and everything is 'pretty', 'merry' or 'generous-hearted'.

The proper feminine of the domestic ideal is further undercut, in both Aurora Floyd and Lady Audley's Secret, through the juxtapositioning of problematic representatives of the improper feminine with equally problematic representatives of the proper or respectable feminine. In Lady Audley's Secret, Clara's capacity to motivate the lethargic Robert Audley is a testimony to the power of the proper feminine, but her dull, enduring passivity and her subjugation to her father's will clearly demonstrate the negative aspects of this version of femininity. The norms of respectable femininity are similarly questioned in the counterpointing of Aurora Floyd's story with that of her virtuous cousin Lucy. Like Braddon's transgressive women, the angelic Lucy is also subjected to the specularity of the narrator's gaze, for example in the treatment of the agonies of her initially unrequited love for Talbot Bulstrode. Bulstrode's dilemma over the competing charms of Lucy and Aurora serves as a focus for a review of the limitations as well as the strengths of the respectable feminine and the domestic ideal. His 'ideal woman' is a powerful cultural stereotype:

> . . . some gentle and feminine creature crowned with an aureole of pale auburn hair; some timid soul with down-cast eyes . . . some shrinking being, as pale and prim as

the mediaeval saints in his pre-Raphaelite engravings, spotless as her own white robes, excelling in all womanly graces . . . but only exhibiting them in the narrow circle of a home.

(AF:34)

Lucy is, in fact, the very pattern of the domestic ideal, 'exactly the sort of woman to make a good wife'.

Purity and goodness had looked over her and hemmed her in from her cradle. She had never seen unseemly sights, or heard unseemly sounds. She was as ignorant as a baby of all the vices and horrors of this big world . . . and if there were a great many others of precisely the same type of graceful womanhood, it was certainly the highest type, and the holiest, and the best.

(AF:41)

Aurora Floyd contrives simultaneously to endorse this ideal and satirise it, but above all to make it seem much duller than its alternative, Aurora.

Lucy and Clara are, of course, common fictional stereotypes, of the kind one expects to find in formulaic fiction such as Braddon's. Perhaps more unusual is the self-consciousness of Braddon's use of stereotypes, and the way in which this self-consciousness foregrounds the ideological power of generic conventions. Braddon's novels also explore, from a variety of perspectives, the hypocrisies, self-deceptions and repressions of the aristocratic, or would-be aristocratic, male, and the social codes over which he presides. These male stereotypes are often used for satirical purposes, but here, as in other matters, the effects of Braddon's satire are complex. Masculine stereotypes or values which are satirically undercut are, in several cases, finally endorsed. Such complexity (even contradiction) is evident in the treatment of Talbot Bulstrode and John Mellish in *Aurora Floyd*: the former, rigidly proud, jealous of his social position and fiercely moralistic; the latter, a more open, frank and generous version of masculinity, a 'big, hearty, broad-chested Englishman' in whom 'the Rev. Charles Kingsley would have delighted' (AF:48). The self-satisfied conservatism of the social code of each of these men is satirised, but both

106

are ultimately vindicated. Partly this is an endorsement of a specifically contemporary masculinity.

Surely there is some hope that we have changed for the better within the last thirty years, inasmuch as we attach a new meaning to this simple title of 'gentleman'. I take some pride, therefore, in the two young men of whom I write, for the simple reason that I have no dark patches to gloss over in the history of either of them.

(AF:51)

Like that of Robert Audley, the fully-formed masculinity of each of these characters is constructed, finally, through complex engagements with various versions of the feminine. Robert Audley, as I have noted, is made as a man by detecting the improper feminine in Lady Audley, by hunting down and containing her secret, and expelling the improper feminine from both himself and the family. In *Aurora Floyd*, where the improper feminine is less alien and masculinity rarely as compromised or threatened as in the earlier novel, Mellish negotiates (rather than confronts) Aurora's secret and domesticates rather than expels the improper feminine. Bulstrode's cold, aristocratic masculinity is challenged and destabilised by his encounter with the dangerous feminine of Aurora, and humanised by learning to accept and forgive feminine transgression (the ministrations of his wife, Aurora's cousin Lucy, are crucial here).

Gender and class are always complexly intertwined categories in Braddon's novels. The focus on specific versions of the masculine and feminine is also a scrutiny of specific versions of class. Ambivalences and anxieties about gender categories and boundaries are, similarly, related to anxieties about class. Braddon's feminised males and transgressive or masculinised women often have ambivalent class positions: they are socially ambitious, their class origins are more lowly than their current or desired social position, or they have not been properly socialised to the class to which they belong. As I noted earlier, Braddon's sensation plots are driven by family secrets, especially women's secrets, which are often connected with lowly social origins and/or social ambition. The typical Braddon novel of the 1860s involves a threat to the family (usually the aristocratic family) from destabilising forces such as a lower-class woman or a socially ambitious male. Such plots serve as a focus for numerous anxieties about the mores of mid-nineteenth-century marriage.

On marriage, as on gender, Braddon's novels offer a range of voices and perspectives. The narrator repeatedly addresses the understanding reader on the way things generally are in marriage in the modern world. This is usually articulated in the woman-to-woman address, which both Braddon and Wood use to position the reader as a feminine subject and as a member of a community which shares common feelings and values. This strategy is used in the address to careless wives, which provides a context for Aurora's predicament.

> Ah, careless wives! who think it a small thing, perhaps, that your husbands are honest and generous, constant and true, and who are apt to grumble because your next-door neighbours have started a carriage . . . stop and think of this wretched girl, who in this hour of desolation recalled a thousand little wrongs she had done to her husband, and would have laid herself under his feet to be walked over by him could she have thus atoned for her petty tyrannies . . . Think of her in her loneliness, with her heart yearning to go back to the man she loved.
>
> (AF:290)

Such writing works to reinforce normative womanly virtues by positioning the reader in a socially or sexually trangressive role, and making her experience vicariously the frisson of having lost the benefits (taken for granted by the ordinary bourgeois wife) of the love of a good man. Although it has the effect of 'talking up' the value of ordinary marriage, this confident pontification is, to some extent, destabilised by the particularities of the situations which the novels dramatise, and by the use of a number of different points of view.

The predicament of the woman who has married into a superior social class is one important focus for Braddon's critique of modern marriage. It is treated satirically in the depiction in *Aurora Floyd* of Eliza Prodder's self-confident negotiations of the snobbery of the County families when she marries the banker Archibald Floyd. Her years as an actress have accustomed her to playing a part and to mixing with stage duchesses, and her fears that 'I shall die of my grandeur, as the poor girl did at Burleigh House' (AF:13) are unfounded. Elsewhere Braddon focuses minutely on the rigours of the role of wife to the upper-middle-class or aristocratic male, and particularly on the wife's learning to play the part expected of her by her husband and the society in which she finds herself. The novels repeatedly focus on a wife's anxieties about being on public view – displayed by her husband to his family and neighbours, or observed or spied on by servants or other members of the household.[15]

Male fears and anxieties about marriage are also explored. They are staged structurally through plots which focus on threats to the patriarchal family by transgressive women. In addition the reader is, from time to time, positioned within a male perspective from which she views male expectations of women and of marriage, and male fears about the social realities of the marriage market. I have already noted Braddon's focusing on the fears and feelings of Mellish and Bulstrode in *Aurora Floyd*; the bathetic scrutiny of Sir Michael Audley's disappointments following his proposal to Lucy is another interesting example:

> He walked straight out of the house, this foolish old man, because there was some strong emotion at work in his heart . . . something almost akin to disappointment; some stifled and unsatisfied longing which lay heavy and dull at his heart, as if he had carried a corpse from his bosom . . . He must be contented, like other men of his age, to be married for his fortune and his position.
>
> (LAS:111–12)

The contradictions inherent in Victorian views of marriage, notably the attempt to hold together a belief in the nobility and sanctity of marital love with a belief in economically prudential alliances, are the source of the narratives of marriage at the centre of most of Braddon's novels. They are seen at their most extreme in the scrutiny of Gilbert Monckton's almost masochistic fantasies about wifely betrayal in *Eleanor's Victory*.

> Yes, Gilbert Monckton had [apparently] discovered the fatal truth that marriage is not always union and that the holiest words that were ever spoken cannot weave the mystic web which makes two souls indissolubly one . . .

109

Did not girls . . . marry for money, again and again, in these mercenary days?

(EV II:140)

In Braddon's fiction marriage is not merely a device of closure but, as in the New Woman fiction of the nineties, a source of story. One of her dominant plots (with the notable exception of *Lady Audley's Secret*) is that in which a wife who has married for prudential reasons (whether these be financial or as a means to some other desired end) learns to love her husband within marriage. Marriage is thus not the goal of romantic love, but *the* site upon which it is constructed.

Braddon's narratives of marriage are usually structured around a series of scenes from a marriage which is threatened by secrecy and lack of understanding between the partners. The most common narrative situation involves the suspicions of one of the partners about the past or present secrets of the other. Although these difficulties are causally linked to specific plot situations, they are also seen as being inherent in the way women and men are socially constructed along rigid lines of difference. Men and women are shown as being foreign countries to each other, largely as a consequence of the fact that they view each other through stereotypes and ideals. In such narratives marriage, the presumed site of union and mutual understanding, is revealed as, in fact, a state of mutual isolation, secrecy and misunderstanding.

Viewing the consequences of such secrecy is a major source of narrative pleasure in Braddon's fiction. Readers are invited to observe and/or participate in the sufferings of characters who have to endure the 'tortures known only to the husband whose wife is parted from him by that which has more power to sever than any . . . wide extent of ocean – a secret' (AF:145). The preoccupation with secrecy in marriage adds another layer of spectating to Braddon's plots. The novels make frequent use of scenes in which a fearful and suspecting spouse watches his or her partner in a scene with another, or others, from which the spectating spouse feels excluded. Such scenes almost always involve the spectating character in misreading what is being seen.

Such misreading is particularly prominent in *Eleanor's Victory*, in which husband and wife are separated by the secrets

110

of their past and by their different social experience. Both habitually misread the signs of each other's behaviour. Gilbert, in particular, misreads a number of scenes in which he is the jealous and masochistic spectator, such as this scene between Eleanor, her friend Richard Thornton, and Launcelot Darrell, the man she suspects of being responsible for her father's death:

> Following every varying expression of her face, Gilbert Monckton saw that she looked at [Thornton] with an earnest questioning appealing glance, that seemed to demand something of him . . . Looking from his wife to Richard, the lawyer saw that Launcelot Darrell was still watched . . . Mr Monckton felt very much like a spectator who looks on at a drama which is being acted in a language that is unknown to him.
>
> (EV II:209)

Such scenes of spectating are even more important in Ellen Wood's novels, and I shall return to the function of this spectatorship in the next section.

Another aspect of secrecy that is foregrounded in Braddon's novels, and in sensation fiction generally, is its ability to transform the home, in Victorian middle-class ideology a domestic shrine, into a prisonhouse of suspicion. Indeed, as in some popular women's genres of the twentieth century, such as the woman's film and the family melodrama of the 1940s and 1950s (and possibly for similar reasons), the domestic setting of the sensation novel is an extremely important part of its message and its pleasures. One of these pleasures is the opportunity afforded by the *mise-en-scène* for a sort of fictional equivalent of a visit to a stately home. Many of Braddon's novels are set in, or involve visits to, rather grand houses, which are described in lavish detail. The use of such settings offers two important sources of narrative pleasure. First it is a kind of voyeurism, allowing the reader to spy on the lives of those in a superior social class. Secondly, and more importantly for the ideological work of sensation fiction, it reconciles the reader to the limitations of her own marriage, home and social circle by means of what one might call the 'Dallas' effect. Like melodramatic television soap opera and cinematic family melodrama, sensation fiction displays to its readers people with

111

money, status and power who, despite their possession of these desired attributes, do not possess happiness. Moreover, since the admired wealth and position are often built on guilty secrets they are insecure and are easily lost. This both articulates social insecurity in a time of rapid change, and also opens a space for the reader to believe that, like femininity, class and social status are a form of masquerade.

Braddon's sensation novels thus play upon their readers' social and material ambitions only to turn them back on themselves and reconcile readers to the mundane securities (however limited) of their own lot. Each portrait of the beautiful, beloved and/or powerful woman is matched by a scene focusing on her misery and powerlessness. Every elaborate description of a lavish interior is matched by a scene of disenchantment in which an aspiring character is pictured in the setting which had previously been the goal of his or her ambitions. Thus Honoria, the child of the gutter (and worse), is pictured surveying the lands and woods she has inherited from her husband only to discover that 'the possession of them means nothing to me' (RE II:32). Similarly, although 'there was a time' when the Bovaryiste Isobel Gilbert in *The Doctor's Wife* 'would have thought it a grand thing to be rich' (347), it has passed when she inherits the house and lands she had once dreamed of.

By juxtaposing the glamorous domestic setting with the scene of disenchantment, Braddon's novels articulate the contradictions of the Victorian view of the home. On the one hand the bourgeois home exists in the public sphere as a sign of social status and site of conspicuous consumption. On the other hand, it belongs to the private sphere of the moral and emotional life. Braddon's sensation novels variously negotiate, resolve, or merely display those contradictions, but in certain cases they work to reposition the woman as a domestic creature. Thus at a key moment in her transformation from racy Girl of the Period to reconstructed domestic woman, Aurora re-views the grand rooms of Mellish Park, not as the potential theatre for her public display but as the setting of a domestic life endangered by revelations about her secret past: 'How pretty the rooms look! . . . how simple and countrified! It was for *me* that the new furniture was chosen . . . Good-bye, dear home, in which I was an impostor and a cheat' (AF:278–9).

When she has repented, and paid for, her transgressive past, Aurora can reoccupy her 'dear home' as a doting wife and mother. However, she does so on new terms. The narrative constructed around Aurora works to translate her marriage and her possession of her home from (to adapt Cixous's terms) the economy of property to the realm of the gift. Anxieties about marriage being a form of prostitution are thus foregrounded by aspects of the sensation plot, but those anxieties are ultimately dispelled as the novel's central marriage is transformed from an economic transaction to a freely given exchange of love. The effect of this process in *Aurora Floyd* (and perhaps in the sensation novel in general) is, in part, simply to mask the real economic relations of marriage, but it also involves an attempt to reassure (male and female) readers that these relations are capable of transformation.

13

Ellen Wood: Secret skeletons in the family, and the spectacle of women's suffering

> Domestic melodrama, situated at the emotional and moral centre of life, is the most important type of Victorian melodrama; it is here that we see primal fears clothed in everyday dress.
>
> (Vicinus 1981:128)

> A small country town in the heart of England was the scene some years ago of a sad tragedy. I must ask my readers to bear with me while I relate it. These crimes, having their rise in the evil passions of our nature, are not the most pleasant for the pen to record; but it cannot be denied, that they do undoubtedly bear for many of us an interest amounting to fascination.
>
> (*Lord Oakburn's Daughters*:1)

> Few of us are without some secret skeleton that we have to keep sacred from the world.
>
> (*Lord Oakburn's Daughters*:339)

These last two quotations from Ellen Wood's now-forgotten *Lord Oakburn's Daughters* contain many of the key elements of her sensation novels (or, more correctly, sensation-influenced novels) from the 1860s. All of these works are tales of 'sad tragedy', set in fairly closed communities on the edges of small English country towns. They are tales of crime and passion involving secret skeletons and the masks and strategies by which those secrets are both generated and concealed. They are all narrated by an intrusive, moralising and gossipy feminine narrator, who, both explicitly and implicitly, acknowledges and panders to a common fascination with the 'evil passions of our nature', while ultimately distancing herself and her readers from them. Wood adhered more closely than did Braddon to the forms of sentimental domestic fiction, and her plot situations, character types and overt moralising more nearly resemble domestic melodrama than do those of her more satirically inclined contemporary.

Wood's novels from the 1860s are, typically, dynastic narratives. They are stories of rivalry within and/or between families, and often have complicated inheritance plots. Both the dynastic rivalry and the inheritance plots turn on issues of transgenerational and class competition. They also involve the exchange of women between men and, quite often, the hero's exchange of one woman for another (morally and spiritually superior) woman. These plots foreground questions of power and authority within the family and society at large, and the means by which they are sustained and legitimated. *Trevlyn Hold*, for example, is the story of the usurpation of an estate from a decaying aristocratic family (the Trevlyns) by an aggressive *rentier* (Chattaway), and its ultimate transmission to its rightful moral heir – the dispossessed yeoman farmer George Ryle – who eventually becomes the manager of the estate and its legally designated heir. Wood's narrative is a version of the family romance, the childhood fantasy, described by Freud, in which the child plays out the Oedipal drama by substituting rich or aristocratic parents for its own. In Wood's narrative, class frequently seems to be a more powerful driving force than sex.

In *Trevlyn Hold* the aristocratic family, the Trevlyns, fractured by rivalry and dispersal, and so physically weak that the male line is about to die out, is renovated by vigorous yeoman stock which espouses all the bourgeois virtues of thrift, hard work and strict conscience. By the end of the novel the new squire's defence of work suggests that the aristocracy has also embraced bourgeois values:

> If the fact of working is to take the gentle blood out of
> a man, there'll not be much gentle blood left for the next
> generation. This is a working age . . . the world has

115

grown wise, and we most of us work with the hands, or
with the head. Thomas Ryle's son is a gentleman if ever
I saw one.

(TH:398)

The plot of *Trevlyn Hold* thus has the effect of squaring legality
with morality and of moralising the idea of the gentleman.
Verner's Pride has a similarly complex, and even more sinister,
inheritance plot turning on intra-familial rivalries. This plot,
like that of *Trevlyn Hold*, works to authorise the claims to
power of the moral heir and true gentleman, Lionel Verner,
but only after he too has experienced dispossession and has
been forced to make his own way in the world.

The role of the aristocratic woman in this renovation of
the aristocracy by bourgeois values is particularly interesting.
George is named as the heir of Trevlyn Hold in his own right,
but he would, in any case, have been likely to inherit through
Maude, a Trevlyn daughter whom he has won for his wife by
the same virtues that have secured him the estate. Similarly
Lionel's confirmation in his possession of Verner's Pride is
accompanied by his marriage to the genteel, upper-class Lucy
Tempest, following a misguided first marriage to Sibylla West,
the socially ambitious daughter of an unscrupulous doctor.

It is clear that such plots both feed on and address profound
anxieties about class and the family at a time of great social
mobility. In *Trevlyn Hold* and *Verner's Pride* Wood fuses
elements of the domestic and the sensation novel to provide
a kind of family melodrama which 'opposes an old order and
a new order through successive generations' (Rodowick
1987:9). In both cases an older feudalism is replaced by a new
social order represented by something that looks very like the
bourgeois family. One of the most striking aspects of Wood's
representation of this process is the way in which her narratives naturalise it. Because both George Ryle and Lionel Verner
are themselves sufficiently closely linked to the old feudal
order, the transition to the new bourgeois world, although
problematic and a source of much narrative complication, is
presented as natural. The social and political implications of
both the story and the transitional process are obscured or
erased; a social process is represented as a personal and familial drama. David Rodowick has suggested that this erasing

116

of the social and the political is characteristic of domestic melodrama as a mode. In such melodrama, he argues:

> [T]he family tries to substitute itself . . . for the global network of authority in which it is implicated; [domestic melodrama] also imagines itself as addressing itself to an audience which does not believe itself to be possessed of social power . . . [I]t is attentive only to the problems which concern the family's internal security and economy . . . The power it reserves for itself is limited to rights of inheritance and the legitimation of the social and sexual identities in which it reproduces its own network of authority.
>
> (Rodowick 1987:270)

Wood's most successful novel, *East Lynne* (like *Lady Audley's Secret* one of the most successful novels of the nineteenth century), also explores the family as a site for the construction and legitimation of social and sexual identities, and reproduces the domestic melodrama's preoccupation with the transfer of power from the aristocracy to the bourgeoisie. However, in this 'dangerous and foolish work' (Oliphant 1862:567) the transfer is effected not by means of an inheritance plot, but through a particular version of the middle-class dream. Richard Carlyle, the industrious and successful country lawyer, purchases an imposing house from a profligate aristocrat, Lord Mountsevern. He also proposes marriage to Mountsevern's daughter, Lady Isabel Vane, in order (partly) to rescue her from the consequences of her father's profligacy. Carlyle's ownership of East Lynne is a public statement of his enhanced social status, which his possession of Isabel confirms. Isabel is also seen as adding grace and charm to his otherwise austere life. This middle-class dream was, of course, also an established social practice in the mid-nineteenth century. Money made in trade, industry and the middle-class professions was used to purchase large houses or country estates, and middle-class money allied itself with aristocratic status through cross-class marriages.

On one level the central narratives of *East Lynne* explode this dream, exposing it as a delusion. From the outset Isabel is a failure as the wife of a middle-class lawyer. She is physically, emotionally and (it would appear) morally frail. Brought up to a life of decorative uselessness, she is incapable of running Carlyle's household and is easily bested by his managing half-sister Cornelia. She is seduced from the path of wifely virtue by an aristocratic rake, with whom she elopes only to be deserted. She is divorced, presumed dead and ultimately replaced as Carlyle's wife by the capable and resourceful middle-class heroine Barbara Hare.

Although this is clearly one powerful narrative pattern which the text would have generated for contemporary readers, the story of Carlyle, Isabel and Barbara also has more diverse and complex meanings. In *East Lynne*, as in Braddon's novels, the reader is offered a shifting range of identifications and reading positions. The female reader in particular is unlikely to see Isabel either as merely the embodiment of aristocratic ineffi-cacy, or the moral exemplum of the 'careless' wife (although she is clearly both of these). The details of the representation of Isabel and her story are greatly in excess of the demands of these specific moral and didactic requirements. Nor is *East Lynne* simply the narrative of the transfer of social and political power from a previously dominant aristocracy to a rising bourgeoisie: a process of renovation (of the aristocracy) and incorporation (of the bourgeoisie). It is also the story of the constantly changing relations of power between men and women, and of the intersections of class and gender. Key aspects of this narrative turn on the ways in which class ident-ities are differently gendered, and the ways in which gender is differently constructed in different classes. Definitions of gender, of masculine/feminine roles and the structure and poli-tics of the family are thus at the centre of this bestseller, which has been dismissed by many critics as a merely conventional and conservative domestic melodrama combining sin and sen-timent in somewhat unequal proportions.[16]

East Lynne is both a story of the feminine and a feminine story. The address of Wood's novels is consistently (and cer-tainly more emphatically than Braddon's) woman-to-woman. The way in which the story is unfolded replicates the rhythms of women's conversation. The pace of the narrative is always leisurely – even when climaxes and crises are at hand – and the narrator habitually refers backwards and forwards in the narrative, reminding the reader of apparently trivial details, or anticipating later developments. For example, when Isabel returns to East Lynne disguised as a governess, the narrator enquires conversationally, 'Shall I tell you what she did? Yes, I will . . .' (EL:410). A little later she notes that Isabel has discarded all her former possessions with the exception of a miniature of her mother and a small golden cross: 'Have you forgotten that cross?' she asks (EL:412), and proceeds to remind the reader of the significance of its earlier appearance in the narrative (when Levison had clumsily broken the doubly sacred object). The narrator persistently addresses the reader directly, assumes a shared experience and a community of values with her readers, or solicits the reader's attention for a particular character's point of view, or a particular moral point of view.

This apparently easy, gossipy address, full of trivia and 'much occupied with servants and the lower classes . . . with explicit details of dress, furnishings and the colour schemes of fashionable carriages' (Hughes 1980:111), positions the reader within a feminine discourse of a specific social register. Similarly the much-noted moralising of the narrator, and even the straining for gentility (attributed by some critics to Wood's own social insecurities as the daughter of a glove manufacturer) are also part of a discourse – the discourse of respectable or proper femininity – which constructs morality along class and gender lines. The social and moral strain and anxiety of Wood's address are integral to that discourse.

East Lynne is not only a feminine narrative, it is also a narrative of femininity. Most of the central characters are women, and each of them is represented at some point as a feminine stereotype to be compared and contrasted with other such stereotypes. Thus Isabel is compared with Barbara Hare, Mrs Hare, Afy Hallijohn and Cornelia Carlyle in her various roles of the aristocratic, childish, dependent wife, the fallen woman, or the suffering mother; Barbara appears as the stereotype of the active middle-class wife and modern mother; Mrs Hare as the tyrannised, invalid wife and devoted mother; Afy as the servant with social pretensions, and fallen woman; and Cornelia as the competent but shrewish old maid.

The central male characters are also, to some extent, feminised. Levison, the seducer, although a sexual predator, is represented as somewhat feminine in his narcissism and sensuality. His cowardice and lack of honour certainly render him 'unmanly' within the terms of the novel's gendered moral discourse. Paradoxically, Carlyle, the very model of 'manly' honour and restraint, also occupies an ambiguous gender position. Initially dominated by his competent, combative and masculinised half-sister, Cornelia, he is consistently blind to the tensions in his own home. This is partly because he is, as a man, presumed to be inherently incapable of fathoming the mysteries of the domestic sphere, and partly because he is frequently absent from it and habitually preoccupied with the concerns of the masculine world of work. In other words, Carlyle demonstrates a structural masculine incomprehension of the domestic: the novel implies that men's position within the family simply does not equip them to read the signs of the domestic sphere. Carlyle thus becomes part of the novel's demonstration and analysis of the way in which different gender roles are produced and function within the family. In this respect he is seen as, to some extent, responsible (through ignorance and inefficacy) for Isabel's dilemma. The well-intentioned, but ignorant and hence unsympathetic husband is, in part, responsible for a difficult domestic situation for which the wife pays the price of banishment and exile.

Carlyle is presented at various stages of the narrative as a failed patriarch in his own household. His gender identity is further problematised (at least in terms of the prevailing stereotypes) by his secret alliance with women (Barbara Hare and her mother) to frustrate the wishes of the domestic tyrant, Justice Hare. Carlyle is thus placed in a very interesting position. On the one hand he is unable to assimilate and accommodate, in his own (first) family, two polarised versions of the feminine: the woman who is all feeling (Isabel), and the aggressive, managing 'phallic mother' (Cornelia). On the other hand, through his involvement with Barbara and Mrs Hare, he himself becomes a kind of super-woman or super-mother. On their behalf he defends the affective family which persists (or subsists) within the stern patriarchal family of Justice Hare. Moreover, through his role in exonerating Richard Hare from wrongful accusations of murder, he effectively strikes the father dead, since on learning of his son's innocence (and thus recognising the harshness of his own conduct) Justice Hare suffers a stroke from which he never recovers: the patriarch is unmanned.

These paradoxes and ambivalences, and, most importantly,

120

Carlyle's confusion about his own position in the dynamics of the various family groupings, are no doubt part of the novel's appeal to both male and female readers. Carlyle's story offers the reader a version of the male experience of the contradictions of the patriarchal family as constituted in mid-Victorian middle-class society, as well as explaining (or rationalising) that predicament to a female audience. In this way it explores some of the anxieties about the bourgeois family which I have discussed in previous sections. The evolution of Carlyle's family history is also important here. He moves between three families: the first is actually run by a martinet spinster (Cornelia), but is supposedly presided over by a dependent child-like woman (Isabel), who combines the characteristics of domestic angel, decorative object and, ultimately, the fallen woman (in this case as victim rather than demon). The second is tyrannically ruled by an old-fashioned patriarch (Hare), who seems more of an eighteenth- than a nineteenth-century figure. In this family women have virtually no influence even in the domestic sphere. (Mrs Hare is afraid to order tea a few minutes before the time prescribed by her husband, even though she is ill and desperately thirsty.) Carlyle ultimately moves beyond these problematic families to a third – a modernised version – presided over by a capable wife with modern ideas of domestic management and motherhood, who actively supports her husband's new career as Member of Parliament. At this level the novel is a narrative about the making of the modern, professional, middle-class family, which inscribes middle-class insecurities about social mobility, warns middle-class men against the growing practice of taking aristocratic wives, and middle-class women against embracing the excessive refinement and susceptibility to feeling of the upper-class woman.

The narrative of Carlyle's two marriages may be read as a staging of the Freudian Oedipal drama by which normative feminine sexuality is constructed. The marriage of Carlyle and Isabel (who represent, in displaced form, the father and mother of the Freudian drama) is threatened by the rebellious daughter (Barbara) who desires the father (Carlyle) and must reject (and in this case replace) the mother (Isabel). However, in its latter stages, as E. Ann Kaplan (1989) has suggested, *East Lynne* also contains an alternative version of this drama. The restaged version articulates precisely what the middle-

121

class family suppresses: an alternative trajectory of feminine sexuality. This second version may be read in two ways. First it could be seen simply as a staging of the Freudian drama from the mother's point of view: thus, Isabel (as disowned wife) painfully yearns for the return of the husband/father who has been 'stolen' by the daughter. Alternatively it could be seen as a quite different story, in which the suffering child's yearning to replace the mother in the father's affections is both sublimated and (infinitely) deferred: sublimated into intense maternal feelings, and deferred for the duration of this earthly life. Adapting Nancy Chodorow's rereading of Lacan's view that it is desire for the lost mother (not the father) that is crucial in the formation of female sexuality, Kaplan (1989) has offered a very persuasive psychoanalytic reading of *East Lynne*, which suggests that Isabel's desire for the child, which dominates the final section, represents a sublimated longing for the mother rather than the father. *East Lynne* thus transforms the Oedipal drama into 'maternal melodrama'.

However one reads it, *East Lynne*'s alternative version of Isabel's role in the Oedipal drama seems to involve the frustration of all feminine feeling within the family: (re)union with the father/husband must be infinitely postponed, the desire for the child cannot be articulated and can only be achieved through death. In this respect, as in others, *East Lynne* follows nineteenth-century melodrama's habitual pattern of articulating both female desire and women's powerlessness.

Apart from the Oedipal drama and the story of the making of the modern middle-class family, the other obvious structural pattern in this novel is its official moral(ising) narrative. This narrative is a parable of the dangers of sexual passion and (female) marital indiscretion, in which the erring wife (Isabel) is fiercely punished, and the patient virtue of the steadfast woman (Barbara) is amply rewarded. Although clearly both morally and socially conservative, it is more complex than has sometimes been suggested. In fact this narrative of conventional sexual morality is another version of the making of the modern middle-class family, which enacts some of the elements that are suppressed in the first version. In both versions the changing roles of Isabel Vane/Carlyle and Barbara Hare/Carlyle are central. The first narrative moves from a woman-dominated (but fractured) family (run by Cornelia), to

122

a companionate affective family (presided over by Barbara), via an excluded third term – the tyrannical patriarchal family of Justice Hare. Similarly, the second version moves from a sexually transgressive wife who is all feeling (Isabel), to a competent, sexually chaste wife (Barbara) who has learned to govern her feelings, via the excluded third term of Afy Hallijohn.

Afy is a stock character of Victorian fiction, in both its high culture and popular modes. She is the saucy servant who apes her superiors and attempts to achieve her social ambitions by sexual means. *East Lynne's* particular treatment of this stereotype demonstrates the ways in which discourses of class and gender intersect in the production of sexual ideology. As in some of Wood's other novels, for example in the depiction of the sexually misused and discarded Rachel Frost in *Verner's Pride*, a sexually exploited female servant is the origin of an important strand of the mystery narrative. Lower-class women are thus figured as a disturbance of the sexual economy of the middle-class family (as in the discourse on the prostitute discussed earlier).

In *East Lynne* the stories of the upstart servant and the aristocratic heroine are carefully juxtaposed. The similarity of their situations is obvious: they are both seduced and abandoned by the same man (Thorn/Levison). However, the effect of the narrative's insistence on the similarities between the sexual transgressions of Afy and Isabel is ultimately to call attention to the fundamental difference between them. Afy is not required to undergo the punitive moral, emotional and physical suffering which is constructed for Isabel. Isabel is harrowed; Afy is ridiculed. Isabel is required to die a lingering and pathetic death; Afy's punishment is a somewhat comic public humiliation at the trial of her father's murderer, and the curtailment of her social ambitions by marriage to a cheesemonger. To be sure, the sexual crimes of Afy and Isabel are different. Afy has merely left her father's home to become Levison/Thorn's mistress, whereas Isabel both enters an adulterous relationship and deserts her husband and children. However, even when this has been take into consideration, significant discrepancies remain.

Afy is required to suffer less than Isabel because of the presumption (heavily underlined by the narrator) that she is less emotionally and morally refined than her social superior. Afy's fall is presented by the narrator as a mixture of folly and wilfulness; if the character reflects upon her situation at all it is to see it as a career move. However, Isabel's is a fall from grace, which is accompanied by exquisite agonies of moral scrupulousness and emotional self-torture, both of which are presented in class terms.

> How fared it with Lady Isabel? Just as it must be expected to fare, and does fare, when *a high-principled gentlewoman falls from her pedestal* . . .
> It is possible that remorse does not come to all erring wives as immediately as it came to Lady Isabel Carlyle – *you need not be reminded that we speak of women in the higher positions of life.* Lady Isabel was *endowed with sensitively refined delicacy, with an innate, lively consciousness of right and wrong.*
>
> (EL:288–9, my italics)

Even though her fall is more serious than Afy's, Lady Isabel remains within the discourse of proper femininity from which Afy is excluded by her class identity. Moreover, Afy plays a crucial role in constructing and sustaining the category from which she is herself excluded. Afy and the class to which she belongs are one means by which proper femininity is maintained.

The ideological work of the narrative which I have been describing may also have provided an important source of narrative pleasure for contemporary readers. Like many of their modern counterparts, these readers no doubt went to fiction (especially their 'lighter reading') not only to find out about the world, but also to have their sense of the world confirmed and their social and sexual fantasies elaborated and enacted. However, both the pleasures and the messages of Wood's bestseller are diverse and contradictory, especially for women readers.

One important source of *East Lynne's* appeal to women was its feminine focus on the family. For the most part it deals with women's experience of the family from a woman's point of view. Like many of Wood's other sensation-influenced novels of the 1860s, but in a more concentrated form, *East Lynne* dwells on women's role and position in the family and

124

household, and on the nature and sources of their domestic power, or lack of it. The novel contains one very powerful example of the ruling domestic woman, in Cornelia, and works towards instating Barbara Hare as the model of commanding household competence, but it also suggests the precariousness of women's domestic power.

Every scene in *East Lynne* that shows a woman reigning in social and/or domestic triumph is matched by at least two that depict women confused, confined and passive. This novel (perhaps to an even greater extent than Braddon's) is full of scenes of domestic entrapment, which represent female characters observing the events of their household and feeling powerless to influence them. Women's power is usually exercised only in relation to children and other women. This subordinated form of power, and the intra-female rivalry it produces, are central to the novel's emotional dynamics.

Rivalry between women within and for the domestic space is a particularly important sub-text of *East Lynne*. Throughout the narrative Isabel is portrayed as being entrapped within the domestic space, in situations that she does not understand, either with or by hostile or unsympathetic women. In marrying Carlyle she exchanges one such situation for another. Carlyle's fortuitous visit to Castle Marling, and his proposal of marriage, come at the climax of Isabel's trials as a dependent female relative in the home of her father's heir, Lord Mountsevern. At Castle Marling she has been falsely accused and mistreated by Mountsevern's wife, who finds Isabel's innocence and beauty a threat to her own power, which is exercised largely through controlled flirtations.

Isabel's sense of confinement within a domestic sphere in which she has no voice, and from which she cannot escape (since she has nowhere else to go), is replicated in somewhat different terms at East Lynne. Her father's former house, refurbished for her occupation, should have been the scene of Isabel's triumphant homecoming. Instead, under the domestic management of Cornelia, it is a place of confusion and impotent suffering (confusion and suffering which Isabel is unable to communicate to anyone else, especially her husband). The point is made very forcefully in the description of Isabel's arrival at her new home, and is underlined by a later narratorial gloss:

125

Isabel would have been altogether happy but for Miss Carlyle . . . She deferred outwardly to Lady Isabel as mistress; but the real mistress was herself, Isabel little more than an automaton. Her impulses were checked, her wishes frustrated, her actions tacitly condemned by the imperiously willed Miss Carlyle. Poor Isabel, with her refined manners and her timid and sensitive temperament, stood no chance against the strong-minded woman, and she was in a state of galling subjection in her own house.

(EL:169–70)

This novel's focus on women within the domestic space exposes the contradictions of the ideology of the separate spheres, at a time when that ideology was undergoing a crisis. Throughout the first half of the nineteenth century, women's lack of public political power was usually justified by the argument that within their own domestic sphere, as wives and mothers, they held complete sway, and from their position of moral, spiritual and emotional superiority they exercised influence over the (male) public sphere. *East Lynne*, on the other hand, exposes the severe limitations of this ideology by depicting wives who are tyrannised within their own households, whether by men or women. The novel also tends to suggest that, since real power resides with men, the separation of the spheres actually works against the interests of those women who conform most closely to prevailing definitions of proper femininity or 'womanliness', especially to those aspects which stress childlike dependence, malleability, and moral and emotional sensitivity, and which cast women in the role of creators (or at least non-disturbers) of domestic peace. Lady Mountsevern (the *femme fatale*) and Cornelia Carlyle (the masculinised old maid) both derive their power and authority from their failure to conform to these versions of the feminine.

If its representation of women's domestic entrapment and subordination speaks to, and for, women readers' own dissatisfaction with their lot, then other aspects of the novel's representation of the family work to contain this dissatisfaction. The family and the domestic sphere, no matter how uncomfortable, are presented as both the protector of women and the agent by means of which excessive female sexuality is con-

126

tained. For example, Isabel is shown as being most vulnerable to sexual temptation during her period of reluctant exile from her home and family when she is sent to France to recover her health.

One of the most important strategies of containment and management of women's familial discontent is the prolonged and intense focus on the sufferings which result from Isabel's (self-induced) exclusion from the household in which she had once felt unhappy and trapped. In the final volume, where Isabel is repeatedly portrayed as a spectator of scenes of domestic intimacy between Carlyle and Barbara, the family becomes for Isabel (and by extension for the reader) the object of desire rather than the cause and focus of discontent. This process works to defuse women's discontent and to reposition them as domestic creatures. However, at the same time, the story of the defence of an affective maternal family within and against the controlling patriarchal family (which is undertaken by Mrs Hare, Isabel, Barbara and the servant Joyce) also offers women a potentially empowering fantasy in which the family is reclaimed as a revitalised women's space.

Perhaps the major and most complex source of narrative interest and pleasure for the first women readers of *East Lynne* derived from its foregrounding and problematising of motherhood. For much of the nineteenth century, and certainly throughout the 1860s, the 'womanly woman' was defined in terms of maternity. *East Lynne* breaks down this single term and offers a range of versions of motherhood. Ironically, the most commanding mother figure in the novel is the childless Cornelia, the epitome of the active controlling phallic mother by whose offices the Law of the father is transmitted and mediated in the domestic sphere. Cornelia would surely have generated conflicting responses in contemporary female readers, who would have been likely to share her common-sense, bourgeois values, but to reject her obstruction of romantic and domestic fulfilment. Mrs Hare, on the other hand, is the vehicle for the articulation of the frustrations of women's role within the patriarchal family, and of resistance to subjugation. In the passive, dependent Mrs Hare (and, later, in Isabel) readers are asked to recognise the maternal bond as the strongest of all bonds, and maternal feelings as a hidden and private space from which women may resist their domestic oppression.

This novel's intense focus on motherhood has led recent critics (such as Kaplan 1989) to describe it as a 'maternal melodrama', a mode which, as Linda Williams (1987) has suggested, has 'historically addressed female audiences about issues of primary concern to women' (305). Such melodramas, Williams argues, habitually place their readers or spectators in a range of feminine subject positions, and 'demand a female reading competence' which derives from the way in which feminine subjectivity is defined and constructed by 'the social fact of mothering' (305). The central narrative of *East Lynne* is certainly structured around maternal experience and competing definitions of motherhood. The novel's double structure involves two heroines, Isabel and Barbara, and turns on a comparison of their roles as mothers and their differing conceptions of motherhood. Barbara, the 'successful' heroine, in many respects represents the type of the modern mother. She is presented as suitably adoring, but also as a woman whose maternal feelings are constrained and contained by her sense of what is due to her husband. She has thoroughly modern ideas on children's place in the domestic economy: 'If I and Mr Carlyle have to be out in the evening, baby gives way. I should never give up my husband for my baby' (EL:418). Barbara is an advocate of women's moral and emotional leadership of the household, a role she considers to be incompatible with (and indeed compromised by) close daily contact with children.

> I hold an opinion . . . that too many mothers pursue a mistaken system in the management of their family. There are some, we know, who lost in the pleasures of the world, in frivolity, wholly neglect them . . . nothing can be more thoughtless, more reprehensible; but there are others who err on the opposite side. They are never happy but when with their children . . . They wash them, dress them, feed them; rendering themselves slaves, and the mother's office a sinecure . . . She has no leisure, no spirits for any higher training: as they grow older she loses her authority . . .
> The discipline of that house soon becomes broken. The

128

children run wild; the husband is sick of it, and seeks peace and solace elsewhere . . . Now, what I trust I shall never give up to another, will be the *training* of my children . . . I hope I shall never fail to gather my children round me daily, at stated periods, for higher purposes: to instil into them Christian and moral duties. . . . *This* is a mother's task . . . A child should never hear aught from its mother's lips but winning gentleness; and this becomes impossible, if she is very much with her children.

(EL:415–16)

This passage deserves close attention since it seems to be an interesting example of the novel's weaving in of an extra-fictional feminine discourse, in this case the discourse of the domestic-conduct book or the woman's or family magazine article. This discourse is itself fractured and contradictory. To read Barbara's set-piece speech against the grain (as perhaps one is encouraged to do by its sharp juxtaposition with the very different version of mothering represented by Isabel) is to see how it reveals the division of labour, and the dependence on servants in the domestic hierarchy which sustains this version of mothering. It also reveals the splitting of the mother herself: her function of moral guardian and guide, and her supposedly natural role as carer, both of which are integral to the 'womanly woman' ideal, are shown to conflict.

Isabel's story is a maternal melodrama or a drama of motherhood. Hers is not simply the story of a fallen woman or an erring wife, it is also, most emphatically, the story of a fallen and hence suffering mother. Isabel's maternal suffering (within the wider context of the novel's representation of mothering) foregrounds the contradictory demands made on women by the equation of true womanhood with maternal feeling. Isabel is a woman, and in particular a mother, who loves too much. Her maternal feelings, like other aspects of her emotional life, are characterised by excess. For approximately the final two-thirds of the novel Isabel is consistently represented and defined as a grieving, sacrificing and suffering mother. Once she begins to entertain jealous doubts about Carlyle and Barbara she channels all her feminine feeling into her children, the only socially sanctioned outlet for female desire, apart from

129

heterosexual love within marriage. Her children are the focus of her anxieties about leaving East Lynne for the continental visit recommended by her doctors (again male authority figures combine to constrain the behaviour of women and compel them to act against their 'natural' desires). The loss of her children is the primary source of both her pain and her repentance following her elopement with Levison. In this respect the novel rehearses what must have been a profound fear for many women at this time. Given the provisions of the divorce laws in cases of female adultery, fear of separation from children was clearly a powerful force in controlling the sexual behaviour of married women.

Following the loss of her husband and lover, Isabel's whole identity (for both the character and the reader) is defined by her motherhood. Within the novel's moral and didactic economy Isabel is thus constructed as an over-invested mother, another version of the improper feminine which must be expelled from the text and replaced by the normative controlled and controlling proper femininity of Barbara Hare. However, within the text's emotional and psychological economy Isabel has quite a different function. Throughout the novel, but particularly in its final volume, the reader is repeatedly invited to identify with Isabel through the text's staging of the spectacle of her maternal suffering. The reader is simultaneously made into a spectator of Isabel's sufferings and drawn into an emotional investment in them through the narrator's rhetorical excess. As is usual in women's sensation fiction, such excess is accompanied by protestations of the narrator's linguistic and representational inadequacies.

I do not know how to describe the vain yearning, the inward fear, the restless longing for what may not be. Longing for what? For her children. Let a mother, be she a duchess, or be she an apple-woman at a stall, be separated for a while from her little children: let *her* answer how she yearns for them. She may be away on a journey of pleasure; for a few weeks, the longing to see their little faces again, to hear their prattling tongues, to feel their soft kisses, is kept under . . . but as the weeks lengthen out, the desire to see them again becomes almost irrepressible. What must it have been, then, for Lady Isabel, who had endured this longing for years.

(EL:397–8)

This passage actively constructs a maternal longing which it expects its readers to recognise as 'natural'. Significantly this longing transcends those differences of class which the novel so carefully establishes elsewhere. There is also a certain irony in the fact that the apparently unbearable maternal deprivation which is created and described is, in a sense, actively sought by the mothers who are escaping from their own maternal and domestic commitments in reading the novel.

The reader's spectating of Isabel's sufferings is not confined to such set-piece scenes of rhetorical excess. The reader is repeatedly positioned as a spectator who watches Isabel silently and feelingly watching painful scenes. In the final volume, Isabel is the frequent spectator of the connubial and familial bliss between Barbara and Carlyle. Through her disguise as a governess she watches her own children and, most poignantly, becomes the helpless and inarticulate spectator of her son's lingering death. This aspect of Isabel's story has been described as masochistic, as a 'prolonged, luxurious orgy of self-torture' (Hughes 1980:115). This so-called masochism of the text is clearly an important source of its pleasures for the middle-class woman reader. Isabel's long-drawn-out suffering not only makes the didactic case against female adultery in an extreme form (and hence confirms the reader's official morality), it also affords the reader the opportunity of spectating feelings of anxiety, separation, loss and claustrophobia which arise from middle-class women's experience of motherhood and domesticity. Thus, although Isabel is redundant insofar as it is her function to be erased from the text and to be replaced by the controlled, competent and controlling Barbara, she also functions as the repository of the text's and the reader's emotional ambivalence and resistance.

In its representation of the masochism of the maternal melodrama, *East Lynne* comprehends (in the sense of both embracing and understanding) women's desire for the child, and their anxieties about the separation from the child – anxieties which according to Lacanian psychoanalysis replicate their own feelings of loss and separation from the mother. The text thus permits its readers to enjoy Isabel's sufferings and longings while, at the same time, requiring them to reject these in favour of properly oriented maternal feelings. However, although readers must finally reject Isabel, their emotional investment in her suffering leads to a questioning of the conditions which produce it.

This discrepancy between the heroine's and the reader's perspective is an important source of the potential subversiveness of the text. The reader's emotional investment in Isabel creates a space for resistance of the text's 'official' morality – that maternal suffering and death are the inevitable and just consequences of female adultery. Recent Marxist–feminist critics have been right to warn of the dangers involved in appropriating literary texts for feminism by over-valuing the space for emotional resistance that they seem to offer. On the other hand, it would seem to be equally misguided to label as conservative or reactionary any text which does not offer a thorough-going structural analysis of capitalist patriarchy, together with a model for changing it. East Lynne tends to leave its readers, like its sacrificial heroine, feeling powerless to change the situation.[17] Nevertheless it has, in the meantime, offered a critique of (or, at the very least, raised serious questions about) that situation.

The subversive sub-text of East Lynne (what Kaplan 1989, following Jameson 1981, calls its political unconscious) derives from the way in which it allows (or even requires) its readers to think two otherwise contradictory things at once; in other words, from what Bakhtinian theory would describe as its dialogism.[18] One of the most prominent aspects of this dialogism can be seen in the novel's manipulation of point of view, and particularly in the way in which it appears to require its readers to condemn a character with whom they are also supposed to identify and sympathise. The middle-class reader (especially the female reader) must ultimately reject Isabel, with whom she has become increasingly involved as the text progresses, in favour of Barbara, a character who is much more like the reader's everyday self-conception, but who is represented as progressively less sympathetic.

These shifts of sympathy and identification depend partly on the way in which the text positions the reader vis-à-vis the characters. In order to see how this works we need to look

more closely at the structural juxtapositioning of the two main
female characters, and more particularly at their changing positions within a triangular relationship with Carlyle. It would
appear that the reader's sympathies usually lie with the character who forms the excluded third term of this triangle. Thus,
the highest point of the reader's sympathetic identification
with Barbara is in the first part of the novel when she is
positioned as the jealous outsider, spectator of Carlyle's and
Isabel's wedded bliss. Indeed, the reader is most closely
involved in Barbara's emotional life in those scenes in which
she transgresses those norms of the proper feminine which
she is later used to exemplify.

In the early stages of the novel Barbara is associated with
silent but active rebellion against her father, and with suppressed passionate feelings for Carlyle, which surface in a
particularly ungenteel scene in Chapter 16 ('Barbara Hare's
Revelation'), which portrays 'one of those moments in a
woman's life when she is betrayed into forgetting the ordinary
rules of conduct and propriety; when she is betrayed into
making a scene' (EL:165). At this stage the reader is also made
into an intimate witness of Barbara's attempts to govern her
emotions so that she may view with equanimity the scenes
between Isabel and Carlyle. However, once Barbara has effectively changed positions with Isabel, she is viewed from a
more distanced perspective and becomes of less emotional
interest. In a similar way the reader's emotional involvement
with Isabel intensifies as she, in turn, becomes the spectator
in the triangle: first, when she suspects the constant têtes-à-
têtes between her husband and Barbara (when they are, in fact,
consulting about Barbara's brother), and (most powerfully) in
the final volume when Isabel is living at East Lynne disguised
as governess to her own children.

Partly as a result of this manipulation of point of view, *East
Lynne* destabilises its own norms. Although the novel ultimately rejects the transgressive, improper femininity of Isabel
in favour of Barbara's proper femininity, it has in the process,
to some extent, destabilised the reader's identification with,
and commitment to, the normative category of bourgeois
femininity. The character who is to become the type of such
femininity is presented most feelingly, and as most feeling
(and the capacity for feeling, after all, is one of the defining

133

characteristics of nineteenth-century femininity) when she transgresses that norm (and is revealed as a barely governable mass of feeling and outrage). On the other hand, the character who becomes the type of the improper, transgressive feminine is presented most sympathetically as the adoring self-sacrificing mother. (Isabel is that striking paradox: the whore as madonna.)

The dialogism, by means of which *East Lynne* subverts its own norms, is also a function of the novel's movements between different sets of generic conventions. This generic slippage, which is found in a great deal of women's sensation fiction, is one of the main sources of the moral and structural ambiguity of the central female characters. The meaning and significance of a particular female character fluctuate according to the generic conventions through which she is mediated at different points in the narrative. Thus Barbara is represented as the villainous 'other woman' of melodrama, but appears as a heroine when the mode is that of sentimental domestic fiction, while Isabel is the suffering domestic heroine, but becomes the fallen woman as villain when positioned by the norms of melodrama.

Despite the apparently conservative morality and sexual politics of its ending, *East Lynne* (like many other sensation novels by women) offers a particularly striking example of the Bakhtinian view of the subversive relationship between popular and official forms.[19] In this case the (originally) popular lower-class form of melodrama subverts, or at least destabilises, the dominant middle-class forms and norms of domestic fiction. The particular mixture of sin and sentiment in *East Lynne* serves to expose the contradictions of the proper feminine, even as the novel works to re-establish it.

Part III

Breaking the Bounds:
The Improper Feminine
and the Fiction of the
New Woman

14

The New Woman

The New Woman is simply the woman of
to-day striving to shake off old shackles, and
the immense mass of 'revolting' literature
cannot have grown out of nothing, or con-
tinue to flourish upon mere curiosity.
(Stutfield 1897:115)

The 1890s was . . . a period in which a
number of women writers, dealing as feminists with the social and sexual rights of
women, secured a prominence which at
times developed into sensation . . . They
helped to wrench English fiction into new
channels.
(Rubinstein 1986:24)

The twin questions 'What is a woman?' and 'What does a
woman want?', and the plethora of answers they provoked,
were even more troubling and pervasive in the culture of the
1890s than they had been in the 1860s. They were given a new
focus in the figure of the New Woman, one of the most widely
and loudly discussed subjects in the public prints of the mid-
nineties. (The year 1894 seems to have been the New Woman's
annus mirabilis.) Who or what was this creature who so powerfully seized the public imagination, and who was analysed,
reviled, caricatured and parodied in fiction and in the words
and images of newspapers and magazines? First and foremost
the New Woman was a representation. She was a construct, 'a
condensed symbol of disorder and rebellion' (Smith-Rosenberg
1985:247) who was actively produced and reproduced in the

137

pages of the newspaper and periodical press, as well as in novels. The New Woman (and the moral panic which surrounded her) was yet another example of the way in which, in the latter half of the nineteenth century, femininity became a spectacle.[1]

This particular version of the staging of the spectacle of femininity, as Terry Lovell (1987) has argued, placed the 'gender order . . . under spotlights', and led to 'a furious debate on what it meant to be a real man, a real woman' (119). Traditional assumptions about the inviolability of these latter categories were also called into question by the new sexual science. In *The Psychology of Sex* (1933, first version published in 1897) Havelock Ellis theorised a fluidity of gender categories which the New Woman dramatised. 'We may not know exactly what sex is', he noted, but 'we do know that it is mutable, with the possibility of one sex being changed into the other sex . . . that its frontiers are mutable, and that there are many stages between a complete male and a complete female' (225). While Ellis analysed and theorised, *Punch's* 'Angry Old Buffer' fulminated against the dissolution of established gender categories, in which the New Woman writer and her 'tales all slang and sin' played a prominent part:

> . . . a new fear my bosom vexes;
> Tomorrow there may be no sexes!
> Unless, as end to all pother,
> Each one in fact becomes the other.
>
> Woman *was* woman, man *was* man,
> When Adam delved and Eve span
> Now he can't dig and she won't spin,
> Unless 'tis tales all slang and sin!
>
> (*Punch* April 27, 1895:203)

The 'New' in New Woman signified not only the supposed novelty of the type, but also (and more ominously for her critics) the type's alleged obsession with novelty. The New Woman was, according to a prominent opponent, 'consumed with a desire for new experiences, new sensations, new objects in life' (Stutfield 1897:105). To the readers of the *Cornhill*, she was represented as a body and a fashion system, both of which violated the code of the proper feminine. Her 'simple', 'close-

138

fitting', 'tailor-made' and 'manly' style of dress 'adds a some-what aggressive air of independence which finds its birth in the length of her stride'; her attitudes are as 'strong and inde-pendent' as her hands; she has a 'discontented mouth, and a nose indicative of intelligence, and too large for feminine beauty'. The *Cornhill's* New Woman is unshockable, 'super-ficially deep', 'crushing' to mild young men, and (most impor-tant of all) 'conspicuously innocent' of any interest in children: 'She has tried to prove that woman's mission is something higher than the bearing of children and the bringing them up. But she has failed' (all quotations Scott and Hall 1894:365–6).

The New Woman was the embodiment of a complex of social tendencies. The title named a beacon of progress or beast of regression, depending on who was doing the naming. To her supporters she was an elevated creature who had been 'sitting apart' from the 'cow-kind of woman', the 'scum' woman, and the 'Bawling Brotherhood' in 'silent contemplation . . . think-ing and thinking, until at last she solved the problem and proclaimed for herself what was wrong with Home-is-the-Woman's-Sphere, and prescribed the remedy' (Grand 1894:270–1). The alternative version, the New Woman as cul-tural demon, had its origins in the 'Wild Women' (Eliza Lynn Linton's sobriquet for the unsuccessful suffrage campaigners) and in the 'Revolting Daughters' (those rebels against parental control and the constraints of prevailing ideas of the proper feminine), whose doings filled the pages of the middle-class periodicals in the early nineties.[2]

Opponents of the New Woman tended to represent the phenomenon in terms of the world-turned-upside-down of rev-olutionary excess, or to associate it with the 'persistent clamor [sic]' of the 'Workingman' (Ouida 1894:610). Linton, who had been an extremely vocal and opinionated commentator on modern woman since the 1860s, viewed the embryonic New Woman through the 'mirror' of recent history in which she saw 'the Parisian woman of the Revolution . . . repeated wherever analogous conditions exist' (1891a:80). She represented late nineteenth-century women's demands for inclusion in political life as both a feminisation and a proletarianisation of the public sphere.

The franchise for women would not simply allow a few

well-conducted, well-educated, self-respecting gentle-
women to quietly record their predilection for Liberalism
or Conservatism, but would let in the far wider flood
of the uneducated, the unrestrained, the irrational and
emotional.

(ibid.)

On the whole, however, the New Woman was represented as
less directly and actively political than the Wild Woman.
Rather she was figured as a symptom or harbinger of social
change, whose 'dominant note . . . [was] restlessness and discontent with the existing order of things' (Stutfield 1897:105).

The New Woman represented a threat not only to the social
order, but also to the natural order. Many doctors believed
that the development of a woman's brain induced infertility
by causing the womb to atrophy, and hence jeopardised the
survival of the race. In addition, the spectre of the 'mannish'
New Woman who refused her biological destiny of motherhood threatened to dissolve existing gender boundaries. Paradoxically the New Woman was represented as simultaneously
non-female, *unfeminine* and *ultra-feminine*. The New Woman's
loss of female characteristics was evident in the 'bearded chin,
the bass voice, flat chest and lean hips of a woman who has
failed in her physical development'. Her lack of femininity was
both the cause and consequence of her resisting traditional
womanly roles – 'a curious inversion of sex, which does not
necessarily appear in the body, but is evident enough in the
mind' (both quotations Linton 1891a:79). The New Woman's
hyperfemininity was signalled by her extreme susceptibility to
feeling; she was a creature whose proper feminine affectivity,
'the dearer, tenderer emotions of the true woman' (83), had
become excessive and degenerate and had thus entered the
domain of the improper feminine.

In the New Woman the self-sacrificially other-directed feeling of the regime of the proper feminine had allegedly become
self-directed and self-absorbed, and manifested itself as 'an
intense and morbid consciousness of the ego' (Hansson
1896:79). The New Woman was also said to be unduly
interested in and familiar with sexual feeling, and the New
Woman writing was supposedly saturated with sex.

Emancipated woman in particular loves to show her inde-

140

pendence by dealing freely with the relations of the sexes. Hence all the prating of passion, animalism, 'the natural workings of sex,' and so forth, with which we are nauseated. Most of the characters in these books seem to be erotomaniacs. Some are 'amorous sensitives'; others are apparently sexless, and are at pains to explain this to the reader. Here and there a girl indulges in what would be styled, in another sphere, 'straight talk to young men.' Those nice heroines of 'Iota' and other writers of the physiologico-pornographic school consort by choice with 'unfortunates,' or else describe at length their sensations in various interesting phases of their lives.

(Stutfield 1895:836)

The 'erotomania' of the New Woman writers was widely held to be part of a general decadence which had infected the culture via contemporary French literature. According to W.F. Barry (1894) the New Woman writing displayed the 'French combination' of 'sensuous introspection . . . the careful Epicurean tasting of life's flavours, and the doctrine of "thrill," which are not only decadent in their origin . . . [but] bring the taint into the book which describes them' (307–8).

The New Woman was persistently represented as an hysteric, whose degenerate emotionalism was both symptom and cause of social change. As symptom, her hysteria was a degenerate form of her natural affections. It was also thought to be a form of brain-poisoning induced by the pressures of modern life and by women's attempts to resist their traditional roles and ape those of men. As cause, hysteria threatened social disintegration and, indeed, the future of the race, by disabling women and preventing them from fulfilling their 'natural' roles of wives and mothers.

The New Woman thus challenged traditional gender boundaries in paradoxical ways. The mannish New Woman threatened such boundaries from one direction by quitting the sphere of the proper feminine, aping masculinity and becoming a new intermediate sex. On the other hand, these boundaries were also eroded by the New Woman's hyperfemininity. The New Woman as hysteric threatened to invade and infect the whole of society with a degenerative femininity, which had the 'inevitable effect of sapping manliness and making people flabby' (Stutfield 1897:842) and 'hysterically susceptible' to 'outside' (i.e., foreign) influences (Linton 1892:457).

The function of the hystericised New Woman in *fin de siècle* representations is thus analogous to the role of the female hysteric in Freudian psychoanalysis. They are both produced as 'the spectacle of femininity in crisis' (Cixous and Clément 1987:9). Since, in the nineteenth century, cultural health was defined in terms of the regulation of the proper feminine, the spectacle of improper femininity represented by the New Woman as hysteric also served as the spectacle of a culture in crisis.

If the New Woman was produced by the multiple contradictions that characterised late Victorian conceptions of the feminine, the New Woman writers (in varying degrees) reproduced those contradictions. However, they also – in different ways and to differing degrees – exposed and explored them. They engaged in a complex negotiation of the available discourses on woman, which challenged, transposed and, on occasions, transformed the terms of the dominant discourse. The New Woman writing, like the New Woman herself, became a site upon which 'the "naturalness" of gender and the legitimacy of the bourgeois social order' (Smith-Rosenberg 1985:245) were contested. Ultimately we may conclude that the New Woman writers, like their earlier Victorian predecessors, 'remained within the terms of the ideology whose discursive rules [they] violate' (Poovey 1989:83), but, as I hope to show in later sections, their writing constantly pushed against and disturbed its boundaries.

15

The New Woman writing and some marriage questions

> It was impossible that the demands of women for freedom should become a feature of modern life without the marriage relation, as at present understood, being called into question.
>
> (Caird 1897:67)
>
> The Woman Question is the Marriage Question.
>
> (Grand 1894:276)

Although sometimes more experimental in form, and almost always more didactic and overtly polemical than the sensationalists, the New Woman writers shared many of their predecessors' preoccupations. Chief among these was a common concern with women's marital and familial roles. Like Braddon and Wood, the New Woman writers of the 1890s focused minutely on the domestic space and, whether writing as feminists or as anti-feminists, engaged in a probing exploration and critique of marriage and the family. 'In almost every case', wrote W.T. Stead in 1894, 'the novels of the modern woman are preoccupied with questions of sex, questions of marriage, questions of maternity' (65). Even those writers who sought to affirm the 'naturalness' of marriage and motherhood (as Mrs Henry Wood had in the 1860s) could only do so within the terms of the renewed contest over those institutions in the 1890s.

Nineteenth-century definitions of femininity and of female sexuality were inextricably linked to contemporary definitions of marriage and to the social and political functions it served.

As the dominant definitions of femininity were more and more fiercely contested in the latter half of the century, the Marriage Question not only appeared to be increasingly problematic, it also became more polarised. At one extreme marriage was seen (by both feminists and anti-feminists) as woman's highest and most natural calling. At the other it was a form of slavery or legalised prostitution. Many, perhaps most, reviewers saw the New Woman fiction as part of a general attack on marriage by fiction writers who, according to Margaret Oliphant (1896), constituted 'The Anti-Marriage League'. Although for Oliphant this league included both male and female writers (Thomas Hardy was singled out for particularly hostile treatment), one of the strongest objections to the anti-marriage fiction (as to the sensation novel) was the prominence of women in its production and mediation. Oliphant clearly saw the New Woman writers as founder-members of the league, and also attacked the part played by women readers in creating a market for anti-marriage fiction. Hugh Stutfield, whose one-man campaign against the 'degeneracy' of contemporary fiction has already been described, was also exercised by the prominence of women writers and the female perspective in the fictional critique of marriage.

> The horrors of marriage from the feminine point of view are so much insisted upon these days, and the husband-fiend is trotted out so often both in fiction and drama, that one wonders how the demon still manages to command such a premium in the marriage market.
>
> (Stutfield 1895:835–6)

The developing debate on the Marriage Question, which was so clearly an important component of the New Woman writing, was given fresh impetus and direction by a series of articles by Mona Caird, which were collected under the title of *The Morality of Marriage* in 1897. Caird's first article on the subject, simply entitled 'Marriage', appeared in the *Westminster Review* (1888), which published numerous essays on marriage and divorce throughout the 1890s. Caird's opening salvo generated widespread commentary and discussion, and was the occasion of a protracted correspondence (some 27,000 letters) in the *Daily Telegraph* throughout the summer of 1888, under

144

the general title *Is Marriage a Failure?* The avowed purpose of Caird's essays was:

> . . . to bring evidence from all sides, to prove that the greatest evils of modern society had their origin, thousands of years ago, in the dominant abuse of patriarchal life: the custom of woman purchase. The essays show that this system still persists in the present form of marriage and its traditions, and that these traditions are holding back the race from its best development. It is proved, moreover, that it is a mere popular fallacy to suppose that our present sex relationship is a natural and immutable ordinance.
>
> (Caird 1897:1)

Caird grounded her case in 'the facts of history, sociology, heredity, and indeed all human experience, rightly understood'. In order to make that case she adopted, by turns, the stance (and the appropriate discourses) of the historian, the anthropologist and the sociologist, as well as engaging with the discourse of post-Darwinian scientific debate. These debates and discourses are also incorporated into her novels on the Marriage Question, seen by some simply as rather crude and inartistic attempts to mix polemic and fiction, and to further the attack on marriage by more accessible and popular means than her periodical essays. Certainly many of Caird's fictional characters appear to be used as mouthpieces for her anti-marriage doctrine. For example, Hadria, the thwarted heroine of *The Daughters of Danaus*, directly echoed the essayist's attack on the 'customs and traditions' of marriage when:

> [She] wondered why it was that marriage did not make all women wicked – openly and actively so. If ever there was an arrangement by which every evil instinct and every spark of the devil was likely to be aroused and infuriated, surely the customs and traditions that clustered around this estate constituted that dangerous combination.
>
> (DD:168)

Caird, however, does not simply translate the rhetoric of the essays into fictional form. She constructs a narrative and develops a rhetoric of feeling which dramatise and explore the dangerous combination produced by a conventionally restrictive and loveless marriage, a sensitive woman, and a particular cultural stereotype of femininity. Like her essays, *The Daughters of Danaus* foregrounds the ideology of female self-sacrifice which conventional middle-class marriage produces, and by which it is reproduced.

Like many other novels of this period *The Daughters of Danaus* is particularly fierce in its indictment of the covert tyranny of the ideology of self-sacrificial motherhood. Recapitulating the 'Revolting Daughter' debates in the *Nineteenth Century* (1894), Caird's novel represents Hadria as the victim of her mother and of her mother's view of marriage and the family, before she herself becomes the victim of marriage. Caird focuses minutely on the social forces which produce Hadria as the latest link in a chain binding women together under the domestic yoke, and makes much of women's complicity in their own subjection and in that of their sisters. (Hadria is duped into an inappropriate marriage and subsequently persuaded to return to her ill-matched husband by his sister's half-truths, misrepresentations and appeals to conventional views of woman's nature and role.) In short, this novel persistently emphasises the lack of fit between the heroine's sense of self, and the versions of proper femininity transmitted via the culture (starting with the mother).

Like the sensation novelists Caird focuses on the constraining and claustrophobic nature of the domestic space. In *The Daughters of Danaus* this is sharply contrasted with the freedom of the moors surrounding Hadria's familial home; with the countryside around her marital home where she roams at liberty; with the free space of The Priory (the usually unoccupied home of Hadria's mentor, Professor Fortescue), which provides the heroine with a refuge of privacy where she may exercise her musical vocation; and with the licensed liberty of the Garret (an attic in the family home) in which Hadria and her siblings construct an alternative world of sexual equality – 'the Preposterous Society'. In the Garret sisters debate on equal terms with their brothers despite their own 'inferior' education. In that private space Hadria is free to articulate her feelings, and to express her musical sensibility and youthful energies in dancing reels, without being prey to the dangers which (as the novel repeatedly emphasises) attend the woman of strong feeling in the sexual politics of the social world. Indeed, one of the more interesting rhetorical devices in this novel is its habitual prefacing of key episodes in Hadria's history with a scene anatomising her sensations in the heightened emotional state induced by her response to music or dancing. Although it repeats the arguments of her essays and, to a great extent, replicates their discourse, Caird's novel puts into play a variety of voices and a variety of views on the Woman and Marriage questions. Ultimately Margaret Oliphant's category of the 'Anti-Marriage' novel proves too limiting for this, as for many other New Woman novels which address the Marriage Question. Like her essays, Caird's novel explores different forms of marriage, and alternatives to marriage. One of the most obvious ways in which she does this is to adapt the contrasting-sisters plot – a staple of women's fiction from the eighteenth century onwards.

In *The Daughters of Danaus* the story of the initially free-thinking Hadria's entrapment by the discourse of proper femininity is juxtaposed with the story of her sister Algitha's rejection of womanliness and the familial role assigned to her by that discourse. Algitha finds fulfilling philanthropic work in London, and ultimately enters into a modern marriage of equals with a socialist New Man. Hadria's decline into a restrictive and frustrating marriage is also compared with the situation of the single woman. A melodramatic sub-plot depicts the emotional sterility and heightened vulnerability of the friendless spinster schoolteacher who is seduced and betrayed by Hadria's would-be lover, Professor Theobald. There is also a sustained examination of the single state which is chosen by Valeria Du Prel as the necessary condition for the exercising of her vocation as a writer. Valeria's sense that her work fails to compensate for the lack of close family ties is contrasted with the frustration of Hadria's musical vocation by the pressures of familial life (an important aspect of the novel, and a point to which I shall return).

The Daughters of Danaus, like many (perhaps most) New Woman novels, does not simply attack marriage, but rather renders it problematic. Much New Woman fiction represents modern marriage as an 'impossible' institution. The impossibility of marriage and (by extension) of women's situation is attributed, both explicitly and implicitly, to the double bind of

147

the contradictory nature of the discourse on woman. As Augusta Webster noted (quoted in Caird 1897:103), 'people think women who do not want to marry unfeminine; people think women who *do* want to marry immodest' (and hence unfeminine, since modesty was one of the defining characteristics of femininity). The heroine of Ménie Muriel Dowie's *Gallia* articulates a similar contradiction when she notes that women are expected to be entirely innocent of sexual desire and ignorant about sexual activity before marriage, and to embrace both wholeheartedly as soon as they marry.

The general effect of the New Woman novel – whether we understand the term to refer to a single text or to a group of texts – is to suggest the 'impossibility' of women's situation. In the New Woman fiction, as in melodrama, women's lives are presented as inherently problematic, and unhappiness is the norm. Whatever path they choose, whether they conform to or break with convention, women are likely to be thwarted and frustrated. For example, George Egerton's two volumes of short stories, *Keynotes* and *Discords*, constitute a frequently depressing catalogue of the impossibilities of women's lives as currently constituted. They are full of contradictory situations and stark contrasts and choices. Stories about women yearning for their lost lovers, their lost illusions about their lovers, or their lost illusions about romantic love itself (such as 'An Empty Frame'), and stories of dreamy unrealised relationships (such as 'Her Share') are contrasted with stories of women trapped in marriage with a brute ('Wedlock', 'Under Northern Sky' and 'Virgin Soil'). The woman who sacrifices all for love is juxtaposed with the equally marginalised, self-possessed working girl who befriends her ('Gone Under'), and a woman's desire for adventure and self-realisation is juxtaposed with the contradictory desire for, and demands of, motherhood ('A Cross Line').

The impossibility of women's lives in the context of modern marriage customs and their attendant gender roles is the central preoccupation of Ménie Muriel Dowie's *Gallia*. This impossibility is, in part, figured as a persistent gap between female desire and the social actuality of women's lives. Whether their desires are those of the traditional, 'womanly woman', or the New Woman (however the 'new' may be expressed or defined), Dowie's female characters are all

148

revealed as pursuing chimeras. Even if they succeed in achieving their ambitions, or realising their desires (and this applies particularly to the various marriage or ménage plots), those ambitions and desires are seen to be hollow and tainted.

The novel's heroine is a case in point. Gallia, the representation of a thoroughly modern young woman of advanced ideas, seeks to rebel against woman's conventional role and take control of her own life. Gallia enjoys some measure of success in redefining what it means to be a woman, or more specifically (as in *The Daughters of Danaus*) a woman of the upper middle classes, by distancing herself from her family, and rejecting her mother and the social and familial duties of her gender and class. Instead of 'coming out' for the London season, Gallia (like a number of her real-life contemporaries) attends lectures at Oxford in an attempt to improve upon the 'home education' usually considered suitable for girls of her class. Although thoroughly disillusioned with modern sex relations, she (like many liberal feminists of the 1880s and 1890s) ultimately becomes convinced that maternity is woman's true and highest vocation, and chooses a husband on the basis of his suitability for procreation. In this last respect Gallia is a version of the New Woman as regenerator of the race. Motherhood is represented not as a mere lapsing back into the traditional role of the womanly woman, but as a freely chosen and newly defined feminine role – that of the reinvigorator or saviour of the race by means of the woman's sexual selection of a non-degenerate male.

However, Dowie's novel deliberately constrains and undercuts its heroine's self-determination by foregrounding her unresolved conflicts and desires. For example, the daughter's unsatisfactory relationship with her mother is not only used as the impetus for her own conversion to the idea of motherhood; it also suggests the potentially limiting conditions of the maternal role she chooses for herself. Similarly Gallia's rational choice of husband leaves a surplus of desire in her unresolved feeling for the rejected and rejecting object of her emotional and sexual desires, Dark Essex. This latter character, whose discovery that he suffers from a heart condition both symbolises and confirms his detachment from social and personal commitment, is almost a parody of a feminised version of modern masculinity. He is an aesthete, cocooned in the world

149

of Oxford colleges: a neurotic New Man, who doesn't know what he wants of either life or women. He is one of the male borderliners classified by Andrew Wynter in *The Borderlands of Insanity* (1877), who inhabit the 'Mazeland', 'Dazeland' and 'Driftland' of a mind which has lost all sense of a 'directing' or 'controlling power' (quoted in Showalter 1991:11).

Dowie's novel further destabilises and problematises the idea of 'woman' by focusing on gender stereotypes. Both the novel and the characters within it habitually represent women (and, to a lesser extent, men) as and through stereotypes. As in so many New Woman novels the female characters in *Gallia* read more like contemporary journalistic sketches of modern female types than complex fictional creations: Gallia herself is the emotionally inconsistent bluestocking, the 'Revolting Daughter' turned race mother; Mrs Leighton, the worldly-wise society woman who uses the influence of the domestic sphere in the public world; Gallia's mother, the self-sacrificial wife and mother, whose sufferings reveal the emotional costs for women of their complicity in the construction and perpetuation of the domestic ideology; Margaret Essex, the pure woman with a spiritual power that is supposed to redeem her future husband's rakish past; Cara Lemuel, the Pre-Raphaelite fleshly woman of the artistic demi-monde; Gertrude Janion, the Girl of the Period (twenty years or so more 'advanced'), whose supremely cynical social climbing is satirised, but whose open cynicism is also used to satirise the pretensions and hypocrisies of modern mores. The appropriation (in some cases a reappropriation), reworking and re-presentation of journalistic stereotypes are in fact strategies found in much New Woman fiction. By exploring such stereotypes and putting them to work in new contexts, the New Woman writers engaged with current discourses on woman and intervened directly in contemporary debates on the Woman Question.

In *Gallia* many of the characters have difficulty in seeing beyond current stereotypes. Indeed, the novel suggests that individual identity has been completely subsumed by accepted gender roles. The debilitating effects of this process have been compounded by the current 'boom of women', in which every new idea, every new version of femininity is rapidly converted into a stereotype, and hence contained and defused. Thus, Gallia declines to write about her eugenicist ideas because:

One would only be grouped with all the other women
who are said to be leading the 'Sexual Revolt,' and that
would do the ideas harm, for no one would take them
seriously . . . What [women] say makes so much noise
that nobody hears properly what it is.

(G:195)

This latter problem is, of course, a central one for the novel
itself, as indeed it is for the New Woman writing in general.
It is the problem of devising ways of ensuring that women's
voices are heard. Gallia resolves it by juxtaposing a multiplicity
of voices on current issues and especially on the Woman and
Marriage questions. This polyphonic effect is both amplified
and problematised by the shifting narratorial tone, particularly
in the representation of Gallia. Never quite sure whether they
are meant to sympathise with, or condemn, the central character, the disorientated readers consequently listen with
increased attentiveness both to the heroine and to the range
of female voices which surround her. The novel's irony and
its brittleness of tone have a further destabilising effect. Just
as Braddon wittily subverts the domestic novel in the 1860s,
Dowie (among others) subverts the 1890s novel of modern life.

Dowie is at her most brittly urbane and ironic (and also
most sensational) in her treatment of the double standard of
sexual conduct, which had become the subject of renewed
controversy in the wake of the campaign for the repeal of the
Contagious Diseases Acts, and other social- and sexual-purity
campaigns. Gallia scrutinises the double standard from a
variety of perspectives, beginning with an early scene in which
its heroine, reading a newspaper article about the state regulation of vice, articulates her perception of the ways in which
the prostitute, or the demi-mondaine who becomes the mistress of the middle-class man, 'assures my class a good deal
of its immunity' (G:54), and underwrites (so to speak) the
proper feminine.

This perception is both reinforced and rendered more complex by the novel's subsequent focusing on the ethical and
sexual politics of a number of triangular relationships, and its
exploration of the different predicaments of the middle-class
male, his mistress, and the respectable woman who is to
become his wife. Dowie uses a conventional narrative pattern,

by means of which the erring middle-class man is 'rescued' by romantic love and marriage to a forgiving, pure woman. However, she puts this narrative to satirical and critical purposes, first by travestying it in her main plot. Here, despite (even partly because of) her knowledge of his earlier sexual adventure with an artist's model (Cara Lemuel), Gallia eugenically selects Mark Gurdon as the husband who will enable her to fulfil the maternal (rather than wifely) function which she comes to regard as woman's central role. The critical focus is also maintained in the sub-plot depicting the triumph of romantic love, in which the angelically pure Margaret Essex rescues the errant artist, Leighton, by forgiving his previous sexual adventures (while striving to remain ignorant of the details). This latter narrative foregrounds the angelic woman's complicity in sustaining the double standard and in exploiting 'fallen women', the precariousness of whose situation is exposed in the novel's frank and detailed portrayal of Cara Lemuel.

In its treatment of the double standard, Dowie's novel not only offers an improperly feminine representation of the demimonde and the sexual sensations of 'respectable' middle-class men and women, it also manifests a similarly improper scepticism about the idea of the proper feminine. *Gallia* puts the complexities of female emotions under the microscope, satirically demystifies the sanctities of romantic love, marriage and motherhood, and adopts a stance of unmasking the network of sexual, economic and psychological exploitation upon which modern marriage is constructed.

Other New Woman writers adopt a more apocalyptic tone in addressing these latter aspects of the Marriage Question. Sarah Grand's novels offer a particularly fierce indictment of genteel society's complicity in the degradation of women through the operations of the double standard. Her bestseller *The Heavenly Twins*, and also *The Beth Book*, focus directly and minutely on the plight of women trapped within degrading marriages. *The Beth Book* depicts its heroine's entrapment in, and ultimate escape from, marriage to a coarse and brutal adulterer, whose exploitation of women extends to his professional life as doctor in charge of one of the Lock hospitals which operated the Contagious Diseases Acts. *The Heavenly Twins* has two parallel degrading-marriage plots. In the first,

Evadne, a woman of independent views and high principles, having learned on her wedding day of her husband's former sexual debauchery, refuses to live with him. She later succumbs to familial pressure and joins him in a marriage of form only, which is used as the vehicle for an exploration and exposure of the sexual politics of the marriage relation. In the parallel plot, Edith, the embodiment of the totally innocent pure woman, fails to heed Evadne's warnings about the past life of her fiancé Sir Moseley Mentieth, and pays the price in bearing him a sickly, syphilitic child and herself succumbing to a syphilis-induced brain fever.

Whether wittily urbane, or apocalyptically admonitory, the New Woman writers' explorations of marriage and their exposure of the double standard not only brought the difference of view to bear on modern marriage and the gender roles it both required and constructed, but also offered an alternative view on gender. They viewed gender difference differently, and their procedures represented a challenge to some of the dominant ideologies.

16

Writing difference differently

Like the sensation novelists, the New Woman writers were
accused of knowing and, more importantly, articulating 'much
that ladies are not accustomed to know' (James 1865:593),
especially about sex and the pathology of sexual disease.
Arthur Waugh (1894) was not alone in holding 'women-writers
. . . chiefly to blame' for 'the latest development of literary
frankness', which 'in fiction . . . infects its heroines with
acquired diseases of names unmentionable' (217–18). In their
overt and explicit treatment of the double standard and the
pathology of sexual disease, the New Woman writers were
involved in a reworking of those discourses on prostitution and
female sexuality within which the sensation novelists wrote.

The sensation novel, as I suggested earlier, was produced
within a polarised discourse in which female sexuality was
represented as either non-existent or all-pervading. The family
was figured as the protector of a feminine purity which was
itself (contradictorily) threatened by an invading female sexuality – that of the prostitute or fallen woman, who was seen
as the bearer of corruption and disease. In contrast, the New
Woman writers figured men as both the physical and moral
corrupters of the family. The sexually threatening woman, the
femme fatale successor of the murderous women of sensation
fiction, remained a potent cultural image in the works of *fin
de siècle* male writers and artists. By the 1890s, however, the
deadly syphilitic male 'had become an arch-villain of feminist
protest fiction, a carrier of contamination and madness, and a
threat to the spiritual evolution of the human race' (Showalter
1986a:88).

In her representations of the diseased male, Sarah Grand,

154

like many of her female contemporaries, appropriated and reversed the terms of male scientific discourse. Throughout the nineteenth century an evolutionary theory of sexual difference was used to account for and perpetuate women's subordination within existing social relations. Particularly in the latter part of the century, scientific discourse figured women's resistance to their conventional social roles as contrary to the laws of nature, and as threatening the health and continuance of the race. The New Woman writers boldly transposed the terms of this discourse, making their male characters serve as both the symptoms of a diseased society and as the carriers of actual disease. 'Proper' (i.e., socially sanctioned) masculine behaviour, not improper femininity, was thus represented as the main threat to the future of the race. Several New Woman writers compounded the irony of this reversal by using doctors – especially specialists in women's ailments – as bearers of disease and disorder, rather than their curers: for example, Grand's Dan Slane (in *The Beth Book*) and Ella Hepworth Dixon's Dunlop Strange (*The Story of a Modern Woman*), who is responsible for the deaths of both the lower-class woman he seduces and the middle-class woman he wishes to marry.

More importantly, many of the New Woman writers transposed the fundamental terms of evolutionary discourse, and in the process transformed that discourse, by valorising its hitherto negative terms. Both Spencerian and Darwinian theory placed women lower in the evolutionary scale than men. For Spencer, woman was undeveloped man; for Darwin, man was developed woman. In either case woman was deemed to be closer than man to the animals and savages. However, although physically and intellectually less highly evolved than man, woman (or more precisely domestic bourgeois woman) was held to be spiritually and morally superior. Like other feminists Grand mobilised this contradiction to form a counter-ideology in which the male of the species was figured as less highly evolved than the female, and hence closer to brute nature. Grand's male villains are portrayed as not only physically diseased, but also as merely appetitive creatures.

Grand's novels represent this male brutishness not by means of a feminist rhetoric of argument, but by a rhetoric of feeling and sensation. By focusing on her heroines' feelings of repulsion, Grand makes the reader also *feel* the brutishness of socially sanctioned masculinity. *The Beth Book*, for example, documents minutely the heroine's pained endurance of her husband's coarse appetites. His sexual attentions are represented as crude, merely self-gratifying, and repulsive, and his excessive interest in food and drink makes meal-times difficult for his wife to endure.

The effects of Grand's focusing on the claustrophobia of the domestic space are thus quite different from those of the sensation novel (and indeed from some other feminist writers), where the focus is on the woman's imprisonment in (and sometimes resistance to) the domestic ideology and the feminine ideal. Instead Grand foregrounds 'the effects of the man's mind upon the woman's, shut up with him in the closest domestic intimacy day and night, and all the time imbibing his poisoned thoughts' (BB:356). Indeed, most of Grand's main female characters are represented as the victims of an atavistic male sexuality which (despite its primitivism) has, and is enforced by, social and cultural authority. In *The Heavenly Twins* the Church and the family (the cornerstones of the State), represented in the person of Edith's father, the Bishop, connive at placing an ignorant young girl in the power of a lecherous and sexually diseased man, while Evadne's first husband, Colquhoun, employs the resources of the culture (Zola's novels) in an attempt to 'educate' her sexual feelings.

Perhaps because it simply reverses the dominant discourse, the feminist counter-discourse retains its contradictions. Many of the New Woman writers, for example, seem actively to (re)construct a biologically essentialist ideology of sexual difference in which woman, as the more highly evolved form, was held to be more civilised and hence more closely associated with the cultural domain than man. This view underwrote the feminists' claims to wrest cultural and political power from the patriarchal institutions in which it was so inappropriately lodged. At the same time, however, because of her maternal function, woman was also closely associated with nature, indeed, was even represented as its embodiment. Many feminists and New Woman writers resolved this contradiction by both spiritualising and moralising maternity and womanhood.

Thus, rather than blurring gender boundaries and gender difference, as many of their critics claimed, some New Woman writers re-emphasised them. At the same time, many of these writers also challenged the customary association between gender difference and biological sex, by focusing on the social construction of gender and of gender roles. Traditional gender stereotypes are certainly viewed differently in Sarah Grand's novels. Both *The Heavenly Twins* and *The Beth Book* devote a great deal of space to the portrayal of wild, idiosyncratic children who enjoy or endure unconventional childhoods. The Heavenly Twins, Angelica and Diavolo, are portrayed in a lengthy period of pre-gendered existence, in which Angelica, the more active, vocal and physically daring, displays most forcefully those characteristics conventionally described as masculine. Grand's narrative focuses on the way in which the twins are educated and produced as differently gendered subjects, and on their resistance to their socially assigned roles (including a sustained episode devoted to Angelica's cross-dressing, to which I shall return). Almost to the end Angelica remains a spirited female devil, while Diavolo resists full cultural masculinisation and remains a sensitive, spiritual, quasi-angelic creature – a sort of asocial (and virtually asexual), feminised and feminist New Man (like the knightly figure of Beth's fantasy at the end of *The Beth Book*).

The contradictions of the counter-discourse on woman are particularly evident in its association of womanhood with maternity (or, more precisely, maternal feeling) and with feeling or affectivity. I want to explore this by looking, first, at the development of a variant of the marriage plot, which was also used in a number of sensation novels: the narrative of a woman who, having married for reasons of expediency, subsequently comes to love her husband. In other words this is a plot in which both romantic love and the domestic narrative are recuperated. In the 1890s this narrative takes on a new meaning, since it often involves the education and transformation of an avowedly anti-domestic, unwomanly heroine who is recuperated for True Womanhood.

17

Feeling, motherhood and True Womanhood

The opposition of the 'womanly woman' and her rebellious or improperly formed 'other' is the site upon which the Girl of the Period, and her successors, the Wild Women, Revolting Daughters and (later) the Shrieking Sisterhood are constructed. 'Womanliness', as Penny Boumelha (1982) has argued, is a 'socially constructed concept', 'an ideal or aspiration' rather than an 'inherent disposition' (74). Linton's 'Girl of the Period' articles, which enjoyed a new currency in the 1880s and 1890s (following their publication in volume form in 1883), were based on the assumption that it was, regrettably (at least as far as Linton was concerned), perfectly possible for any particular woman to be unwomanly. Certainly, most of the feminist writers of the 1880s and 1890s openly rejected the concept of womanliness. Their fiction is full of restless, searching women who have either deliberately rejected this socially constructed womanliness, or who have been imperfectly socialised. The rejection of womanliness is sometimes figured in a female character's rejection of her mother. Imperfect socialisation (i.e. social feminisation) is also attributed to inadequate mothering, sometimes by a woman disabled by her immersion in the self-effacing, self-sacrificial role of the proper feminine ideal, and sometimes by a woman disabled by her failure to conform to this ideal.

In the late nineteenth century the rejected womanliness was replaced by 'Womanhood' or 'True Womanhood', terms which denoted 'an immanent natural disposition, originating in a pre-determining physiological sexual differentiation' (Boumelha 1982:86). In some 1890s writers (Egerton, for example) True Womanhood is distinguished from, and opposed to, the tra-

158

ditional womanly role. In others the heroine's discovery of her
True Womanhood coincides with her acceptance of a womanly
role; the discredited or problematic concept of womanliness is
thus recuperated by a revitalised concept of womanhood.
Sarah Grand's *The Heavenly Twins*, and *A Yellow Aster* by Iota
(K.M. Caffynn) both represent this latter process, albeit from
different points of view, since Grand's sympathies were with
the feminists while Iota was an avowed anti-feminist.

In *The Heavenly Twins* the recuperative narrative is reworked
in an extravagant, even parodic form. Angelica, who transgresses all the norms of proper femininity, proposes marriage
to a longstanding family friend who, she believes, will let her
do as she likes. She is a prototypical 'Revolting Daughter',
who enters a chaste marriage in order to escape the constant
social pressure to marry, and thus obtain the freedom from
social constraints which middle-class marriage afforded to
women, without accepting the social and domestic burdens
and obligations which usually accompanied it. Angelica's
unconventional marriage provides the arena for her experiments in life, the chief of which forms the strange 'Interlude'
of 'The Tenor and the Boy'. In this episode Angelica, disguised
as her brother, throws off the shackles of her feminine identity
and embarks on a series of night-time visits to the Tenor who
admires and idealises her (as Angelica) from afar. For the
female character (and perhaps for the female reader) this
period of cross-dressing serves to enact a fantasy of liberation
from the constraints of her gender. As Angelica remarks when
her deception is uncovered:

'I had the ability to be something more than a young
lady, fiddling away her time on useless trifles, but I was
not allowed to apply it systematically, and ability is like
steam – a great power when properly applied, a great
danger otherwise . . . This is the explosion,' – glancing
round the disordered room, and then looking down at
her masculine attire.

(HT:450)

For the reader the hallucinatory writing of the Interlude
conjures up a dream-world where gender boundaries dissolve
and reform in disconcerting ways. The whole episode is
charged with the frisson of ambiguous sexuality: the Tenor is

159

clearly attracted to the Boy, but it is unclear whether this is a homoerotic attraction, or an attraction to Angelica's essential femininity. The episode also offers a strange (and, because of the disguise, displaced) version of a narrative more common in the novels of male writers in this period, in which a male character is destroyed by the experiments and whims of a New Woman (Hardy's Jude and perhaps also Giles Winterbourne spring most readily to mind). In this case the Tenor's slide towards death coincides with his discovery that the 'Boy' is a woman.

Angelica's response to the Tenor's death and, more particularly, the maternal sympathy she feels for the choirboy who mourns him, inaugurate the birth of her True Womanhood, and also her movement towards acceptance of her womanly role.

> All that was womanly in Angelica went out to the poor little fellow. She would have liked to have comforted him, but what could she say or do? *Alas! alas! a woman who cannot comfort a child, what sort of woman is she?*
>
> (HT:519, my italics)

Angelica's journey to full womanhood proceeds by a series of epiphanies of feeling until, in a rewriting of George Eliot's conversion narrative, she 'awoke to the consciousness . . . that she herself was an insignificant trifle on the face of the earth' (HT:542). It is, however, worth noting that the consciousness to which Angelica awakes is not Gwendolen Harleth's consciousness of her human insignificance and indeterminate future, but Dorothea Casaubon's recognition of her proper womanly role.

Angelica's recuperation is completed when she acknowledges her need of a loving husband. Like the Interlude of the Tenor and the Boy, this phase of the narrative is also marked by a melodramatic excess which verges on the parodic and comic. Angelica's return from the wilder shores of unwomanly eccentricity is represented by means of wild dreams ending in a tableau of reconciliation in which traditional gender roles appear to be re-established, as she falls on her knees and, in effect, thanks 'heaven, fasting, for a good man's love' (*As You Like It*:III, iv).

Iota's *A Yellow Aster* offers a somewhat different, although

160

no less melodramatic, version of this recuperative narrative. The heroine, Gwen Waring, one of two children of a pair of unworldly scientists who live entirely for their work, grows up deficient in proper womanly feeling and possessed of eccentric ideas. She is a strange, hybrid creature, as unnatural as the yellow aster of the title. Gwen's unnaturalness is directly attributed to her mother's unwomanly abstraction, self-absorption and immersion in her companionable intellectual rapport with her husband. To use the terminology of Nancy Chodorow (1978) – who argues that existing gender relations in western societies are reproduced through the reproduction of female mothering – Gwen is a character in whom mothering has failed to be reproduced.

Inadequately mothered, Gwen embarks on adult life with an unwomanly sense of herself as an active agent, a knight-errant with her own quest to pursue, rather than the object of some one else's quest. 'I will attain like Paracelsus' (YA:78), she avers. However, her knightly quest comes to an early conclusion when, 'as an experiment' and 'because I like new sensations' (YA:29), she marries Humphrey Strange. In this narrative one set of textual signals telegraphs the presence of the febrile New Woman, wandering between two worlds, while the practised reader of romantic fiction also recognises the signs of a woman waiting to discover her true identity through love.

> Love is a mere name to me . . . I must be honest too, and tell you that I shouldn't know how to dispose of a whole heart full of love . . . in the face of all this I want to accept your offer. I don't know why; I really believe it is not I . . . who wants this, it is something outside me that wants it for me. I never felt so impersonal in all my life.
>
> (YA:129)

As the novel goes on to suggest, that impersonal 'something outside me' is the True Womanhood that is waiting to claim her. This essential womanhood is figured in the portraits and sketches which her husband's friend Brydon makes of her; these representations, from the outset, suggest aspects of Gwen's nature which are as yet unapparent to the ordinary eye. As in *Lady Audley's Secret*, the secret of Gwen's essential feminine identity is staged for the reader as a spectacle pro-

161

duced by the privileged gaze of the male artist. Brydon's portraits keep one step ahead of Gwen's development until portrait and character coalesce in a final *tableau vivant* in which Humphrey (newly returned from an exile to which Gwen had banished him) awakes from a feverish sleep to see Brydon's last portrait apparently come alive, as Gwen steps out from in front of it.

Before she discovers her True Womanhood and her womanly role, the unredeemed Gwen sees marriage as legalised prostitution. Her discovery that she is expecting Humphrey's child is used as the occasion of a feeling attack on 'unnatural' loveless marriage and conventional moral values which is typical of New Woman writing.

> Now I must sit under those deep, all-pervading eyes of his and feel myself ten thousand times his chattel . . . Talk of the shame of those women who have children out of the pale of marriage, it's nothing to the shame of those who have children and don't love. Those others, they have the excuse of love – that's natural, that purifies their shame; this – our life – the portion of quite half the well-to-do world – this is unnatural.
>
> (YA:247)

The sanctification of motherhood which emerges in the above passage to link prostitute, kept woman and wife in a community of True Womanhood is the key to the novel and to the development of its central female characters. In an interesting variant of the maternal melodrama noted in the sensation novel, Gwen's mother undergoes a crisis in which she discovers her maternal feeling in and as a drama of suffering. Paradoxically, maternal feeling is represented as at once natural (a disposition awaiting discovery), and as acquired through the experience of suffering. Gwen's mother's story hinges on the discovery of a lack which she first learns to acknowledge and name, and then to rectify through observing, and learning from, the maternal behaviour of other (more conventionally socialised) women.

Gwen's own rebirth into womanhood begins with a moment of revelation in which she simultaneously affirms her link to her mother and her own unborn child.

As her mother kissed and bit, and mumbled over her hand, and half sang little quaint snatches of baby song . . . her own baby 'leapt in her womb', and the scales fell from her eyes, and her heart melted within her, and the breast of her dying mother was as an open book to her.

(YA:273–4)

This melodramatic passage provides a graphic account of the reproduction of mothering as a process in which daughters are perpetually reproduced as affective creatures, and as the nurturers of the next generation, through the bond with the mother. Gwen (like Angelica and a host of other female characters in the fiction of this period) is recuperated for True Womanhood through the birth of proper feminine feeling, which is associated with the biological fact of maternity and the social practice of mothering. True Womanhood is thus defined as affectivity. It is the New Woman writing's engagement with this equation of feeling and the feminine that I want to explore next.

18

Woman's 'affectability' and the literature of hysteria

The rhetoric of feminists, anti-feminists, misogynists and the proponents of the womanly woman coincided in its identification of woman with feeling. This equation of feeling and the feminine should hardly be surprising to readers of the novel, since throughout the nineteenth century (and, arguably, from its inception), the novel was preoccupied with women and feeling. Indeed it could be argued that the novel has always tended to represent woman *as* feeling. The fiction of the 1890s, whether written by men or by women, was both produced by and engaged with a complex and contradictory discourse on woman's supposedly affective nature, a discourse which, by equating woman with feeling, assigned her either to the domain of the irrational, or to that of the supra-rational.

In the first case woman was represented as a pre-logical being, existing outside of rationality in a state of nature; she was like a child, and hence dependent and in need of nurturing and guidance. This was precisely the view that had been rejected by the earliest feminist campaigners.[3] When sexual feeling was included in this particular equation, woman became the embodiment of a danger which had to be controlled. (Both of these versions of feminine 'affectability' were central to the strategies of containment of the domestic ideology.)

On the other hand, when associated with the supra-rational, woman was represented as being *above*, rather than *beyond*, rationality. She was associated with the order of nature, but was held to transcend both nature and rationality by means of her spirituality and intuitive powers. This latter view is clearly an important component in the construction of both

domestic woman with her feminine influence, and the feminists' regenerative woman with her mission to rescue a degenerate civilisation. The equation of woman with supra-rational
feeling also usually involved associating her with an emotionality which transcended sexuality. Woman *as* feeling was thus
either humanity in a state of nature, or nature in its most
highly evolved form. This contradiction is evident in many late
nineteenth-century popularisations of post-Darwinian science.
George Romanes (1887), for example, attributed the 'Mental
differences between men and women' to a female emotionalism which is at once disabling and the source of women's
superior spirituality. '[W]oman as contrasted with men', he
argues, is disabled by her emotions, which 'are almost always
less under control of the will – more apt to break away, as it
were, from restraint of reason, and to overwhelm the mental
chariot in disaster' (657–8), but this same emotionality – in its
guise of 'intuitive insight' (655) – is also the source of woman's
moral and spiritual superiority.

This contradictory view of feminine affectivity is central to
the writing of George Egerton, best known for her two collections of short stories, *Keynotes* and *Discords*. These stories,
together with her curiously fragmentary (and now little-
known) novel, *The Wheel of God*, represent feeling as the key
to 'the enigma of woman', what Egerton called that *'terra incognita'* of the female self (quoted in Gawsworth 1932:58),
which was her central concern. Virtually all of her fictions
stage the drama of the heroine's grappling with the riddle of
her femininity and the mystery of 'what it is we [women] need
to complete us' (D:198). In this drama, as in the psychoanalytic
discourse which developed in the late nineteenth century (and
in its Lacanian revisions), feminine affectivity, indeed femininity itself, is defined as a lack.

> Perhaps we seek a key to the enigma of our own natures,
> we try man after man to see if he holds it . . . [but]
> perhaps we are merely the playthings of circumstances.

Femininity is also contradictory and duplicitous. It is feared,
repressed and concealed.

> [We are] contradictions, leading a dual life . . . our vary-
> ing moods bound up with the physiological gamut of our

165

being. We have been taught to shrink from the honest expression of our wants and feelings as violations of modesty, or at least of good taste. We are always battling with some bottom layer of real womanhood that we may not reveal; the primary impulses of our original destiny keep shooting out mimosa-like threads of natural feeling through the outside husk of our artificial selves, producing complex creatures.

(Both quotations D:198)

Egerton's stories undertake an investigation of that 'bottom layer of real womanhood', posited on the existence of 'the primary impulses of our original destiny' which precede socialisation. This process involves the excavation or unmasking of 'the untrue feminine of man's making', and the discovery of the 'strong, the natural, the true womanly [that] is of God's making' (K:42).

Egerton's representation of the feminine tends to align itself on the nature side of the nature/culture debate. Her 'true womanly' is 'woman's witchcraft', 'the eternal wildness, the untamed primitive savage temperament that lurks in the mildest, best woman . . . [which] may be concealed but is never eradicated by culture' (K:22). Anticipating the version of the feminine celebrated by some late twentieth-century feminists (particularly by French theorists of the feminine, such as Hélène Cixous and Luce Irigaray), Egerton tends to represent woman as a pre-cultural primitive, bound to the mysteries and cycles of nature. Woman is the sorceress who contains within herself the repressed past of a culture, 'who in the end is able to dream Nature', and who 'incarnates the reinscription of the traces of paganism that triumphant Christianity repressed' (Cixous and Clément 1987:5). Thus, in a passage which also anticipates D.H. Lawrence's *The Rainbow*,[4] *The Wheel of God* stages its heroine, Mary, enacting a rite of spring in which she is said to feel the call of the spring as 'the primitive in her, untouched by its passage through all the centuries . . . closer to the forces of nature than man – genetic woman' (WG:95).

The most sensational (in several senses) aspect of Egerton's primitivism, as far as her first readers were concerned, was her insistence on the primacy and autonomy of women's sexual feeling, and her detailed representation of an eroticised feminine sensibility. Egerton's writings directly challenged the repressive hypothesis of the dominant discourse on female sexuality, focusing instead on the deforming or explosive consequences of a social repression which contradicts woman's 'nature' (the idea of 'woman's nature' does not seem to have been problematic for Egerton). As the first-person narrator of the framed narrative 'Now Spring Has Come' remarks, women 'repress and . . . repress, and then some day we stumble on the man who just satisfies our sexual and emotional nature, and then there is shipwreck of some sort' (K:57).

Egerton's challenging of the dominant discourse (as the last quotation suggests) comes from within the terms of that very discourse. Her version of woman and of female sexuality is itself produced by a polarised (and contradictory) discourse in which woman is either asexual, or omni-sexual. In several stories this polarisation is foregrounded by Egerton's use of contrasting paired characters: the self-controlled (indeed self-repressed), respectable working woman and the fallen woman, 'Mrs Grey', who has given all for love in 'Gone Under', or the struggling, self-contained woman writer and her misused, drunken landlady (whose situation as an unmarried mother has resulted in an unsuitable marriage) in 'Wedlock'.

Although Egerton's stories also offer a range of shrewd, reflective and self-reliant women (see, especially, the heroine of 'A Psychological Moment'), most of her women are represented as hypersensitive creatures possessed of unnameable desires and inexpressible yearnings. They are so many stringed instruments whose strings, tautened to breaking point, await the touch of the right circumstances, or man. (Mary's ritual dance of spring, for example, is made even more electric by her longing for a male partner.) All too often instrument and player are kept apart (by the adverse circumstances of contemporary woman's lot) and, 'like a harp that has lain away . . . the strings are frayed, and no one ever call[s] out [the woman's] music' (D:170).[5] Alternatively, many of Egerton's stories contrive to suggest that the man has not yet been born who is sufficiently attuned to the delicate instrument of female sensibility and sexuality.

If an autonomous sexuality is one key to the enigma of woman, maternal *feeling* (as opposed to the mere fact of physical reproduction) is the other.

167

[T]he only *divine* fibre in woman is her maternal instinct
. . . Every woman ought to have a child, if only as a
moral educator . . . a woman who mothers a bastard,
and endeavours bravely to rear it decently, is more to be
commended than the society wife who contrives to shirk
her motherhood. She is at heart loyal to the finest fibre
of her being, the deep underlying instinct, the 'mutter-
drang,' that lifts her above and beyond all animalism,
and fosters the sublimest qualities of unselfishness and
devotion.

(D:100–1)

Here, as in the dominant discourse, woman is identified with
nature: if she suppresses the maternal instinct 'it turns to a
fibroid sapping all that is healthful and good in her nature'
(D:100). However, since Egerton (in common with many late
nineteenth-century feminists) also spiritualises maternity,
woman, in fulfilling her natural function, is held to transcend
merely brute nature.

By fusing together an autonomous female sexuality and a
sublime maternity Egerton's stories appear to wrest woman
from the familiar whore/madonna dichotomy of the dominant
discourse. However, paradoxically, her identification of
woman with nature, and even her apparently disruptive insistence on the primacy of female sexual feeling, combine to reinscribe woman in an essentialist discourse in which women's
lot is determined by physiology, and woman is a creature who
is *by nature* affective and 'affectible'. In practice, however, the
effect of her writing is rather more complex: Egerton does not
simply reproduce this essentialist discourse, she also appropriates and interrogates it. Although she may ultimately remain
within it, she puts it to new uses by attempting to reclaim
autonomous feeling as a source of power, and by dwelling on
the destructive effects of feminine self-sacrifice.

In Egerton's fictions, like those of many of the New Woman
writers, the conventional association of feeling and the feminine is not merely a topic of the narrative, it is also part of
the narrative texture. Like a number of New Woman writers
Egerton developed an aesthetic practice in which, at its most
highly charged moments, writing became equated with feeling.
In fact, to some of its earliest readers and critics the New

168

Woman writing simply was feeling; it was an hysterical literature, written (and read) on the nerves.

George Egerton['s] . . . perceptions are of the nerves . . .
she personifies our modern nervousness, and her best
characters are quivering bundles of nerve . . . [W]riters
of this type . . . are always purely subjective . . . Like all
introspective work . . . Egerton appeals to women far
more than to men, for her instinct enables her to perceive
the fundamental traits of woman's nature.

(Stutfield 1897:109–10)

In other words, Egerton's writings were read as the discourse
of the hysteric. Indeed, like Cixous and Irigaray (and with
some of the same problems), Egerton sought to appropriate
the culturally ascribed role of hysteric and to use it actively,
rather than merely to bear it as the mark of the wounded
victim. Egerton's fictions reverse the negative associations of
feeling and the feminine, and instead analyse and celebrate
the vitality and complexity of a specifically feminine feeling.

An excellent example of this can be found in 'A Cross Line',
a story which is structured around the changing currents of the
restless desires of its central character, who is, as in virtually all
of Egerton's stories, an unnamed woman. In this case (again,
not untypically) the central character bears all the signs of the
New Woman and her contradictions. She is both self-sufficient
and 'a creature of moments' (K:24), unwomanly and hyperfeminine. Her unwomanliness is signalled by her brown hands,
her skill in the 'masculine' pursuit of fishing, and the fact that
she roams the countryside freely, has a frank mode of address
(friendship with her is 'like chumming with a chap', says her
husband), is sexually tolerant, and tends to take the sexual
initiative. Most unwomanly of all is her apparent lack of
maternal feeling, which is signalled by her disgust at small
things (in sharp contrast to her husband's 'maternal' delight
in the ducklings on their smallholding). On the other hand,
hyperfemininity is signalled by her restless nerviness and
emotionality: 'One speculation chases another in her quick
brain . . . There is a look of expectation in her quivering nervous little face' (K:13). Her highly charged eroticism is another
sign of the hyperfeminine; she is represented as both erotic
object (the object of the desiring gaze of the stranger whom

169

she meets on one of her rambles), and as powerfully desiring subject.

The plot of this story (insofar as any of Egerton's stories can be said to have a plot) appears to be conservative and essentialist: a woman fantasises about and contemplates escape from the constraints and tedium of domestic life, but becomes resigned to her lot when she discovers (or belatedly acknowledges) that she is expecting her husband's child, and accepts the maternal role. Woman is once more defined by her biological reproductivity. However, the conservative narrative trajectory of this story is apparently subverted by aspects of its narration. This is particularly true of the much-discussed 'clouds' passage.[6] This interior monologue, semi-detached from the narrative, forms an extended piece of lyrical writing which writes the unconscious, defines the feminine as and through feeling, and explores and celebrates the energy and complexity of a particular woman's feeling and fantasies. It is an extraordinary passage, and worth quoting at length:

> Summer is waning and the harvest is ripe for ingathering, and the voice of the reaping machines is loud in the land . . . Overhead a flotilla of clouds is steering from the south in a north-easterly direction. Her eyes follow them. Old time galleons, she thinks, with their wealth of snowy sail spread, riding breast to breast up a wide blue fjord after victory . . . Somehow she thinks of Cleopatra sailing down to meet Antony, and a great longing fills her soul to sail off somewhere too – away from the daily need of dinner-getting and the recurring Monday with its washing; life with its tame duties and virtuous monotony. She *fancies* herself in Arabia on the back of a swift steed. Flashing eyes set in dark faces surround her, and she can *see* the clouds of sand swirl, and *feel* the swing under her of his rushing stride. Her thoughts shape themselves into a wild song. . . . to the untamed spirit that dwells in her.
>
> (K:18, my italics)

The energy and extravagance of this opening passage of the 'clouds' section enact (rather than merely describe) a fantasy of escape from mundane domestic duties. It is an example of that feminine economy of excess, that overflow of eroticism which (for Cixous) characterises *l'écriture féminine*. The reader is caught up in the character's asocial fantasy of female power, and is co-opted to her point of view as she moves from revelling in sensuous and sensual feeling to delighting in her power over the audiences she invents for the scenes of her performance.

Then she *fancies* she is on the stage of an ancient theatre out in the open air, with hundreds of faces turned towards her . . . *Her arms are clasped by jewelled snakes, and one with quivering diamond fangs coils round her hips. Her hair floats loosely* . . . and the delicate breath of vines and the salt freshness of an incoming sea seem to fill her nostrils. *She bounds forward and dances,* bends her lissom waist, and gives to the soul of each man what he craves, be it good or evil. *And she can feel now, lying here in the shade of Irish hills . . . the grand intoxicating power of swaying all these human souls to wonder and applause. She can see herself with parted lips and panting, rounded breasts . . . sway voluptuously to the wild music that rises . . . She can feel the answering shiver of feeling that quivers up to her from the dense audience . . . And the men rise to a man and answer her, and cheer, cheer till the echoes shout from the surrounding hills.*

(K:19–20, my italics)

Elaine Showalter (1991) has read this passage in terms of the *fin de siècle* preoccupation with the veiled woman who 'stood as a figure of sexual secrecy and inaccessibility for Victorian men', and also signified 'the quest for the mystery of origins, the truths of birth and death' (145). Egerton's heroine (in Showalter's reading) 'autoerotically imagines herself' (156) in the role of that most famous of *fin de siècle* veiled women, Salome. The fantasy version of herself that Egerton's nameless heroine projects is, like Oscar Wilde's Salome, a Medusan figure whose 'hair floats loosely', and whose 'arms are clasped by jewelled snakes'. Freud (as Showalter points out) 'interpreted the myth of the Medusa's head as an allegory of the veiled woman, whose unshielded gaze turns men to stone' (145). However, unlike this castrating Medusa, Egerton's Salome activates her male audience, makes them share in her feeling and acknowledge the power of her performance with cheers. This particular act of female unveiling 'substitutes

171

power for castration' (Showalter 1991: 156). Egerton's Salome is an image of female power, the laughing Medusa envisaged by Hélène Cixous (1981): 'she's not deadly. She's beautiful and she's laughing' (255).

In this passage, Egerton stages her heroine in the process of staging herself as a combination of the sorceress and that 'Newly Born Woman' who will, in Cixous's phrase, live beyond the 'character' assigned to her by the patriarchy.[7] For a brief moment, the language of the 'clouds' section celebrates the magic and power of the woman as sorceress or hysteric, whilst avoiding the burdens of guilt which are conventionally attached to these roles. Like Cixous's and Clément's (1987) Newly Born Woman, Egerton's heroine's fantasy version of herself is 'innocent, mad, full of badly remembered memories . . . she is the seductress, the heiress of all generic Eves' (6).

The dreamlike nature of the 'clouds' section, and its lack of causal connection with the rest of the story, are used to figure the feminine as a 'wild zone',[8] 'the imaginary zone' which every culture has 'for what it excludes' (Cixous and Clément 1987: 6). However, I think it would be a mistake to see this piece of writing as simply offering what some late twentieth-century feminists might see as a liberating carnival of the hysteric's fantasy.[9] The clouds passage also disrupts its own disruption. It distances the reader from the character's fantasy, as it slides into a more discursive analysis of 'the problems of [woman's] complex nature' (a complexity which the passage also articulates). It examines women's habitual denial of their own power and desire, and their collusion with man's 'chivalrous, conservative devotion to the female idea he has created'.

And her thoughts go to other women she has known. . . . joyless machines for grinding daily corn, unwilling maids grown old in the endeavour to get settled, patient wives who bear little ones to indifferent husbands until they wear out . . . She busies herself with questioning. Have they, too, this thirst for excitement, for change. . . . And she laughs. . . [B]ecause of the denseness of man, his chivalrous, conservative devotion to the female idea he has created blinds him, perhaps happily, to the problems of her complex nature . . . Deep in through ages of convention [a] primeval trait burns, an untameable quan-

tity . . . [I]t is there sure enough, and each woman is
conscious of it in her truth-telling hours of quiet self-
scrutiny – and each woman in God's wide world will
deny it, and each woman will help another to conceal it
– for the woman who tells the truth and is not a liar
about these things is untrue to her sex and abhorrent to
man, for he has fashioned a model on imaginary lines,
and he has said, 'so I would have you,' and every woman
is an unconscious liar, for so man loves her.

(K:21–3)

The clouds section offers an interesting variant of that staging of the feminine that I identified in the sensation novel.
Whereas in the sensation novel this is done by means of various scenes or melodramatic tableaux, in the clouds passage a
woman is staged in the process of staging her own femininity.
In each case acting is used in a different way and signifies
differently. As I suggested earlier, the sensationalists' staging
of the feminine reproduces or engages with the pervasive fear
that femininity is itself a form of acting – a masquerade. At
first glance it might appear that the woman's imaginary performance in the clouds passage is being used to signify the
truth (or essential femininity) that underlies the mask of social
femininity. However, ultimately the elliptical and evasive
nature of Egerton's narrative (and its refusal to analyse or
disclose motivation) has the effect of disrupting the idea of a
stable feminine identity. Instead the story presents us with a
multiplicity of selves, or a self in process.

More generally, Egerton's tendency to reproduce an essentialist discourse of 'True Womanhood' is repeatedly undercut,
and rendered more complex by her preference for episodic
forms and fragmented narrative. The effect of the varied view-
points afforded by her choice of the short-story form, and
by her use of shifting perspectives within those stories, is to
emphasise multiplicity and to focus on differences (between
women) as well as difference (as a universal, essentialist
gender category). The same might be said of her fragmentation
of narrative in her episodic novel *The Wheel of God*.

Moreover, although Egerton's fiction foregrounds feminine
affectivity, it also problematises and interrogates the dominant
discourse on woman's 'affective nature'. By persistently

173

focusing on the problems which affectivity poses for particular women, Egerton's stories open up a space for resistance to it. In Egerton's work sexual and maternal feeling are both woman's glory and her curse. Such feelings trap women in 'Wedlock' (the title of a story in Discords, my italics), bind them to violent, drunken, lecherous, or simply boring and unresponsive men, make them emotionally vulnerable and subject to drink, despair and derangement. At a time when women were bombarded from all sides with cultural messages (often contradictory) seeking to persuade them of the glory of their womanly feeling, it was perhaps salutory to be offered a series of representations of the depressing consequences of such feeling, and to be asked to consider the possibility that the 'crowning disability of my sex' is 'affection', and that 'affectability' is one of 'the tragedies of her sex' (WG:95).

Several other New Woman writers simultaneously celebrate the feminine and/as feeling, and problematise the conventional association of woman with feeling. Grand's The Heavenly Twins both recuperates the 'deviant' Angelica for proper womanly feeling and, at the same time, depicts the destruction of another woman (Edith) by that same socially sanctioned womanliness. However, perhaps the most interesting example of the way in which the novel interrogates the conventional view of women is its representation of Evadne. In this case, as in Egerton's writings, a woman's feelings (or woman's feeling) are not simply a topic of the narrative, they are also a narrative medium, since Evadne is persistently represented through sensation and feeling.

The nature and status of Evadne's feelings become particularly important in the novel's final section, in which the impersonal third-person narrator is replaced by the first-person narrative of Galbraith, Evadne's doctor and subsequently her husband. In this final book, the feeling female subject becomes the object of the male, medical gaze. The third-person narration, with its privileged access to the character's subjectivity, invites the reader's sympathetic identification with, and intuitive understanding of, Evadne's feelings as suffering. The first-person narrative of Galbraith, on the other hand, scrutinises those feelings as hysterical symptoms. The third-person narrative offers the reader a subjective understanding of the character's feelings as the history of her interiority; Galbraith views the character from the outside and through the lens of the nascent science of psychology, which claims a privileged knowledge of women's interiority.

The sign she made was deceptive, and probably only a man of my profession, accustomed to observe, and often obliged to judge more by indications of emotions than by words, would have recognised its true significance.

(HT:573)

One of the effects of this shift of narrative perspective is to problematise the female hysteric. As Carroll Smith-Rosenberg (1985) has pointed out, nineteenth-century medical discourse represented the hysteric as 'the embodiment of a perverse or hyperfemininity' (198). To Grand's medical men, hysteria is perverse femininity, or feminine perversity. They suspect their patients of 'extraordinary systems of fraud and deceit' (HT: 573), equate 'these female illnesses' with 'depravity', and seek to 'cure' them by moral management: 'steady moral influence will do all that is necessary. The great thing is to awaken the conscience' (HT:375).[10] Grand's third-person narrative, however, tells the hysteric's story differently, and from the woman's point of view. Seen from this perspective, hysteria may appear to be less a disease or psychopathology than a social role produced by the nineteenth-century family, a form of withdrawal or resistance by means of which 'women, to escape the misfortune of their economic and familial exploitation, chose to suffer before an audience of men' (Cixous and Clément 1987:10).

The discourse of woman's affectivity which is developed in the third-person narrative of The Heavenly Twins represents Evadne's 'hysteria' as both withdrawal and resistance. It is a form of hyperfemininity, which even as it disables the character also marks her out as a moral heroine who is superior to the men who seek to diagnose and treat her. In the feminised moral economy of Grand's novel, Evadne's nervous symptoms are the embodiment and barometer of her superior feminine sensitivity to the evils of a degenerate world. Evadne is an example of what Juliet Mitchell (following Cixous) describes as the hysteric as creative artist, one who 'suffer[s] from reminiscences' and who has heard, or seen, something that has made her ill (Mitchell 1984:298).

175

The narrative form of *The Heavenly Twins* thus restages the contest, which was being waged more widely in the New Woman fiction and in the culture at large, about how and by whom 'woman' and women's feelings might be defined. In the next section I shall explore the figure of the creative woman as one of the sites upon which this contest was waged.

19

Writing women: writing woman

[L]ate-Victorian readers had become accustomed to novels by women which were as much about the problems of being a woman writer as about the problems of women in society.

(Showalter 1985:viii)

I realised that in literature, everything had been better done by man than woman could hope to emulate. There was only one small plot left for her to tell; the *terra incognita* of herself, as she knew herself to be, not as man liked to imagine her – in a word to give herself away, as man had given himself in his writing.

(Egerton, quoted in Gawsworth 1932:58)

If women's sensation novels had proclaimed themselves women's texts by focusing on women's sensations, adopting a woman-to-woman address and working within what was perceived to be a feminine genre, many New Woman novels situated themselves as women's texts by making writing women and women's writing their subjects. By foregrounding the figure of the woman writer, such novels foreground the problems of their own production. In addition, the woman writer, or more generally the woman artist (Caird's Hadria, for example, is a musician), is repeatedly used as a way of figuring the lack of fit between women's desire, the socially prescribed norms of the woman's lot, and the actuality of women's lives. In some New Woman fiction the writing or creative woman was also a vehicle for *celebrating* female desire. Writing the woman writer's sensations and consciousness became a form of writing the woman as a feeling, experiencing subject, rather than as merely the victim of her affectivity, or as the object of a specular gaze (as is the case in the work of most male authors of the 1890s). Several of the New Woman writers also used the figure of the woman writer or artist as a means of exploring and interrogating the medical discourse on hysteria.

Sarah Grand's *The Beth Book* offers one of the most sustained representations of the sensibility of the woman artist. The childhood and adolescence of Grand's heroine, Beth, comprise a kind of portrait of an artist as a young woman. Much of the earlier part of the novel focuses on the minute details of the myriad sense impressions that constitute the history of Beth's coming to self-consciousness, as she emerges from being 'as unconscious as a white grub without legs' (BB:10) into an awareness of self and of her relationship to, and separateness from, the world she inhabits. Many of the passages which involve this process function as both representations of the character's consciousness, and celebrations of the writer's self-consciousness. The language of these passages is frequently in excess of the demands of the mere portrayal of character; writing itself is foregrounded.

The young Beth is depicted as a 'fine instrument, sensitive to a touch' (BB:43), whose senses are unusually acute, and whose memory 'from the first . . . helped itself by the involuntary association of incongruous ideas' (BB:17). She is a dreamer and a visionary, possessed of a 'further faculty', beyond mere intellect, which enables her to look upon life 'as if from a height, viewing it both in detail and as a whole' (BB:28). The subjectivity which Grand constructs for her character is partly that of the Wordsworthian infant, trailing clouds of glory, and partly a late nineteenth-century version of the Kristevan semiotic – that domain of instinctual, psychosexual drives which, according to Kristeva, precedes language and is repressed as the child enters the realm of the symbolic and of social communication.[11]

Grand's Wordsworthian infant is a 'natural' poet seeking to name the sights and sounds of the world around her and to articulate a pre-intellectual sense of the world. This vision of the poet is expressed in Beth's description of the genesis of her 'song of the sea in the shell':

It just came to me . . . I used to listen to the sea in the shell in the sitting-room, and I tried and tried to find a name for the sound, and all at once *song* came into my head – *The song of the sea in the shell*. Then I was lying out here on the grass when it was long . . . and you came out and said, 'There's a stiff breeze blowing.' And then it blew hard and then stopped, and then it came again; and every time it came the grass went – swish-h-h! *The swish of the grass in the breeze* . . . Then the leaves – it *was* a long time before anything came that I could sing about them. I used to try and think it, but you can't sing a thing you think. It's when a thing comes, you sing it.

(BB:68)

Beth is also celebrated as a kind of infant witch, connected by a pre-conscious, pre-linguistic race-memory to a mysterious ancestry and a world of dream and the irrational, from which she becomes separated only by her entry into phallocentric language and the workaday world of her historic self.

Beth had the sensation of having been nearer to some-thing in her infancy than ever she was again – nearer to knowing what it is the trees whisper – what the murmur means . . . It may have been hereditary memory, a knowledge of things transmitted to her by her ancestors . . . the recollection of a condition anterior to this, a condition of which no tongue can tell, which is not to be put into words.

(BB:27–8)

Kristeva's version of the semiotic, whatever reservations one might have about its essentialism, does provide a useful lens through which to view Grand's representation of Beth. Femin-ist exponents of Kristeva have explicitly linked the semiotic to the feminine because of its association with the mother's body before the child's entry into the 'male' symbolic order. As Alice Jardine writes (1981), 'This space before the sign, the *semiotic*, has been and continues to be coded in our culture as feminine: the space of privileged contact with the mother's female body' (228). Beth's 'further faculty', the source of both her indepen-

179

dence and her creativity, is similarly associated with her connection with the body of the mother (notwithstanding the fact that she has a distant and difficult relationship with her actual mother) through her 'recollection' of the birth process. This 'recollection' also prefigures her later rebirth into feminist activism.

> One other strange vision she had which she never forgot. With her intellect she believed it to have been a dream, but her further faculty always insisted that it was a recollection. She was with a large company in an indescribable, hollow space, bare of all furnishments because none were required; and into this space there came a great commotion, bright light and smoke, without heat or sense of suffocation. Then she was alone, making for an aperture; struggling and striving with pain of spirit to gain it; and when she had found it, she shot through, and awoke in the world. She awoke with a terrible sense of desolation upon her, and with the consciousness of having traversed infinite space at infinite speed.
>
> (BB:28)

Beth is, in part, a portrait of the artist as young romantic, set apart by a super-sensitivity which gives access to a vision which can never be fully articulated in language. Gender, however, adds another problematic dimension to the romantic artist's predicament. Historically, women writers have had even greater difficulty than their male counterparts in articulating their inner visions, because they have not had equal access to language. Beth's story, like that of most nineteenth-century women, is shaped by her inadequate education (her own education is sacrificed for that of her brother), and also by prevailing notions of the proper feminine. In order to become a writer Beth must learn, from life as well as from books, much that women are not accustomed to know: 'you can't write if you don't know how everyone talks' (BB:190). *The Beth Book* repeatedly emphasises the fact that the attributes which make Beth a writer are precisely those that unmake her as the conventionally socialised woman, and thus consign her to the improper feminine of the unwomanly woman.

As I suggested in the first part of this book, contemporary discourses of art and of woman rendered the phrase 'woman artist' a contradiction in terms. A number of the women writers of this period not only engaged with this discursive problem, but also focused on the practical problems that follow from it, and from the nature of women's social situation. Mona Caird (1897), for example, invited 'anyone [who] wishes to know why many women have not written Shakespeare's plays (as it is generally quaintly expressed)', to consider the inhibiting effects of 'the weary detail of domestic duties, of the unending petty responsibilities, the constant call "to give small decisions and settle minute emergencies" ' (5–6). In *The Daughters of Danaus* Caird wrote feelingly, as Mary Cholmondeley was later to do in *Red Pottage*, of the erosion of female creativity by the constant demands of domestic and familial duties.

Cholmondeley's heroine, Hester Gresley, suffers physical and nervous breakdown as a consequence of being forced to rise at daybreak in order to secure a period for uninterrupted writing. A similar (this time non-fictional) story is told by Alys Pearsall Smith in her contribution to the 'Revolt of the Daughters' controversy. In 'A reply from the daughters II' she rehearses the history of a girl with an insatiable desire for study whose family 'strongly objected to her taking time from the family life for this purpose'. The girl developed the habit of rising several hours before anyone else in order to pursue her studies, and consequently needed to sleep in the afternoon.

> Not knowing the cause, no one objected to this. It was considered in the family that she was delicate, and must on no account be disturbed in this daily nap. Whereas had she wished to . . . study [in this nap period] she would have been indignantly reproved for her selfishness. For her surface need of a nap she found sympathy and consideration, for her vital need of study she found only reproof.
>
> (Smith 1894:445)

This practice of secret study was one of the 'symptoms' documented by Freud and Breuer in their *Studies in Hysteria* (1895). Hysterical girls, they noted, were likely to be 'lively, gifted, and full of intellectual interests'. Among the 'hysterical' women they treated were 'girls who get out of bed at night so as secretly to carry on some study that their parents have

forbidden for fear of overworking' (quoted in Showalter
1991:40).
The musical vocation of Caird's Hadria is not merely constrained by parental and (later) husbandly dictates, and her
womanly duties; it is, ultimately, destroyed.

> [H]er greatest effort had to be given, not to the work
> itself, but to win an opportunity to pursue it . . . [her
> mother] opposed her daughter's endeavours . . . It was
> not good for a girl to be selfishly preoccupied . . .
> If Hadria yielded the point on any particular occasion,
> her mood and her work were destroyed, through the
> nervous disturbance and the intense depression which
> followed the winning of a liberty too dearly bought . . .
> [This] process told upon her health . . . The injury was
> insidious but serious. Hadria, unable to command any
> certain part of the day, began to sit up at night.
>
> (DD:109)

Both Caird and Cholmondeley give an interesting twist to
the conventional view of the female artist (especially the 1890s
woman writer) as hysteric. Instead of representing artistic work
as the product of the hysteria or nerves of the aspiring woman
artist, both authors represent 'hysteria' (or breakdown) as produced by artistic effort in adverse circumstances, or by the lack
of an outlet for creative desire. *Red Pottage* stages this process
particularly melodramatically, by having its writer-heroine suc-
cumb to a complete breakdown induced by her evangelical
brother's destruction of the manuscript of the novel which she
has produced at such great physical and emotional cost.

Cholmondeley's own work, as her journals suggest, may
well have been produced by the frustrations and constraints
of her life as a daughter of the vicarage. Vicarages have, of
course, been a productive breeding ground for women novelists in England, and Cholmondeley appears to have an acute
awareness of the painful ironies of this fact when she makes
her otherwise sympathetic Bishop articulate the repressive
hypothesis of Hester's creativity.

> [T]he best thing that could happen to Hester is to be
> thrown for a time among people who regard her as a
> nonentity, who have no sense of humour, and to whom

she cannot speak of any of the subjects she has at heart
. . . She is so susceptible [to sympathy and admiration],
so expansive, that repression is positively necessary to
her to enable her, so to speak, to get up steam. There is
no place for getting up steam like a country vicarage.

(RP:87)

Several of the New Woman writers anticipated Virginia
Woolf's sense that the woman artist might best 'get up steam'
if she had £500 a year and a room of her own. They also
dramatised the problems for women of acquiring the necessary
mental, as well as physical, space for creative production.
Caird's Hadria sets up (with some difficulty) a room of her
own in Paris, but she is unable to free herself from 'the peculiar
claims that are made, by common consent, on a woman's
time and strength [which] weave their tiny cords around her'
(DD:322). Her vocation as a composer is destroyed by a combination of these external constraints and the self-suppression
which results from her internalisation of them.

Sarah Grand provides another perspective on 'a room of
one's own' by constructing for her heroine a secret room that
is not simply a private place, but is, in effect, her secret,
private self. Beth's discovery of the secret room in her marital
home is both the realisation of a wish-fulfilment fantasy
(shared by the author and the character, and also implicating
the reader) and a way of figuring the character's interiority.
Beth's wish for 'some corner where she could be safe from
intrusion' (BB:345) is answered a few lines later by the discovery of 'a narrow door flush with the wall', scarcely percep-
tible to the eye, which leads into 'a charming little room'. The
narration of this episode and the description of the room are
suffused with a sense of homecoming.

Everything about her was curiously familiar, and her first
impression was that she had been there before. On the
other hand, she could hardly believe in the reality of
what she saw, she thought she must be dreaming, for
here was exactly what she had been pining for most in
the whole wide world of late, a secret spot, sacred to
herself, where she would be safe from intrusion.

(BB:347)

The room is a feminine space. It is, in part, another of Beth's 'recollections', since it closely resembles the room of her aunt and mentor, Victoria. Showalter (1978a) reads this episode as a 'feminist fantasy' and a 'housewife's dream' (208, 209), and dismisses as 'improbable' the process of self-education to which it leads. It is an example of what Showalter takes to be a radical failure of the women's writing of the 1880s and 1890s: 'Given the freedom to explore their experience, they rejected it, or at least tried to deny it. The private rooms that symbolize their professionalism and autonomy are fantastic sanctuaries closely linked to their own defensive womanhood' (215). Of course, Grand's secret room *is* both improbable and fantastic, but it is also utopian, and utopianism has always been an important element in revolutionary or progressive political movements such as feminism. The secret room serves not as a means of escape *from* reality and the self, but as a route *to* reality and the self. This is not to say that the episode is not problematic. In fact its structural relationship to what precedes and follows takes us back to some of the central contradictions about feeling and the feminine to which I referred in the previous section.

In her apparent endorsement of Beth's period of self-disciplining and self-education, the narrator would seem to dismiss the aesthetic realm which is valorised both in and by the writing in the earlier part of the novel.

> Wholesome consideration of the realities of life took the place of fanciful dreams . . . purposeful thought was where the mere froth of sensuous seeing had been; and it was thought that now clamoured for expression instead of . . . verses and stories.
>
> (BB:356–7)

This might be viewed either as a positive turn to the practical and the political, or alternatively (and more negatively) as a turning back to a self-sacrificial conception of the feminine, and a consequent rejection of self-directed and self-expressive feeling and sensation. In the end the novel merges these two perspectives. Ultimately, Grand's narrative requires its heroine to abandon the (so to speak) absence of writing in the secret room, for the presence of the speaking body. By the end of the novel Beth is made to undergo a quasi-religious conversion, as a result of which she discovers her vocation as a public speaker who has the power to act upon the feelings (as well as the minds) of her audience. Grand's descriptions of Beth's public speaking bear an interesting resemblance to Hélène Cixous's descriptions of the privileging of the voice in feminine writing: *'writing and voice* . . . are woven together'; woman 'physically materializes what she's thinking; she signifies with her body' (quoted in Moi 1985:114).

The secret room itself also undergoes a transformation; it is transplanted to London, and in the process it is put to work in two distinct aesthetic modes. On the one hand it is transformed from its initial role of scene and product of (feminine) fantasy, and is reconstructed as a London garret in the New Realist narrative of hardship and struggle (in the manner of Gissing), in which Beth attempts to make a life as an independent woman. On the other hand, the garret itself becomes the secret room of romance, the site of the enactment of an aesthetic fantasy of romantic love which reworks Tennyson's 'The Lady of Shalott'. In effect the New Realist narrative is captured for Romance through the figure of Brock, the young artist whom Beth befriends. Brock becomes merged with the visionary Sir Lancelot figure which originally appears to Beth in a dreamlike sequence as she contemplates the emptiness of life in her marital home:

As he came abreast of the window, the rider looked up, and Beth's heart bounded at the sight of his face, which was the face of a man from out of the long ago, virile, knightly, high-bred, refined . . . It was as if he had recognised her; and she felt herself as if she had seen him before, but when or where, in what picture, in what dream, she could not tell.

(BB:432)

In reworking Tennyson's allegory, Grand also domesticates it. Tennyson's Lady drifts beautifully and mysteriously towards death when she leaves the lonely room in which she weaves her web, and pursues Sir Lancelot. Grand's heroine, on the other hand, performs her self-sacrificial, self-immolating act by nursing her Lancelot (Brock) from the brink of death, at the cost of her own health, before they are both reborn into a new life. Ultimately, like so much of the New Woman

185

writing, *The Beth Book* is unable to break free of the discourse of the proper feminine. Within this discourse it proves impossible to write the woman writer. The portrait of the artist as a young woman is replaced by the portrait of the mature woman as public speaker, and as the womanly woman who sacrifices her own health to nurse the struggling male artist. The sensuous becomes spiritualised; individual rebellion is ultimately reincorporated into the traditional attributes of the proper feminine: duty, self-sacrifice and suffering. However, as in the sensation novel, there remains a surplus, a residual challenge to the proper feminine, in the excess (often a melodramatic excess) of the writing, not only of the early scenes, but also of the final dreamlike stages of the recuperative narrative.

Another favourite character in the New Woman writing is the struggling professional writer who pursues her vocation as much out of economic need as from the need for self-expression. Financial hardship, following the death of her father, forces Mary Erle, the heroine of Ella Hepworth Dixon's *The Story of a Modern Woman*, to abandon her early artistic vocation. She sacrifices her ambitions to be admitted to the Royal Academy School to study painting and begins a career as a hack writer in order to support herself and to maintain her brother in the educational pattern considered appropriate for a young man of his class. Like many women writers throughout the nineteenth century, Mary turns to fiction writing because this was one of the few careers available to a partially educated but completely untrained middle-class woman.

Dixon uses Mary's initiation into literary production and London literary life as a means of satirising the contemporary literary market-place. However, as in Gissing's anatomisation of New Grub Street, satire is progressively replaced by a bleaker vision as Dixon's heroine is portrayed succumbing to the physical and psychological pressures of maintaining the level of literary output necessary to meet her financial commitments. The most concentrated piece of satire is found in Chapter 10 ('In Grub Street'), which recapitulates Gissing's attack on the metropolitan literary machine with an admirable economy and lightness of touch. Dixon uses Mary's experience of Grub Street as a means of focusing on its coarse masculinity, its sexism (depicted in the vignette of Mary's morning in the offices of *The Fan*), and its systematic marginalisation of women writers and women's writing. These attitudes are summed up by the editor of *Illustrations*, whose view of the scope of the woman writer and of writing for women is summarised in his advice that 'with practice, you may be able to write stories which other young ladies like to read' (SMW:107).

The clash between Mary's developing experience and her encounter with the values of the literary market-place becomes the focus for an exploration and questioning of certain ideas about acceptable forms of literary representation, particularly representations by and for women. Like many of the novels of this decade, *The Story of a Modern Woman* is extremely 'self-conscious about its own textual status' (Flint 1990:vii). It is a realistic novel about the lives of women which is, in part, about the impossibility of writing (or, more specifically, publishing) realistic novels about women's experience. Its heroine's desire to write and publish a novel that 'would be a bit of real life' and 'have twenty-seven years of actual experience in it' is constantly thwarted by the exigencies of a market-place which 'would take anything in a newspaper' but demands a fiction 'fit to go into every parsonage in England', a fiction for 'healthy English homes' (SMW:181). To some extent Dixon's novel transcends the conditions of its own production, since it does succeed, however obliquely, in telling the story of the young woman in Regent's Park of whom Mary observes: 'If that tawdry-looking girl could write down her story . . . we should have another masterpiece! It is because they suffer so that women have written supremely good fiction' (SMW:122).

The relationship between female suffering and literary production, and the conflict between the demands of the writer's vocation and those of the woman's vocation (as defined by the regime of the proper feminine) are also examined (admittedly more obliquely) in George Egerton's 'Wedlock'. In this story, an unnamed woman writer observes the developing tragedy of the woman in whose house she lodges. The writer is introduced immediately following a scene depicting the landlady's collapse in a drunken stupor.

> The woman lay . . . with her feet thrust out in her half-buttoned boots, and her hands hanging straight down. The sun crept round the room, and at length a clock

chimed four . . . A woman sitting writing at a table . . .
looks up with relief, and moistens her lips; they are dry.
A pile of closely written manuscript lies on the floor
beside her . . .
She is writing for money, writing because she must,
because it is the tool given to her wherewith to carve her
way; she is nervous, overwrought, every one of her fin-
gers seems as if it had a burning nerve-knot in its tip;
she has thrust her slippers aside, for her feet twitch; she
is writing feverishly now, for she has been undergoing
the agony of a barren period for some weeks, her brain
has seemed arid as a sand plain . . . she has felt in her
despair as if she were hollowed out, honeycombed by
her emotions as she has cried over her mental sterility.
(D:123–4)

Two pictures of female suffering are here carefully anatomised
and sharply juxtaposed. In the first, a lower-class woman has
rendered herself insensate in an effort to avoid the emotional
consequences of her economic dependence on a man who
mistreats her. In the second, a middle-class woman is rendered
hypersensitive by the isolation and emotional harrowing of the
vocation which she pursues in order to remain economically
independent.

The passage I have quoted links these women together and
focuses on their common suffering, but the rest of the story
focuses on the ways in which they are separated from each
other by the contradictions of the proper feminine. The writer
is ultimately separated from her landlady *by* the proper feminine, even as she herself is separated *from* it. She is separated
from the proper feminine by the demands of the writer's
vocation, which conflict with the proper feminine's demands
that a woman should be self-sacrificing and sympathetic to the
emotional needs of others. Thus, although the writer feels a
sympathy for her landlady's predicament, her need for quiet
and calm conditions in which to undertake her work leads her
to withdraw from the scene of suffering; sympathy is replaced
by detached observation.

The . . . [writer] observes her closely as she does most
things – as material. It is not that her sympathies are less
keen since she took to writing, but that the habit of

188

analysis is always uppermost. She sees a voluptuously made woman, with a massive milk-white throat . . . she is attractive and repellent in a singular way.

(D:129)

As the concluding sentence of this quotation begins to suggest, the female writer is also separated from the landlady *by* the proper feminine. Her own genteel, middle-class sensibilities are both fascinated and appalled by the lower-class woman's physical presence and her lack of control.

The woman writer's brief appearance in this story is also used to explore and make explicit the role of class in the construction of the proper feminine. In fact this story seems to disrupt conventional boundaries of gender difference precisely at the point of class difference; it is the working-class man (a bricklayer working nearby) who becomes sympathetically engaged in the landlady's tragedy (and attempts to avert it), while the genteel female writer distances herself from it. This disruption is, however, a double disruption: the writer's self-distancing is the product of both her middle-class sensibility and that suppression of 'proper womanly' feeling which is a function of her need for economic survival.

In fact the complex interrelationship and interdependence of women's emotional and economic situations are recurrent concerns in all of Egerton's writing. Egerton's New Women, like those in Jean Rhys's novellas of the 1930s, are 'new' only in their refusal or inability to fit easily or silently into established gender roles and social patterns. They are, for the most part, trapped by economic or emotional neediness (or by a combination of the two), and escape their dependence on a man, if at all, by various routes of desperation – the death of the oppressive male ('Under Northern Sky'), madness ('Wedlock'), decline and death ('Gone Under').

On the whole, Egerton offered a sharply polarised view of the female predicament. On the one hand, her women can seek self-realisation, or follow their own desires, with all the attendant risks of increased economic and emotional vulnerability and social ostracism. On the other, they are left with the boredom, meanness and restriction of the conventional female lot. Alternatively they can write a different story, or at least they can choose to turn to the blank page on which a new kind of story might be written. One version of this blank page is presented at the end of 'Virgin Soil', which pictures its heroine standing 'once more on the platform where she stood in the flush of her girlhood' (D:162), when she had embarked on her wedding journey; she then takes the train in the opposite direction to an unknown destination. Similarly the heroine of 'A Psychological Moment' removes herself from the melodramatic novelette of the degrading liaison into which she has been blackmailed by a dissolute cynic, and embarks on the path of silence and exile (and possibly cunning), undeterred by the dragons of fear and convention.

> 'There are no dragons in the world nowadays that one cannot overcome, if one is not afraid of them, and sets up no false gods.' [. . .]
> She . . . sits watching. One great star blinks down at her like a bright glad eye, and hers shine steadily back with the sombre light of an undaunted spirit waiting quietly for the dawn to break, to take the first step of her new life's journey.
>
> (D:66)

This disruptive, quasi-utopian vision of a brave new world in which women might make their way undeterred by dragons does indeed break the bounds of the proper feminine. It also, apparently, approaches the limits of what can be written. Egerton's brave New Woman is frozen in a tableau which prefigures but does not embody action. *The Story of a Modern Woman* also ends with its heroine's vision of the future, but Dixon, unlike Egerton, not only plots the future, she also writes it. However, when the mode is realistic, the mood tends to be pessimistic.

> It was London that lay stretched out at her feet; majestic, awe-inspiring, inexorable, triumphant London.
> Standing alone, there on the heights, she made a feint as if to grasp the city spread out before her, but the movement ended in a vain gesture, and the radiance of her face was blotted out . . .
>
> (SMW:271)

Whereas D.H. Lawrence's young male thought-adventurer Paul Morel, in a similar scene at the end of *Sons and Lovers*, strides off 'towards the faintly humming, glowing town', Dixon's New Woman writer 'plod[s] homewards in the twilight of the suburban road' (SMW: 271).

20

New Woman: new writing

> Now that woman is conscious of her own
> individuality as a woman, she needs an
> artistic mode of expression, she flings aside
> the old forms, and seeks for new.
> (Hansson 1896:78–9)

> [T]he language is seldom choice; and the
> manner is self-conscious, or even pedantic
> . . . [D]eclamation, argument, caricature,
> interminable prosing of everyone to his
> neighbour, and absolute farce, make amends
> for the absence of genuine humour, of wit
> and comedy, of refinement and ease in the
> dialogue.
> (Barry 1894:295, on *The Heavenly Twins*)

Late nineteenth-century reviewers and many late twentieth-century feminist literary historians have concurred in finding the New Woman writing aesthetically flawed. It is said to buckle under the weight of its feminist rhetoric, its 'ethical propagandism' and 'abstract intellectualism' (Williams 1925:436). It is accused of lapsing into formal conventionalism and ideological conformity, or alternatively of collapsing inwardly into aesthetic dead ends, or the dead end of aestheticism. Elaine Showalter has found the New Woman writers and their successors guilty of both of these apparently contradictory failings. Turn-of-the-century women writers, she has argued, were trapped in the aesthetic dead end of a conservative ideology.

While male writers explored the multiplicity of the self, the myriad fluid lives of men, women were limited by the revived biological essentialism of post-Darwinian thought. The unchanging nature of woman as pure spirit made good politics but bad fiction.

(Showalter 1986a:110)

On the other hand the New Woman writers, and more especially their immediate successors, were 'confined' by what Showalter describes, elsewhere, as the 'self-annihilation' of 'the female aesthetic' (1978a:240). I have tried to suggest throughout this part of my study that the reinsertion of some of the New Woman writers and their texts into their socio-aesthetic contexts yields a more complex picture.

The 1880s and 1890s were a significant 'moment of change in fiction' (Boumelha 1982:93). It was a period of great experimentation in fictional practice, and of acrimonious debate about the appropriate form and content of fiction. Following the 1870 Education Act, which produced a larger and more socially differentiated constituency for the novel, there was a significant increase in the number of outlets for fiction. The role of the circulating libraries was greatly diminished, removing one powerful pressure for formal conformity and decorous subject-matter. Both the fiction market and the novel itself became more stratified into the commodified medium of mass entertainment and instruction, and the increasingly fetishised aesthetic object of an intellectual high culture.

Gaye Tuchman has recently argued that this stratification of the novel was part of a process of 'edging woman out' of the serious high-art novel. She describes the period 1880–99 as one of 'redefinition' of the novel, 'when men of letters, including critics, actively redefined the nature of a good novel and a great author . . . [preferring] the new form of realism that they associated with "manly" – that is great – literature' (Tuchman 1989:8). As I have suggested in Part I of this book, late nineteenth-century men (and women) of letters were a great deal more divided and confused about both the desirability and 'manliness' of realism than Tuchman suggests. Moreover, hers is a history written from the perspective of the supposed victors, and tends to lose sight of the nature of the particular battles. To look again at the women writers of the 1890s is to see the importance of the part they played in the period of redefinition of fiction. Whether reviled or admired, their work was taken very seriously by critics. It was also in great demand with readers. The attempts of the New Women writers to write for women, to write about women and, in some cases, to write woman herself, led them to use the available forms in new ways and to look for new (often self-consciously modern) ways of writing.

As I have suggested, writing the New Woman involved a negotiation not only of the discourse of the proper feminine, but also of the discourses of fiction – language, form and genre. To write the New Woman and to write woman (or women) anew was to write the, as yet, unwritten. It was, in effect, to write the unwritable in terms of 'the weary ways of fiction' which 'make a pivot of the everlasting love story . . . as if there was nothing else of interest in life but our sexual relations' (BB:373).

It is no mere coincidence that this latter critique of the conventional nineteenth-century novel (voiced by Sarah Grand's Beth in *The Beth Book*) should echo George Eliot's 'Silly novels by lady novelists' (1856), for Eliot is clearly a model for some of the New Woman writers (most notably Grand), who sought to emulate the large scale, high seriousness and visionary tone that the earlier writer had brought to the woman's novel. In the 1890s, however, the sage utterances of Eliot's meditative, masculine narrators were usually replaced by a visionary and hortatory feminist (or anti-feminist) rhetoric which disrupts the narrative and undermines the authority of the univocal omniscient narrator.

In the hands of the New Woman writers the massive, multiplotted, panoramic Eliotean novel increasingly became fragmented into episodes, or abandoned in favour of the developing new form of the short story. Many of the New Woman novels (for example, Sarah Grand's *The Beth Book* and the massive and unwieldy *Heavenly Twins*, and George Egerton's *The Wheel of God*) are so fragmented and episodic, and employ such a wide variety of fictional modes (naturalism, documentary, romance, allegory, satire and melodrama) that they are more like collections of short stories than novels. Indeed *The Wheel of God* is less the novel it claims to be than a collection of episodes in the life of a modern woman. There

194

is little narrative pressure. The central female character (Mary Desmond) is viewed from various angles and in a variety of situations in relation to a number of representative modern types. The narratorial medium ranges from the coolly forensic to the effusively lyrical, as Egerton attempts to write the modern woman in (to adapt D.H. Lawrence's phrase) the process of becoming self-responsible.

The grand synthesising vision of the traditional realist novel was, it seemed, not an appropriate – or indeed possible – medium for writers who were seeking to question and redefine woman's place in the world. Instead the New Woman writers sometimes adopted a proto-modernist form, using a proliferation of voices and perspectives to challenge fixed views. Grand's changing narrative distance in *The Beth Book*, the move from the third-person to the first-person narrator in *The Heavenly Twins*, and her persistent mixing of modes (realism, dream, allegory) are examples of this. Perhaps this polyvocality and multi-perspective approach are best seen, however, in George Egerton's stories, with their habitual use of multiple narrators, framed narratives and dramatised consciousness (often in combination). Indeed, although Egerton's stories put women under the microscope by focusing minutely on a succession of particular (though usually unnamed) female characters, they employ a range of narrative techniques that tend to evade explanation and dissolve causation. The effect, as in much of the New Woman writing, is to problematise moral and behavioural categories and, more particularly, to problematise the category of woman.

Their efforts to write the New Woman and engage with her situation led the New Woman writers, by various routes, away from the old realism (both the miniaturistic detail of the domestic novel, and the ethical high realism of George Eliot). Sometimes they abandoned realism altogether. Sometimes, like their male contemporaries, they articulated their sense of the modern world through the new naturalism imported from France and Scandinavia. On the whole, however, the New Woman writers developed an impressionistic and intuitive, rather than a pathological, forensic, categorising naturalism. Indeed many of these writers might perhaps best be seen not (as their contemporaries often saw them) as failed masculine realists, or incomplete pathological naturalists, but as experimental writers who anticipated the attempts of Dorothy Richardson and Virginia Woolf to develop a specifically feminine voice and form for fiction.

The experiments of the New Woman writers were part of that redefinition of realism that took place in the late nineteenth and early twentieth century – a redefinition which disrupted the gendered discourse on realism with its privileging of the (supposedly) generalising and scientific masculine imagination. Many of the New Woman writers were exponents of the feminine New Realism such as those described by R.Brimley Johnson in 1920, who sought 'with passionate determination, for that reality which is behind the material, the things that matter, spiritual things, ultimate Truth' (xiv–xv).

In their various and varying ways the New Woman writers broke the bounds of the proper feminine by moving away from their permitted role as the observers and recorders of surface minutiae. They refused to stay within the usual scope permitted to women writers – the anodynely domestic, the gently didactic, the uplifting and improving, and, above all, the private – and engaged in 'debate upon economic, religious and sexual questions' (Williams 1925:436). Several of them also appropriated the conventional idea that 'Woman is the most subjective of all creatures', and focused minutely on subjective realities. This self-conscious reversal of the negative association of femininity and subjectivity challenged both the gendered discourse on the form and content of fiction, and the dominant forms themselves. As Laura Marholm Hansson observed:

> Formerly women's writings were, for the most part, either directly or indirectly the expression of a great falsehood. They were so overpoweringly impersonal . . . Now that woman is conscious of her individuality as a woman, she needs an artistic mode of expression, she flings aside the old forms, and seeks for new.
>
> (Hansson 1896: 78–9)

Although many of the New Woman writers found that the old forms were not to be easily thrown aside, they nevertheless appropriated the idea that feeling was woman's special province. They developed a rhetoric of feeling, often articulated in a language of melodramatic excess which 'implicitly insists that the world can be equal to our own most feverish expectation of it' (Brooks 1976:40). The New Woman writing, like that of the women sensationalists, addresses its audience (as Christine Gledhill argues melodrama does) 'within the limitations of the status quo, of the ideologically permissible', and articulates 'demands inadmissible in the codes of social, psychological or political discourse'. Both the contemporary cultural significance of these two groups of writers, and their continuing importance in the late twentieth century, lie in 'this double acknowledgement of how things are in a given historical conjuncture, and of the primary desires and resistances contained within it' (Gledhill 1987:38).

Conclusion: reading out women's writing

Despite the fact that both the women's sensation novel and the New Woman writing caused a sensation in their own day, and were widely discussed as examples of new and often disturbing trends in fiction, they nevertheless rapidly disappeared from view, leaving (according to the critical consensus) little lasting impression upon the history of fiction. Thus Patrick Brantlinger, re-examining the sensation novel in 1982, drew attention to its ephemerality, describing it as 'a minor subgenre of British fiction that flourished in the 1860s only to die out a decade later' (37). Similarly, David Rubinstein, an historian who writes interestingly and sympathetically about the New Woman fiction, concludes that it was 'in decline by 1896 or so' (1986:25), and that the female New Woman writers 'contributed little of permanent value to the development of English fiction' (33–4). Many of the feminist critics who have rediscovered the New Woman writing in the wake of post-1960s feminism have been moved to ponder the question of 'why it was that the men who took up the themes of feminism in their fiction were the ones who had literary survival value, and not the women' (Lovell 1987:107). A similar question might be asked about the sensation novel. Why has interest in the work of Braddon and Wood lagged so far behind the revival of interest in Wilkie Collins?

The rapid disappearance from critical view of both the women's sensation novel (and perhaps the sensation novel in general) and the New Woman writing may, in part, be seen as a function of their topicality. They were both very much of their own time. They registered the pulse of contemporary feeling and were deeply implicated in the immediate social and political issues of their day. Many of the sensation novels grew out of specific concerns about women's social and familial roles. Many of them, too, were directly inspired by historical events, notably the sensationally reported criminal trials which filled the newspapers in the 1850s and 1860s. Henry James's (1865) observation that 'Modern England – the England of today's newspapers – crops up at every step' (593) in the sensation novel might also be applied to the New Woman writing, since it too shared this journalistic quality. The New Woman fiction of the 1890s both derived from, and became part of, specific press campaigns, and it also arose from and intervened in specific political debates.

The very immediacy and contemporaneity of the fiction discussed in this book were clearly important factors in its disappearance from view once the immediate historical conditions of its production had passed away. Looked at another way, however, the historical oblivion and critical neglect suffered by the women sensationalists and New Woman writers are not untypical of the fate of women's writing more generally. A closer examination of some of the reasons for this neglect may shed interesting light on the processes by which women's writing is read out of (literary) history.

Both the hostile contemporary reception and the later critical neglect of the women's sensation novel and the New Woman fiction may be connected with the fact that these novels were associated with – to (mis)appropriate Raymond Williams's terms – residual or emergent forms,[1] rather than with a dominant form of fiction. The literary status of both groups of writers was also compromised by their association with 'low art'. The women's sensation novel was connected with residual popular forms, such as melodrama with its low-art and working-class associations, and with other low discursive forms, such as sensational newspaper journalism. On the other hand, the most successful of the women's sensation novels also shared some of the characteristics of emergent (and, significantly, 'feminised') forms of 'high art', such as the fleshly school of poetry and painting pioneered by the Pre-Raphaelites and their followers. The female sensationalists' interest in marriage as a source of narrative, rather than as merely a device of closure, also anticipated the development of the marriage-problem novel by 'high-culture' novelists such as George Eliot (in *Middlemarch* and *Daniel Deronda* in the 1870s), Thomas Hardy, George Moore and George Meredith, as well as the New Woman writers.

Similarly the New Woman writers' subject-matter and their eclectic mixing of styles and forms linked them to both residual and emergent forms. In their preoccupation with unconventional, socially and sexually trangressive women, they looked back to the middle-brow fiction and journalism of the 1860s, to the 'fast women' and 'Girls of the Period' who filled the pages of the newspaper and periodical press and generated so many of the concerns of the sensation novel. Their depictions of such contemporary types as the 'Wild Women', 'Revolting Daughters' and the New Woman also connected them with non-literary, low discursive forms, most notably journalism. As I suggested in an earlier section, the New Woman writers, to an even greater extent than the women sensationalists, were part of an extra-literary cultural and political formation. Their own claims to literary status were and undoubtedly are compromised by this association. Moreover, like those of the sensation novelists, their novels were further tainted by their reputation as bestsellers.

Their preoccupation with sexuality, and their sexual frankness, also caused the New Woman writers to be linked to the residual forms of 'pernicious literature' and French naturalism of the 1870s and 1880s, while also linking them to the emergent forms of 'Ibscenity' and sex-problem literature that developed around the turn of the century. Their interest in gender identity, and the various ways in which they articulated or demonstrated gender confusion, also led them to be associated with another emergent formation, that of the *fin de siècle* decadence. The subjectivity of some New Woman writing produced a fiction of feminine self-consciousness which anticipated the feminine New Realism of Dorothy Richardson and Virginia Woolf in the opening decades of the twentieth century. The New Woman fiction was thus marginalised as both a residual and debased form of French decadence, and an inferior and ancillary form of an emergent avant-gardism and modernism.

Perhaps the most important factors in the lack of literary survival power of the writers I have looked at are connected with issues of gender. Terry Lovell (1987) has identified a set of 'loosely defined rules or codes, which have tended to work against' (131–2) the literary survival of women writers. The concepts of the *auteur* and the *œuvre* are central to these codes. Lovell argues that, with a few notable exceptions such as *Wuthering Heights*:

> [I]t is authors rather than books that survive . . . It is the *auteur* who is constructed in literary criticism rather than the text. A single text is seldom enough to establish that status. Once it is established, however, *all* the author's texts become worthy of study however flawed any particular one may be.
>
> (Lovell 1987:132)

Clearly this 'rule' or 'code' of acceptance tends to disadvantage the New Woman writers, many of whom produced a very small fictional *œuvre*. The reasons for this varied from writer to writer. In some cases it was connected with a heavy involvement in other (non-fictional) forms of writing, and other kinds of work – especially political work of various types. This small fictional output can also be explained, as Lovell notes, by the fact that 'women in the nineteenth century typically began their literary apprenticeships later in life than their male colleagues. If and insofar as they were also encumbered with pressing domestic duties, they would have been additionally handicapped' (132).

The situation is, however, more complex and contradictory than Lovell's model allows. The women sensationalists, for example, seem to have been handicapped in the literary survival stakes not by the fact that they wrote too little but, on the contrary, by the fact that they wrote too much. In the case of these writers more was clearly taken to mean worse: because they produced much that was merely meretriciously potboiling, *all* of their work is labelled as inferior, unlike the work of an *auteur*, whose inferior productions are treated seriously as the flawed works of a master.

Mass-production by the chief of the women sensationalists introduces the catch-22 of the 'professionalism' of women writers. Writing, as Nigel Cross points out in *The Common Writer* (1985:166), was one of the few professions open to women in the nineteenth century. Female drudges (to use Cross's term) such as Mary Elizabeth Braddon, Ellen Wood, Rhoda Broughton, Ouida, etc. were clearly 'professional' in the sense that they earned their living from producing fiction. As applied to these women writers, 'professionalism' was invariably a denigratory term. The (female) 'professional' wrote to order, according to set formulae, in order to satisfy markets. The (male) 'artist', on the other hand, exercised a vocation and wrote out of an inner (rather than pecuniary) need. However, because they were women, Braddon and others had, paradoxically, also to be regarded as amateurs. They were women first, and writers second. Thus, the memoirs of Braddon and Wood written by their sons both emphasise the fact that their mothers' professional avocations never diverted them from their familial and domestic duties.[2] In fact, in terms of the available discourses, women could be neither fully-fledged professionals nor amateurs who followed a calling: they could not be truly professional because their womanly duties must always come first, and they could not have a writer's vocation because being a woman was in itself a woman's true vocation.

Another of Lovell's 'codes' that has clearly played an important part in the 'reading out' of women's sensation fiction and the New Woman writing is that of 'address': 'Woman-to-woman forms', Lovell argues, 'are not permitted to become part of the general stock of "cultural capital" ' (1987:132). Although neither the women's sensation novel nor the New Woman fiction is addressed exclusively to women, on the whole each assumes a culturally constructed 'feminine' awareness in its readers, and claims a privileged access to feminine interiority. Both are deployed and perceived as feminine genres.

The single most important factor in the filtering out of these women writers from the literary tradition is the gendered discourse on fiction explored in Part I, which privileges gender-neutral or 'masculine' forms. Throughout the nineteenth century, debates about the novel seem to have been pervaded by a fear that fiction might be inherently feminine, oscillating between the constricted, aesthetically and intellectually limited, domestic sentimentality of the proper feminine, and the promiscuous profusion and abandoned sensationalism of the improper feminine. The habitual association of the 'lower', deviant or subversive forms of fiction with a negatively defined version of the feminine played a crucial part in the production and mediation of novels by both men and women. This

202

association was also instrumental in the contemporary marginalisation and subsequent disappearance from the tradition of much fiction by women.

The gendered discourse on fiction has proved remarkably persistent. Nina Baym (1986), for example, has attributed the absence of women novelists from the American canon – despite the fact that 'Commercially and numerically they have probably dominated American literature since the middle of the nineteenth century' (64) – to 'gender-related restrictions' that do not necessarily arise out of 'the cultural realities contemporary with the writing women, but out of later critical theories . . . which impose their concerns anachronistically, after the fact, on an earlier period'. Baym argues that some of the most influential of these theories have been based on strongly masculine assumptions, and cites as evidence Harold Bloom's *Anxiety of Influence* and Edward Said's *Beginnings*. The former plots literary history as an Oedipal drama in which sons struggle to free themselves from their literary fathers, while the latter rereads the history of nineteenth-century British fiction as a story of 'filiation'. The apparent persuasiveness of these models, even to feminist critics (Bloom's influence on the theory of literary creation developed in Gilbert and Gubar's *The Madwoman in the Attic* has been much discussed), thus served to counteract the effects of the substantial work of recovering women writers which was undertaken by feminist scholars in the 1970s. As Nina Baymn writes, 'just at the time that feminist critics [were] discovering more and more important women [writers], the critical theorists . . . seized upon a theory that allows the women less and less presence' (78–9).

The terms of the gendered discourse on fiction, and particularly its privileging of the masculine, have not gone unchallenged. From the late nineteenth century onwards, feminists and their sympathisers have sought to redefine these terms and appropriate them for their own ends. From Virginia Woolf in the early years of the twentieth century to the French theorists of the feminine, and writers such as the American poet and critic Adrienne Rich, women have sought to revalue the feminine, and to reclaim it as a cultural positive. Thus Virginia Woolf (1966 II: 204), in one of the earliest attempts to articulate a positively evaluated feminine practice of writing, argues for the 'difference of view, the difference of standard' of women's writing (and, by implication, of women's reading).

[I]n both life and art the values of a woman are not the values of a man. Thus when a woman comes to write a novel, she will find that she is perpetually wishing to alter the established values – to make serious what appears insignificant to a man, and trivial what is to him important.

(Woolf 1966 II:145-6)

In this book I have tried to demonstrate that when readers and literary historians apply this particular difference of view and difference of standard (rather than that difference of standard which masquerades as a universal), the women's writing that has hitherto been consigned to the dustbin of history can be relocated in history and reinserted into literary history.

Clearly the feminist (and anti-feminist) debates of the later twentieth century have been one important source of such a 'difference of standard'. Current debates in and around feminism have made visible the women writers whose work is the subject of this book and have also provided the conditions for a more sympathetic valuation of that work. The second-wave revitalisation of feminist politics has made readers more responsive to the political concerns of the New Woman writers. Some of the fictional experiments of second-wave feminists might also have created a climate in which readers are less likely to dismiss New Woman fiction as merely inartistic propaganda. Similarly, the feminist-inspired interest in the determinants and effects of popular women's genres has made literary historians more alert to the aesthetic politics of the production and consumption of bestseller fiction by and for women. It has also made readers more inclined to look for, and discover, the possibly subversive complexities which may be woven into the formulaic surfaces of the women's sensation novel.

Another important source of this changing viewpoint has been the French theorists of the feminine, one of whose main concerns has been *difference* in writing and the difference of women's writing. Although the theories of Luce Irigaray, Julia Kristeva and Hélène Cixous (to take only the most prominent of the French theorists) differ from each other in important respects, each of these writers, at least implicitly, has exposed the operation of a gendered discourse on and in writing, in which the masculine is the privileged term. They have sought, in different ways, to demonstrate how the linguistic and discursive systems of western culture have systematically repressed, managed and marginalised the feminine voice, the female body and women's experience. Each of them has also suggested different ways of using and/or combatting this process. On the whole they have been more interested in developing a feminine writing practice than in re-examining the writing of the past. Nevertheless many of their ideas provide interesting new perspectives on the forgotten women writers of the nineteenth century whose work has been the focus of this study, and on the gendered critical discourse which was a key determinant of both the production and the suppression of the women's sensation novel and the New Woman fiction.

The style, form and main concerns of the writers discussed in this book, and also the discourse of the im/proper feminine, may be interestingly reread through Kristeva's concept of the discourse of the hysteric. For Kristeva 'femininity' is a term which evades definition; the feminine is a relational category denoting what the patriarchal symbolic order marginalises. Kristeva argues that because women write as outsiders from the point of view of masculine-dominated patriarchal society, theirs is a discourse of the hysteric, and their style is likely to involve (as Ann Rosalind Jones glosses it) 'repetitive, spasmodic separations from the dominating discourse, which, more often, they are forced to imitate' (Jones 1986:363). Certainly the female sensationalists and the New Woman writers have been treated (and dismissed) as hysterics by a gendered criticism which has relegated their writings to the realm of the improper feminine. However, as I have tried to show throughout this study, not only are both groups of writers formed by the discourse of the hysteric, they also (to different degrees) interrogate this discourse. They appropriate the concept of hysterical writing as a way of finding a form in which to discuss and articulate women's experiences, desires and frustrations. In other words, they do not simply *repeat* the discourse of the hysteric, they also explore, exploit and develop it.

In Kristeva's account, the marginality of woman's social

205

position and her outsider relationship to the dominant discourse also produce another significant point of difference: the absence of a fixed and authoritative subject and speaking position. This lack of fixity and authority was exploited in both the women sensationalists' and the New Woman writers' use of the shifting point of view, in the 'inconsistency' and moral ambivalence of the sensation heroine, in the development of the feminine subject in process, and in the more fluid styles of writing found in some of the New Woman fiction.

As I have suggested in earlier sections, the 'muted', marginalised voice which was assigned to the feminine by both the nineteenth-century discourse on gender and the gendered critical discourse sometimes made it difficult for women's writing to be heard. However, it also provided a way of undermining and finding gaps in the dominant discourse. The muted feminine voice offered a challenge for the woman writer to overcome if she was to make herself heard on her own terms. The women sensationalists and the New Woman writers both, on occasion, rose to this challenge by developing the stylistic and linguistic excess which I have noted at several points in this study. Writers as different from one another as Mary Elizabeth Braddon and George Egerton display the tendency to 'mimic' masculine forms that Luce Irigaray has observed in women's writing. In their representation of women, and particularly of the female body, both Braddon and Egerton, for example, mimic the specular erotic gaze of masculine writing. In both cases, however, this is taken to excess and becomes a distinctive feminine style, rather than a mere imitation of the dominant masculine. Braddon's and Egerton's use of the gaze in staging woman as spectacle thus tends to destabilise, rather than merely repeat, the discourse it is mimicking.

It is this idea of a distinctive feminine mode of writing, an *écriture féminine*, which offers the most important 'difference of view' and has provided perhaps the single most important perspective through which to re-view the writers at the centre of this study. I have not sought, nor would I wish to claim, that the women sensationalists and the New Woman writers developed a revolutionary *écriture féminine* a century before the French theorists did. I would also want to avoid the biological essentialism and bio-cultural (over)determinism which seem to be a problematic aspect of some of the pronouncements of Cixous and Irigaray. However, if the women's fictions of the 1860s and 1890s have been erased from view by the operations of a gendered critical discourse which has regarded them either as failed or inferior versions of the dominant (masculine) forms, or as examples of trivial or marginal feminine forms, then the idea of an *écriture féminine* provides a very useful way of bringing them back into view and arriving at a difference of standard by which to re-view them.

When used flexibly and with due regard for the historical specificities of both women's socio-cultural position and of genre, this concept of a feminine mode of writing enables us to see the women's sensation novel and the New Woman writing as attempts to appropriate and transform the subject-matter and styles of fiction, and to extend the possibilities of particular genres beyond their culturally ascribed limits. It also affords a view of these much-decried women writers as experimenters in form, style and/or subject-matter, whose work – even when it falls back on devices of closure which reinforce traditional gender stereotypes – can usefully be seen as oppositional feminine forms, written in the margins of the dominant discourse, produced by and engaging with the contradictions of that discourse.

Whether as the result of a conscious resistance, or as a consequence of the pressure of cultural and generic contradictions, the women sensation novelists and the New Woman writers refused or failed to stay within the culturally prescribed bounds of proper feminine writing. As a woman 'you are supposed', as Christiane Rochefort (1981) has observed, 'to write *about* certain things: house, children, love' (373), and for the most part this is what the writers I have examined did. However, they did so in unusual, sometimes challenging and often unacceptable ways. Stylistically, the female sensationalists and the New Woman writers certainly did not remain within the culturally and generically prescribed bounds of proper feminine writing. Their excess, their emotionalism and sensationalism, their penchant for melodrama and, in the case of some of the New Woman writers, their intellectualism, took them beyond the confines of the proper feminine of 'women's writing', and into the domain of what Alfred Austin designated the improper feminine, or what Hélène Cixous has

207

described as a feminine libidinal economy of writing. To a large extent, Cixous's concept of masculine and feminine libidinal economies of writing repeats the terms of the gendered critical discourse of the nineteenth century, but it does so in ways which offer the possibility of rethinking that discourse. The crucial difference, of course, lies in the different values attached to the gendered terms: in the nineteenth-century discourse the masculine is the positive term, whereas the feminine is the positive term in Cixous's model.[3] Cixous's feminine economy – the Realm of the Gift which she elaborates in *The Newly Born Woman* – bears a remarkably close resemblance to the domain of the 'improper feminine' which Alfred Austin defines as 'the feminine element . . . unrestrainedly rioting in any and every area of life in which an indiscriminating imagination chooses to place it' (1869:468–9). It is precisely this lack of restraint and 'indiscriminating imagination' that Cixous values in 'feminine' writing (and urges upon women writers).

The Realm of the Gift is characterised by abundance, generosity, openness and multiplicity. These are also the characteristics of *écriture féminine*:

> [Woman's] libido is cosmic, just as her unconscious is worldwide. Her writing can only keep going, without ever inscribing or discerning contours . . . She alone dares and wishes to know from within, where she, the outcast, has never ceased to hear the resonance of forelanguage. She lets the other languages speak – the language of 1,000 tongues which knows neither enclosure nor death.
>
> (Cixous 1981:259–60)

Cixous's masculine economy – *l'Empire du Propre* – is structured around concepts such as property, propriety, regulation, classification, systematisation and hierarchism; in other words, around those terms which are the positively evaluated masculine ones of the nineteenth-century gendered critical discourse. The colonisation or enfeebling of this masculine Realm of the Proper by the promiscuous disorder of the improper feminine, or by that inferior, debased version of the masculine economy which was the proper feminine, was what Austin and others feared. Many of the contemporary objections to the work of the female sensationalists and the New Woman writers were rooted precisely in such fears about this process of (supposed) contamination and colonisation. Such fears have also, undoubtedly, played a significant part in what we might call (without having recourse to anything so crude as a patriarchal-conspiracy theory of literary history) these writers' prolonged period of suppression.

If a complex of thinking about gender and sexual difference has effectively written these women writers out of history, then a feminist awareness of this process and its categories enables us to write them back into literary history. What we have seen at work in the gendered critical discourse of the nineteenth century is a desire to fix gender categories, particularly the feminine term. We have also seen how the regime of the im/proper feminine worked to define the feminine as either subversive or subordinate. The contradictions in nineteenth-century conceptualisations of the feminine rendered it an impossible, permanently unstable, constantly shifting term. As a subordinate term the (proper) feminine stood for order, control, regulation, propriety, domesticity, the maternal, spirituality, morality, asexuality, and a careful concern for minutiae. In its subversive form of the improper feminine, it signified chaos, uncontrollability, impropriety, sexuality, carnality, immorality, the non- or anti-maternal, and a promiscuous profusion (and confusion) of minutiae and detail. I have tried to show that, although they were undoubtedly formed by this discourse of the im/proper feminine, neither the female sensationalists nor the New Woman writers were contained by it. Their negotiations or disruptions of its contradictions are themselves contradictory and, on occasion, contorted. This makes a smooth recuperation of their work for feminism difficult (even if it were desirable), but it is also major source of their interest to a late twentieth-century reader.

Notes

INTRODUCTORY NOTE

1 See, for example, Penny Boumelha's (1982) rereading of Hardy in the context of the fiction by women writers in the 1880s and 1890s.

PART I

1 See Pykett 1985.

2 See Showalter 1978a, Boumelha 1982 and Bjørhovde 1987.

3 This irruption of the feminine in the work of late nineteenth-century male writers is explored in Boumelha 1982, Stubbs 1979 and Showalter 1991.

4 See Hughes 1980 and Taylor 1988 for a discussion of the sensationalists, and Boumelha 1982, Stubbs 1979 and Cunningham 1978 for the writers of the 1890s.

5 For example in Barry 1894.

6 The concept of negotiation, which is borrowed from cultural studies (see Hall et al. 1980), is extremely useful for analysing the relations between cultural products, ideologies and audiences. 'The value of this notion', Christine Gledhill (1988) argues, 'lies in its avoidance of an overly deterministic view of cultural production . . . for the term "negotiation" implies the holding together of opposite sides in an ongoing process of give-and-take . . . Meaning is neither imposed, nor passively imbibed, but arises out of a struggle or negotiation between competing frames of reference' (67–8).

7 The Saturday Review's polemic on woman gained even wider currency with the publication of Modern Women and What is Said of Them (1868), which reprinted thirty-seven essays from the Saturday, including ten by Linton and ten by J.R. Green.

8 For a full and interesting discussion of the development of the middle-class family in the early nineteenth century see Davidoff and Hall 1987.

9 See Davidoff and Hall 1987 and Smith-Rosenberg 1985.

10 The importance of conduct books in constructing Victorian notions of womanhood and controlling female behaviour is discussed

(*passim*) in Armstrong 1987, Armstrong and Tennenhouse 1987 and Strachey 1978:46.

11 See Geddes and Thompson 1889 and Allan 1869. The scientific debates about the nature of woman are discussed in Conway 1980, Helsinger *et al.* 1983, Jacobus *et al.* 1990 and Russett 1989.

12 Krafft-Ebing (1892) and Ellis (1894 and 1895) both developed the idea of an intermediate sex (the mannish woman) to account for women's deviation from conventional gender and sex roles.

13 See Bram Djikstra 1986:15.

14 It is materialist insofar as it sees the sensation novel as the product of certain material conditions, and anti-materialist or idealist insofar as it derives from a prescriptive view of art as transcending material conditions.

15 See also 'Novels of the day', *Fraser's* 1860. Tony Davies (1983) writes interestingly about the phenomenon of railway reading.

16 The most prominent of the Spasmodic poets were Philip James Bailey and Alexander Smith. They affected an amalgam of the styles of the younger Romantics, producing an extravagant, egotistical poetry, which was castigated by Arnold and the more austere reviewers of Victorian poetry for its disorganised, sensuous, emotional and formal excess. Jerome Buckley provides quite a lively account of the Spasmodics in Chapter 3 of *The Victorian Temper* (Cambridge, Mass., 1951).

17 See Kristeva 1974 and Moi 1985:163ff.

18 The *fin de siècle* revival of romance by male writers was another such attempt. See Showalter 1991:78 ff.

19 D.H. Lawrence similarly claimed (in a letter to Sallie Hopkin, December 23, 1912) that his fiction would 'do my work for women, better than the suffrage' (*Letters*, 1979, I:490).

PART II

1 This problem is discussed in Harris 1990:21.

2 Ray (1865) notes that sensation novels were sometimes recommended as 'good stimulants in these days of toil and worry . . . well-fitted for relieving over-taxed brains by diverting our thoughts from the absorbing occupations of daily life.' (202).

3 Kalikoff (1986) discusses a variety of these forms and explores the sensation novel's links with them.

4 See Boyle 1989 and Altick 1970.

5 See Holcombe 1983 for details.

6 See Weeks 1981:20.

7 See the film and television journal *Screen* and also Gledhill 1987, Kaplan 1987 and 1990, Kuhn 1985, de Lauretis 1984 and 1987, and Pribram 1988.

8 See Kemble 1838.

9 Showalter (1987) suggests that this association of madness and the

feminine is endemic 'within our dualistic systems of language and representation', and that 'madness, even when experienced by men, is metaphorically and symbolically represented as feminine: a female malady' (3–4).

10 The resemblance between Braddon's plot and a contemporary case study of this condition has been much commented upon. Showalter quotes from John Connolly's *Physiognomy of Insanity* the case of a 'sensitive woman whose mother had been insane . . . [and who] became deranged and melancholic almost as soon as her poor little child came into this world of want' (Showalter 1987:71–2).

11 The terms of this description closely resemble those in which M. Héger recalled Emily Brontë: 'She should have been a man – a great navigator . . .'(quoted in Gérin 1972:127).

12 The Medusan snakes are losing themselves in Aurora's clothing rather than turning outwards towards the spectator.

13 See, for example, *Lady Audley's Secret*, pp. 294–5: 'If Mr. Holman Hunt could have peeped into the pretty boudoir I think the picture [of Lady Audley in thoughtful pose before the fire] would have been photographed upon his brain to be reproduced by-and-by upon a bishop's half-length. My lady in that half-recumbent attitude, with her elbow resting on one knee, and her perfect chin supported by her hand, the rich folds of drapery falling away in long undulating lines from the exquisite outline of her figure . . . Beautiful in herself, but made bewilderingly beautiful by the gorgeous surroundings which surround the shrine of her loveliness.' The passage continues with an elaborate inventory of the gorgeous objects.

14 This is a recurring situation in Braddon's novels. Both Paul Marchmont (JML) and Victor Carrington (RE) are feminised men who seek to defend a version of the family which they identify closely with their mother. While Robert Audley polices the (improperly) 'feminised' family to protect it from the criminality of Lucy, Paul Marchmont and Victor Carrington turn to crime to wrest the family from (what they perceive to be) usurping females.

15 The role and significance of the 'household spies we call servants' (AF:19) are discussed in Trodd 1989.

16 Hughes (1980) argues that 'The unbeatable combination of sin and sentiment, the unrestrained emotional wallowing, ultimately depend on an unquestioning acceptance of conventional morality and conventional standards' (112).

17 Moretti (1988) argues that 'moving literature' always functions in this way. 'Tears are always the product of *powerlessness*. They presuppose two mutually opposed facts: that it is clear how the present state of things should be changed – and that this change is *impossible*' (162).

18 See Bakhtin 1963 and 1981.

19 See Bakhtin 1981 and 1984.

PART III

1 David Rubinstein (1986) suggests that the New Woman was first named by Sarah Grand in the *North American Review* (1894). Carroll Smith-Rosenberg attributes the title to Henry James in the 1880s. As was the case with the 'fast woman' and the 'Girl of the Period' in the 1860s, the cultural image of the New Woman was made and remade as stereotypes were constructed, exchanged and recirculated in and between novels, short stories and newspaper and periodical articles. The fact that the image of the New Woman acquired a greater cultural force than some of the earlier representations of modern woman may be attributed (in part) to its proliferation and diffusion through a newly enlarged and more powerful system of print media.

2 See (*inter alia*) Sarah M. Amos 1894, Blanche Crackanthorpe 1894 and Susan M. Jeune 1894.

3 See Frances Power Cobbe 1868.

4 It is interesting to compare this passage with Lawrence's depiction of Anna dancing to the moon in 'Anna Victrix' in *The Rainbow*. In fact, both thematically and stylistically, *The Wheel of God* anticipates the Lawrence of *The Rainbow* and *Women in Love*. When read alongside Egerton's novel Lawrence's fictions appear less stylistically innovatory, and his representation of women less radically new, than has sometimes been claimed.

5 See also 'Her Share'.

6 See Bjørhovde 1987: 142–5 and Showalter 1991:145ff.

7 See Cixous 1974 and Cixous and Clément 1987.

8 Showalter (1982) discusses this term, which she borrows from the anthropologists Edward and Shirley Ardener.

9 See, for example, Claire Wills 1989.

10 Smith-Rosenberg (1985) points out that many nineteenth-century medical men feared that hysteria might not be a disease at all, and that 'hysterics' might simply be 'clever frauds and sensation seekers – morally delinquent and, for the physician, professionally embarrassing' (204). Showalter (1987) also writes extensively on the moral management of female hysterics in the nineteenth century.

11 See Toril Moi 1985 and 1986.

CONCLUSION

1 I have borrowed these terms from Raymond Williams (*Marxism and Literature* 1977), who uses them in a much more sophisticated way in developing a model for analysing and accounting for 'the dynamic interrelations, at every point in the process, of [the] historically varied and variable elements' of a culture (121).

2 Charles Wood (1894) wrote that 'No home duty was ever put aside for literary labours' (228), and Braddon's son William Maxwell (1938) affirmed that his mother 'got through her immense amount

of work as if by magic. She never seemed to be given any time in which to do it. She had . . . no part of the day to be held sacred from disturbance and intrusions' (281).

3 The feminine libidinal economy (as defined and used by Cixous) is not necessarily connected to the female body, nor is it exclusively the property of writing by women. However, it should be noted that Cixous' terminology is prone to some slippage between the 'feminine' and the biologically female.

Works referred to

In the case of the novels of the 1860s and 1890s I give full bibliographical details of the edition cited in the text. Wherever possible I have cited editions that are currently in print. When the first edition has not been used I give the date of first publication in parentheses at the end of the reference. I have also adopted this practice for other nineteenth-century texts of which I do not cite the first edition. In the case of fictional works which are referred to frequently, the following abbreviations have been used in the text:

AF	*Aurora Floyd*
BB	*The Beth Book*
CUF	*Cometh Up as a Flower*
D	*Discords*
DD	*The Daughters of Danaus*
DW	*The Doctor's Wife*
EL	*East Lynne*
EV	*Eleanor's Victory*
G	*Gallia*
HT	*The Heavenly Twins*
JML	*John Marchmont's Legacy*
K	*Keynotes*
LAS	*Lady Audley's Secret*
RE	*Run to Earth*
RP	*Red Pottage*
SMW	*The Story of a Modern Woman*
TH	*Trevlyn Hold*
WG	*The Wheel of God*
YA	*A Yellow Aster*

Unless otherwise stated the place of publication is London.

NOVELS OF THE 1860s

Braddon, M.E. (1987) *Lady Audley's Secret*, Oxford, Oxford University Press (1862).
—— (1984) *Aurora Floyd*, Virago (1863).
—— (1863) *Eleanor's Victory*, Tinsley Brothers.

215

—— (1863) *John Marchmont's Legacy*, Tinsley Brothers.
—— (1864) *The Doctor's Wife*, Tinsley Brothers.
—— (1868) *Run to Earth*, Ward, Lock and Tyler.
—— (n.d.) *Henry Dunbar*, Maxwell (1864).
Broughton, R. (1898) *Cometh Up as a Flower*, Macmillan (1867).
—— (1967) *Not Wisely but Too Well*, Cassell (1867).
Ouida (Marie Louise de la Ramée) (1896) *Under Two Flags*, Chatto and Windus (1867).
Wood, E. (1984) *East Lynne*, Dent (1861).
—— (1893) *Verner's Pride*, Richard Bentley (1863).
—— (1895) *Lord Oakburn's Daughters*, Richard Bentley (1864).
—— (1886) *Trevlyn Hold; or Squire Trevlyn's Heir*, Richard Bentley (1864).

NOVELS OF THE 1890s

Caird, M. (1894) *The Daughters of Danaus*, Bliss, Sands, Foster.
Cholmondeley, M. (1985) *Red Pottage*, Virago (1899).
Dixon, E.H. (1990) *The Story of a Modern Woman*, Merlin (1894).
Dowie, M.M. (1895) *Gallia*, Methuen.
Egerton, G. (Mary Chavelita Dunne) (1983) *Keynotes and Discords*, Virago. First published in two separate volumes by John Lane: *Keynotes* in 1893 and *Discords* in 1894.
—— (1898) *The Wheel of God*, Grant Richards.
Grand, S. (1893) *The Heavenly Twins*, Heinemann.
—— (1979) *The Beth Book*, Virago (1897).
Iota (K.M. Caffynn) (1894) *A Yellow Aster*, Hutchinson.

OTHER NINETEENTH-CENTURY TEXTS

Unattributed periodical and newspaper articles are included under the entry for the relevant journal.

Acton, W. (1857) *The Functions and Disorders of the Reproductive Organs in Childhood, Youth, Adult Age, and Advanced Life Considered in their Physiological, Social and Moral Relations*.
Allan, J.M. (1869) 'On the differences in the minds of men and women', *Journal of the Royal Anthropological Society of London*, vol. 7, pp. cciv–ccxix.
Amos, S.M. (1894) 'The evolution of the daughters', *Contemporary Review*, vol. 65, pp. 515–20.
Austin, A. (1869) 'The poetry of the period: Mr. Swinburne', *Temple Bar*, vol. 26, pp. 457–74.
—— (1870a) 'Our novels: the fast school', *Temple Bar*, vol. 29, pp. 177–94.
—— (1870b) 'Our novels: the sensational school', *Temple Bar*, vol. 29, pp. 410–24.
Barry, W. (1892) 'The French decadence', *Quarterly Review*, vol. 174, pp. 479–504.
—— (1894) 'The strike of a sex', *Quarterly Review*, vol. 179, pp. 289–318.

Besant, W. (1890) 'Candour in English fiction', *New Review*, vol. 2, pp. 6–9.

Buchanan, R (1862) 'Society's looking-glass', *Temple Bar*, vol. 6, pp. 129–37.

Caird, M. (1892) 'A defence of the so-called "Wild Women" ', *Nineteenth Century*, vol. 31, pp. 811–29.

—— (1897) *The Morality of Marriage and Other Essays on the Status and Destiny of Woman*. Originally published in *Westminster Review*, 1888–94.

Christian Remembrancer (1863) 'Our female sensation novelists', vol. 46, pp. 209–36.

Cobbe, F.P. (1868) 'Criminals, idiots, women and minors: is the classification sound?', *Fraser's*, vol. 78, pp. 777–94.

Collins, W. (1858) 'The unknown public', *Household Words*, August 21, pp. 217–22.

Crackanthorpe, B. (1894a) 'The revolt of the daughters', *Nineteenth Century*, vol. 34, pp. 23–31.

—— (1894b) 'The revolt of the daughters', *Nineteenth Century*, vol. 35, pp. 424–29.

—— (1895) 'Sex in modern literature', *Nineteenth Century*, vol. 37, pp. 607–16.

Crackanthorpe, H. (1894) 'Reticence in literature', *The Yellow Book*, vol. 2, pp. 259–73.

Dallas, E.S. (1862) '*Lady Audley's Secret*', *The Times*, November 18, p. 8.

—— (1866) *The Gay Science*.

Drysdale, G. (1860) *The Elements of Social Science*.

Eliot, G. (1856) 'Silly novels by lady novelists', *Westminster Review*, vol. 66, pp. 442–61.

Ellis, H. (1888) *Women and Marriage; or Evolution in Sex*.

—— (1894) *Man and Woman: A Study of Human Secondary Sexual Characters*.

Ellis, S. (1843a) *The Mothers of England, their Influence and Responsibility*.

—— (1843b) *The Wives of England, their Relative Duties, Domestic Influence and Social Obligations*.

—— (1845) *The Daughters of England, their Position in Society, Character and Responsibilities*.

Ferrerro, G. (1893) *The Problem of Woman from a Bio-Sociological Point of View*, Turin.

Fraser's Magazine (1860) 'Novels of the day: their writers and readers', vol. 62, pp. 205–17.

—— (1863) 'The popular novels of the year', vol. 68, pp. 253–69.

Geddes, P. and Thompson, J.A. (1889) *The Evolution of Sex*.

Gosse, E. (1892) 'The tyranny of the novel', *National Review*, vol. 19, pp. 163–75.

Grand, S. (1894) 'A new aspect of the woman question', *North American Review*, vol. 158, pp. 271–6.

Greg, W.R. (1850) 'Prostitution', *Westminster Review*, vol. 53, pp. 448–506.

—— (1859) 'The false morality of lady novelists', *National Review*, vol. 8, pp. 144–67.

—— (1862) 'Why are women redundant?', *National Review*, vol. 14, pp. 434–60.

Hansson, L.M. (1896) *Modern Women*, trans. Hermione Ramsden.

Hardy, T. (1890) 'Candour in English fiction', *New Review*, vol. 2, pp. 15–21.

Hutton, R.H. (1858) 'Novels by the authoress of *John Halifax*', *North British Review*, vol. 29, pp. 466–81.

James, H. (1865) 'Miss Braddon', *The Nation*, November 9, pp. 593–5. Reprinted in *Notes and Reviews* (Cambridge, Mass., 1981), pp. 108–16.

Jeune, S.M. (1894) 'The revolt of the daughters', *Fortnightly Review*, vol. 61, pp. 267–76.

Kemble, J.M. (1838) 'Custody of Infants Bill', *British and Foreign Quarterly Review*, vol. 7, pp. 269–411.

Krafft-Ebing, R. von (1892) *Psychopathia Sexualis with Especial Reference to the Antipathic Sexual Instincts* (first German edition 1886).

Lang, A. (1887) 'Realism and romance', *Contemporary Review*, vol. 52, pp. 683–93.

Lee, V. (Violet Paget) (1885) 'A dialogue on novels', *Contemporary Review*, vol. 48, pp. 378–401.

Lewes, G.H. (1850) 'A gentle hint to writing women', *Leader*, vol. 1, pp. 929–30.

—— (1852) 'The lady novelists', *Westminster Review*, vol. 58, pp. 129–41.

—— (1865) 'The principles of success in literature (ii)', *Fortnightly Review*, vol. 1, pp. 185–96.

Linton, E.L. (1868a) 'The Girl of the Period', *Saturday Review*, March 14, pp. 339–4.

—— (1868b) 'Feminine affectations', *Saturday Review*, June 13, pp. 776–7.

—— (1868c) 'La femme passée', July 11, pp. 49–50.

—— (1890) 'Candour in English fiction', *New Review*, vol. 2, pp. 10–14.

—— (1891a) 'The Wild Women as politicians', *Nineteenth Century*, vol. 30, pp. 79–88.

—— (1891b) 'The Wild Women as social insurgents', *Nineteenth Century*, vol. 31, pp. 596–605.

—— (1892) 'Partisans of the Wild Women', *Nineteenth Century*, vol. 30, pp. 455–64.

London Review (1860) 'Female novelists', vol. 1, pp. 137–8.

McCarthy, J. (1864) 'Novels with a purpose', *Westminster Review*, vol. 82, pp. 24–49.

Mansel, H.L. (1863) 'Sensation novels', *Quarterly Review*, vol. 113, pp. 481–514.

Maudsley, H. (1874) 'Sex in mind and education', *Fortnightly Review*, vol. 21, pp. 466–83.

Moore, G. (1976) *Literature at Nurse, or Circulating Morals: A Polemic on Victorian Censorship*, ed. P. Coustillas, Sussex. This edition reprints Moore's 'A new censorship of literature', *Pall Mall Gazette*, December

10, 1884, and the ensuing correspondence, plus *Literature at Nurse* (1885).

Noble, J.A. (1895) 'The fiction of sexuality', *Contemporary Review*, vol. 67, pp. 490–8.

Norman, H. (1883) 'Theories and practice in modern fiction', *Fortnightly Review*, New Series, vol. 34, pp. 870–86.

Oliphant, M. (1856) 'The laws concerning women', *Blackwood's*, vol. 76, pp. 379–87.

—— (1862) 'Sensation novels', *Blackwood's*, vol. 91, pp. 564–84.

—— (1863) 'Novels', *Blackwood's*, vol. 94, pp. 168–83.

—— (1867) 'Novels', *Blackwood's*, vol. 102, pp. 257–80.

—— (1896) 'The anti-marriage league', *Blackwood's*, vol. 159, pp. 135–49.

Ouida (Marie Louise de la Ramée) (1894) 'The new aspect of the woman question', *North American Review*, vol. 158, pp. 610–19.

—— (1895) *Views and Opinions*.

Parkes, B.R. (later Belloc) (1865), *Essays on Women's Work*.

Ray, W.F. (1865) 'Sensation novelists: Miss Braddon', *North British Review*, vol. 43, pp. 180–204.

Romanes, G. (1887) 'Mental differences between men and women', *Nineteenth Century*, vol. 21, pp. 654–72.

Ruskin, J. (1880) 'Of Queen's Gardens' in *Sesame and Lilies* (1865).

Saturday Review (1860) 'The literature of the social evil', October 6, pp. 417–18.

—— (1868a) 'Woman and her critics', January 25, pp. 108–9.

—— (1868b) 'What is woman's work?', February 15, pp. 107–8.

—— (1871) 'The British mother taking alarm', September 9, pp. 334–5.

Scott, H.S. and Hall, E. (1894) 'Character note: the new woman', *Cornhill*, vol. 70, pp. 365–8.

Smith, A.P. (1894) 'A reply from the daughters II', *Nineteenth Century*, vol. 35, pp. 443–50.

Smith, B. Leigh (later Bodichon) (1854) *A Brief Summary in Plain Language of the Most Important Laws Concerning Women, Together with a Few Observations Thereon*.

Stead, W.T. (1894) 'The novel of the modern woman', *Review of Reviews*, vol. 10, pp. 64–73.

Stutfield, H.M. (1895) ' "Tommyrotics" ', *Blackwood's*, vol. 157, pp. 833–45.

—— (1897) 'The psychology of feminism', *Blackwood's*, vol. 161, pp. 104–17.

Taylor, H. (later Mill) (1851) 'Enfranchisement of women', *Westminster Review*, vol. 55, pp. 289–311.

Walker, A. (1840) *Woman Physiologically Considered as to Mind, Morals, Marriage, Matrimonial Slavery, Infidelity and Divorce*.

Waugh, A. (1894) 'Reticence in literature', *The Yellow Book*, vol. 1, pp. 201–19.

Westminster Review (1866) 'Belles lettres', vol. 20, pp. 269–70.

Wood, C. (1894) *Memorials of Mrs Henry Wood*.

WORKS FIRST PUBLISHED AFTER 1900

Abel, E. (ed.) (1982) *Writing and Sexual Difference*, Sussex.

Altick, R.D. (1970) *Victorian Studies in Scarlet*.

Armstrong, N. (1987) *Desire and Domestic Fiction*, New York.

—— and Tennenhouse, L. (eds) (1987) *The Ideology of Conduct: Essays in Literature and the History of Sexuality*.

Bakhtin, M.M. (1963) *Problems of Dostoevsky's Poetics*, ed. and trans. Caryl Emerson, Minneapolis.

—— (1981) *The Dialogic Imagination*, trans. C. Emerson and M. Holquist, Austin.

—— (1984) *Rabelais and His World*, trans. H. Iwolsky, Bloomington.

Basch, F. (1974) *Relative Creatures: Victorian Women in Society and the Novel, 1837–67*, trans. A. Rudolf.

Baym, N. (1986) 'Melodramas of beset manhood', in Showalter, E., *The New Feminist Criticism*.

Bevington, M.M. (1941) *The Saturday Review 1855–1868: Representative Educated Opinion in Victorian England*, New York.

Bjørhovde, G. (1987) *Rebellious Structures: Women Writers and the Crisis of the Novel, 1880–1900*, Oxford.

Boumelha, P. (1982) *Thomas Hardy and Women: Sexual Ideology and Narrative Form*, Sussex.

Boyle, T. (1989) *Black Swine in the Sewers of Hampstead: Beneath the Surface of Victorian Sensationalism*.

Brantlinger, P. (1982) 'What is sensational about the sensation novel?', *Nineteenth-Century Fiction*, vol. 37, pp. 1–28.

Brooks, P. (1976) *The Melodramatic Imagination*, New Haven.

Chodorow, N. (1978) *The Reproduction of Mothering: Psychoanalysis and the Sociology of Gender*, Berkeley.

Cixous, H. (1974) 'The character of character', *New Literary History*, vol. 5, pp. 384–402.

—— (1981) 'The laugh of the Medusa', in Marks, E. and Courtviron, I., *New French Feminisms* (1976).

—— and Clément, C. (1987) *The Newly Born Woman*, trans B. Wing, Manchester.

Cominos, P.T. (1963) 'Late Victorian sexual respectability and the social system', *International Review of Social History*, vol. 8, pp. 18–48, 216–50.

Conway, J. (1980) 'Stereotypes of femininity in a theory of sexual evolution' in Vicinus, M., *Suffer and Be Still*.

Courtney, W.L. (1904) *The Feminine Note in Fiction*.

Cross, N. (1985) *The Common Writer: Life in Nineteenth-Century Grub Street*, Cambridge.

Cunningham, G. (1978) *The New Woman and the Victorian Novel*.

Davidoff, L. and Hall, C. (1987) *Family Fortunes: Men and Women of the English Middle Classes, 1780–1850*.

Davies, T. (1983) 'Transports of pleasure: fiction and its audiences in the later nineteenth century', in Burgin, V. and Kaplan, C., *Formations of Pleasure*.

Djikstra, B. (1986) *Idols of Perversity: Fantasies of Feminine Evil in Fin-de-Siècle Culture*, Oxford.

Edwards, P.D. (1971) *Some Mid-Victorian Thrillers: The Sensation Novel, Its Friends and Foes*, St. Lucia, Queensland.

Ellis, H. (1933) Studies in the Psychology of Sex, New York. An earlier version of this work was published in London in 1897.

Fahnestock, J. (1981) 'Bigamy: the rise and fall of a convention', *Nineteenth-Century Fiction*, vol. 36, pp. 47–71.

Feuer, J. (1984) 'Melodrama, serial form, and television today', *Screen*, 25:1, pp. 4–16.

Flint, K. (1986) 'The woman reader and the opiate of fiction', in Hawthorn, J., *The Nineteenth-Century British Novel*.

—— (1990) Introduction to *The Story of a Modern Woman*.

Foucault, M. (1979) *The History of Sexuality: An Introduction*, trans. R. Hurley.

Fowler, B. (1991) *The Alienated Reader: Women and Popular Romantic Literature in the Twentieth Century*.

Gawsworth, J. (Terence Armstrong) (ed.) (1932) *Ten Contemporaries*.

Gérin, W. (1972) *Emily Brontë: A Biography*, Oxford.

Gilbert, S. and Gubar, S. (1978) *The Madwoman in the Attic: The Woman Writer and the Nineteenth-Century Literary Imagination*, New Haven.

—— (1988) *No Man's Land: The Place of the Woman Writer in the Twentieth Century*, vol. 1: *The War of the Words*, New Haven.

—— (1989) *No Man's Land*, vol. 2, *Sexchanges*, New Haven.

Gledhill, C. (1987) *Home Is Where the Heart Is: Studies in Melodrama and the Woman's Film*.

—— (1988) 'Pleasurable Negotiations' in Pribram, E. D., *Female Spectators: Looking at Film and Television*.

Hall, S. et al. (1980) *Culture, Media, Language*.

Harris, S.K. (1990) *Nineteenth-Century American Women's Novels: Interpretative Strategies*, Cambridge.

Helsinger, E.K. et al. (1983) *The Woman Question: Society and Literature in Britain and America, 1837–1883*, three vols., Manchester.

Higson, A. and Vincendeau, G. (1986) 'Melodrama: an introduction', *Screen*, 27:6, pp. 2–5.

Hirschkop, K. and Shepard, D. (1989) *Bakhtin and Cultural Theory*, Manchester.

Holcombe, L. (1980) 'Victorian wives and property: reform of the married women's property law, 1857–1882', in Vicinus, M., *A Widening Sphere: Changing Roles of Victorian Women*.

—— (1983) *Wives and Property: Reform of the Married Women's Property Law in Nineteenth-Century England*, Oxford.

Hughes, W. (1980) *The Maniac in the Cellar: The Sensation Novel of the 1860s*, Princeton.

Huyssen, A. (1986) *After the Great Divide: Modernism, Mass Culture, Postmodernism*.

Jacobus, M., Fox Keller, E. and Shuttleworth, S. (1990) *Body/Politics: Women and the Discourse of Science*.

Jameson, F. (1981) *The Political Unconscious: Narrative as a Socially Symbolic Act.*

Jardine, A. (1981) 'Pre-Texts for the "transatlantic" feminist', *Yale French Studies*, vol. 62, pp. 220–36.

Johnson, R.B. (1920) *Some Contemporary Novelists (Women).*

Jones, A.R. (1986) 'Writing the body: towards an understanding of *l'écriture féminine*', in Showalter, E., *The New Feminist Criticism.*

Jordanova, L. (1980) 'Natural facts: a historical perspective on science and sexuality', in McCormack, C. and Strathern, M., *Nature, Culture and Gender*, Cambridge.

Kalikoff, B. (1986) *Murder and Moral Decay in Victorian Popular Literature*, Ann Arbor, Michigan.

Kaplan, E.A. (1987) 'Mothering, feminism and representation: the maternal melodrama and the woman's film 1910–40', in Gledhill, C., *Home Is Where the Heart Is.*

—— (1989) 'The political unconscious in the maternal melodrama: Ellen Wood's *East Lynne* (1861)', in Longhurst, D., *Gender, Genre and Narrative Pleasure.*

—— (1990) *Psychoanalysis and Cinema.*

Kent, S.K. (1990) *Sex and Suffrage in Britain, 1860–1914.*

Kersley, G. (1983) *Darling Madam: Sarah Grand and Devoted Friend.*

Kristeva, J. (1974) 'La femme, ce n'est jamais ça', *Tel Quel*, vol. 59, pp. 19–24.

Kuhn, A. (1985) *Power of the Image: Essays on Representation and Sexuality.*

—— (1987) 'Women's genres: melodrama, soap opera and theory', in Gledhill, C., *Home Is Where the Heart Is.*

Lauretis, T. de (1984) *Alice Doesn't: Feminism, Semiotics, Cinema.*

—— (1987) *Technologies of Gender.*

Lawrence, D.H. (1913) *Sons and Lovers.*

Light, A. (1986), 'Writing fictions: femininity in the 1950s', in Radford, J. (ed.) *The Progress of Romance: The Politics of Popular Fiction.*

Loesberg, J. (1986) 'The ideology of narrative form in sensation fiction', *Representations*, vol. 13, pp. 115–38.

Lovell, T. (1987) *Consuming Fiction.*

Marcus, S. (1969) *The Other Victorians: A Study of Sexuality and Pornography in Mid-Nineteenth-Century England.*

Marks, E. and Courtviron, I. (1981) *New French Feminisms*, Sussex.

Maxwell, W. B. (1938) *Time Gathered.*

Mitchell, J. (1984) *Women: The Longest Revolution.*

Mitchell, S. (1977) 'Sentiment and suffering: women's recreational reading in the 1860s', *Victorian Studies*, vol. 21, pp. 29–45.

Modleski, T. (1984) *Loving with a Vengeance: Mass-produced Fantasies for Women.*

Moi, T. (1985) *Sexual/Textual Politics: Feminist Literary Theory.*

—— (1986) *The Kristeva Reader*, Oxford.

Moretti, F. (1988) *Signs Taken For Wonders.*

Nield, K. (1973) *Prostitution in the Victorian Age.*

Pollock, G. (1988) *Vision and Difference: Femininity, Feminism and the Histories of Art*.

Poovey, M. (1989) *Uneven Developments: The Ideological Work of Gender in Mid-Victorian England*.

Pribram, E.D. (1988) *Female Spectators: Looking at Film and Television*.

Pykett, L. (1985) 'George Eliot and Arnold: the narrator's voice and ideology', *Literature and History*, 11:2, pp. 229–40.

Radway, J. (1987) *Reading the Romance: Women, Patriarchy and Popular Literature*.

Rochefort, C. (1981) 'Are women writers still monsters?', in Marks, E. and Courtviron, I., *New French Feminisms*.

Rodowick, D.N. (1987) 'Madness, authority and ideology: the domestic melodrama of the 1950s' in Gledhill, C., *Home Is Where the Heart Is*.

Rose, J. (1986) *Sexuality in the Field of Vision*.

Rubinstein, D. (1986) *Before the Suffragettes: Women's Emancipation in the 1890s*, Sussex.

Russett, C. E. (1989) *Sexual Science: The Victorian Construction of Womanhood*, Cambridge, Mass.

Schor, N. (1987) *Reading in Detail: Aesthetics and the Feminine*.

Showalter, E. (1978a) *A Literature of their Own*.

—— (1978b) 'Family secrets and domestic subversion: rebellion in the novels of the eighteen-sixties', in Wohl, A., *The Victorian Family: Structure and Stresses*.

—— (1982) 'Feminist criticism in the wilderness', in Abel, E., *Writing and Sexual Difference*.

—— (1985) Introduction to *Red Pottage*.

—— (1986a) 'Syphilis, sexuality, and the fiction of the *fin de siècle*', in Yeazell, R.B., *Sex, Politics and Science in the Nineteenth-Century Novel*, Baltimore.

—— (ed.) (1986b) *The New Feminist Criticism: Essays on Women, Literature and Theory*.

—— (1987) *The Female Malady*.

—— (1991) *Sexual Anarchy: Gender and Culture at the Fin de Siècle*.

Smith-Rosenberg, C. (1985) *Disorderly Conduct: Visions of Gender in Victorian America*, New York.

Spencer, J. (1986) *The Rise of the Woman Novelist*, Oxford.

Strachey, R. (1978) *The Cause: A Short History of the Women's Movement in Great Britain* (1928).

Stubbs, P. (1979) *Women and Fiction: Feminism and the Novel, 1880–1920*.

Taylor, J. B. (1988) *In the Secret Theatre of Home: Wilkie Collins, Sensation Narrative and Nineteenth-Century Psychology*.

Tillotson, K. (1969) 'The lighter reading of the eighteen-sixties', introduction to Wilkie Collins, *The Woman in White*, Boston.

Todorov, T. (1984) *Mikhail Bakhtin: The Dialogical Principle*, trans. W. Godzich.

—— (1990) *Genres in Discourse*, trans. C. Porter, Cambridge.

Tompkins, J. (1985) *Sensational Designs: The Cultural Work of American Fiction, 1790–1860*, Oxford.

Trodd, A. (1989) *Domestic Crime in the Victorian Novel.*

Trudgill, E. (1976) *Madonnas and Magdalens: The Origins and Development of Victorian Sexual Attitudes.*

Tuchman, G. with Fortin, N. (1989) *Edging Women Out: Victorian Novelists, Publishers and Social Change.*

Vicinus, M. (1980a) *Suffer and Be Still: Women in the Victorian Age.*

—— (1980b) *A Widening Sphere: Changing Roles of Victorian Women.*

—— (1981) ' "Helpless and Unfriended": nineteenth-century domestic melodrama', *New Literary History*, vol. 13, pp. 127–43.

Walkowitz, J. (1982) *Prostitution and Victorian Society*, Cambridge.

Weeks, J. (1981) *Sex, Politics and Society: The Regulation of Sexuality since 1800.*

White, T. de Vere (1958) *A Leaf from* The Yellow Book: *The Correspondence of George Egerton.*

Williams, H. (1925) *Modern English Writers: Being a Study of Imaginative Literature, 1890–1914.*

Williams, L. (1987) ' "Something else besides a mother": *Stella Dallas* and the maternal melodrama', in Gledhill, C., *Home Is Where the Heart Is.*

Williams, R. (1977) *Marxism and Literature*, Oxford.

Wills, C. (1989) 'Upsetting the public: carnival, hysteria and women's texts', in Hirschkop, K., *Bakhtin and Cultural Theory.*

Wolff, R.L. (1979) *Sensational Victorian: The Life and Work of Mary Elizabeth Braddon*, New York.

Woolf, V. (1966) 'Women and fiction' reprinted in *Collected Essays*, vol. 2 (1929).

224

Index

Acton, William, 15–17, 19; and
  Grand, 20; and proper
  feminine, 15–17
affectivity, 25, 27, 164–7;
  containment, 164; Egerton,
  165, 173–4; Grand on, 175; lack,
  165; women, victim of, 178
angel in the house, 12, 16; in *Lady
  Audley's Secret*, 92
Armstrong, Nancy, 23
Aurora Floyd, 98–9; criminality,
  87; discourse on women, 88;
  girl of the period, 88, 112;
  improper feminine, 88;
  marriage, 108–9; plot, 86–7;
  sales, 7; secrets, 86; spectacle,
  99–100, 105; stereotypes,
  105–6; transgressive past,
  86–8, 102, 112–13
Austin, Alfred, 24; and proper
  feminine, 25, 207–8; women
  and art, 9

Bakhtin, Mikhail, 132, 134
Baym, Nina, 203
Besant, Walter, 39–40
Beth Book, The, 194; feminism,
  180; and 'The Lady of Shalott',
  185–6; mother of Beth, 180;
  proper feminine, 185–6; secret
  room, 183–6; spiritualising,
  186; woman artist, 178–80,
  183–6
Bethell, Sir Richard, 59
Bevington, Merle, 69
Blackstone, William, 57–8

Bloom, Harold, 203
body: and medical discourse, 95;
  and sensation fiction, 35, 79;
  see also: spectacle; woman
Boumelha, Penny, 41, 158
Braddon, Mary Elizabeth,
  83–113, 201; address, 32, 108;
  amateur, 202; concealed pasts,
  84; defies rules, 33; *The Doctor's
  Wife*, 112; and domestic
  melodrama, 75; and domestic
  novel, 151; female body, 35;
  feminine spectacle, 91–3,
  97–102; femininity, 91–102;
  feminisation of heroine, 85;
  gender boundaries, 102–3;
  gender and class, 107; hair, 98;
  Henry Dunbar, 85; on heroines,
  82; improper feminine, 84, 88,
  92–3, 107; interest in, 198;
  interiority, 91–2, 101; *John
  Marchmont's Legacy*, 95–7;
  madness in, 89–90, 93–6;
  marriage, 108–13; masculinity
  in, 102–4, 106–7; mimicry of
  masculine form, 206; mother,
  lack of, 86–7; and New Woman
  writing, 143, 151; plots, 85, 110;
  points of view, 80–1; private
  female spaces, 91–2, 101;
  proper feminine, 84, 95–6; *Run
  to Earth*, 85; secrets, 83–4, 86–7,
  89, 91–2, 107, 110, 111; on
  sensation fiction, 53; success,
  6–7; suspicion, 111;
  techniques, 97, 108, 111–12,

225

149, 168; and New Woman,
137; and New Woman writing,
156, 192, 198, 204; regenerative
woman, 165; rhetoric and New
Woman writing, 192; second
wave, ix–x, 203, 204; sensation
fiction, 48–51; and utopianism,
184; and womanliness, 158
feminists: and gender, 10; liberal
and maternity, 149; marriage,
144; and New Woman writing,
156, 204
femininity: in Braddon, 91–102;
contradictory, 165–6; as lack,
165; Linton on, 71–2; and
madness, 89; and New
Woman writing, 5; and
realism, 26, 40; in sensational
novel, 5
femininization: of culture, 23; of
heroine, 85; of masculinity,
149–50; and the novel, 9
Feuer, Jane, 97
fiction: as feminised form, 22–9;
feminine forms marginalised,
36; gendered discourse, x,
22–9, 32, 38–43, 196, 202–5;
improper feminine, 24–5,
202–3; and men, 26; proper
feminine, 24–5, 202–3; separate
sphere, 39–40
filiation, 203
Fortin, Nina, 36
Foucault, Michel, 13–14
Fowler, Bridget, 77
Fraser's, 53–4
French literature, 37–8, 42, 195,
200; naturalism, 200; and New
Woman writing, 141
Freud, Sigmund: on hysteria,
142, 181–2; Medusa's head,
171–2; Oedipal drama, 115,
121–2

Geddes, Patrick, 13
gender: anxiety, x, 21, 23, 51;
boundaries, 102–3, 138–42,
159–60; categories, 10, 14,
19–21, 81, 82, 138–42, 153,

156–7, 159–60, 161, 195, 200;
class, 107; cultural authority,
38–9; discourse on, 67–8;
gender and writing, 3–10
gendered discourse, 202–9;
detailism, 28; erasure of
women, 206, 207; on fiction, x,
22–9, 32, 36, 38–43, 196, 202–5;
masculine privileged, 205;
New Woman writing, 205; and
nostalgia, 43; realism, 196;
sensation fiction, 205; sexual
stereotypes, 43; and women,
206, 207
genre: concept of, 73–4;
historicised, 47–54, 73–82; New
Woman writing, 202; and
popular narrative forms, 73–82
Gilbert, S., 203
Girl of the Period, 20, 158, 200;
Aurora Floyd, 88, 112; defined,
69–71; on marriage, 69–70; in
New Woman writing, 150; in
sensation novel, 69
Gissing, George, 3, 185, 186; on
sexual anarchy, x
Gledhill, Christine, 78, 197
Gosse, Edmund, 36
gothic novel, 74
gothic romance, 77
Grand, Sarah: and Acton's
woman, 20; domestic space,
156; feeling, 174–5; gender,
157, 159; hysteria, 174–5; male
characters, 155–6, 157;
marriage question, 152–3, 157;
maternity, 157; Noble on, 41;
proper feminine, 159; and
scientific discourse, 154–5;
success, 7; womanliness, 159;
see also: *The Beth Book*; *The
Heavenly Twins*
Greg, W.R., 65
Gubar, S., 203

Hansson, Laura Marholm, 196
Hardy, Thomas, 3, 200; on
censorship, 39; anti-marraige,
144; and New Woman, 160

separate spheres, 12–13, 60, 68,
69; and *East Lynne*, 126; of
fiction, 39–40; and sensation
novels, 68–9
servants, 129; in *East Lynne*,
123–4; proper feminine, 124
sexology, 20
sexual difference and science,
13–14
sexual diseases, 151–3, 154–7
sexuality, 151–3; anxiety about,
51; definition and marraige,
143–4; Drysdale on, 17–18; in
East Lynne, 118, 122–5; Egerton
on, 167–8, 170–2; fear of
female, 15–16; in Grand, 41;
and marriage, 18, 143–4; and
New Woman, 140–1; in New
Woman writing, 7–8, 10, 200;
representation of, 36–7; and
sensation fiction, 7–8, 10, 34–5;
and women, 8, 14–15
Showalter, Elaine: on *The Beth
Book*, 184; on Egerton, 171; on
Gissing, x; on New Woman
writing, 192–3; on sensation
fiction, 48–50, 80, 83–4; on
women's writing, 177
Smith, Alys Pearsall, 181
Smith-Rosenberg, Carol, 175
Spasmodic poetry, 31
spectacle, 178; in Braddon, 91–3,
97–102, 105, 161–2; in Egerton,
173, 206; and New Woman,
138; in sensation fiction, 173;
woman as public, 67
Spencer, Herbert, 13; on women,
155
Spencer, Jane, 23
Stead, W.T., 5; on New Woman
writing, 143; and social change,
41
Stutfield, Hugh, 42–3; on
interiority, 20; on marriage,
144
suffragism and 'Wild Women',
139
Swinburne, Algernon, 24
syphilis, 153, 154

Taylor, Harriet, 56–7
Temple Bar, 9, 24
Tennyson, Alfred, Lord, 185
Thackeray, W.M., 66
Thompson, J. Arthur, 13
Tillotson, Kathleen, 47
Times, The, 32
Todorov, T., 47
Tompkins, Jane, 73
Trodd, Anthea, 83–4
Trollope, Anthony, 24; and
proper feminine, 24
True Womanhood, 157, **158–63**;
in Egerton, 158–9, 166, 173; in
Grand, 160; in Iota, 162–3
Tuchman, Gaye, 36, 193

utopianism, 184

Vicinus, Martha: on domestic
melodrama, 114; on
melodrama, 75
Vincendeau, Ginette, 73
Vizetelly, Henry, 37–8

Waugh, Arthur, 40, 154
Westminster Review, 51, 52, 56–7;
and marriage, 144–5; and
prostitution, 65; and sensation
fiction, 51, 52; on women's
wrongs, 60–1
'Wild Women', 20, 139–40, 158,
200
Wilde, Oscar, 171
Williams, Linda, 128
Williams, Raymond, 199
Woman Question, 7
Womanhood, True, 157, **158–63**;
Egerton on, 158–9, 166, 173;
Grand on, 160; Iota, 162–3; and
maternity, 162–3
womanliness, 158–63;
constructed, 158; and
feminism, 158; in Grand, 159;
in Iota, 159
women: affectivity, 25, 27, 164–7,
173–4, 175, 178; angels in the
house, 12, 16, 92;
characterised, 43; Cixous and

Lightning Source UK Ltd.
Milton Keynes UK
UKOW030951221112

202593UK00001B/11/A